Electronic Safety and Soundness

Securing Finance in a New Age

Thomas C. Glaessner
Tom Kellermann
Valerie McNevin

THE WORLD BANK
Washington, D.C.

ISBN: 0-8213-5759-X
eISBN: 0-8213-5760-3
ISSN: 1726-5878

Thomas C. Glaessner is Lead Financial Economist in the Financial Sector Operations and Policy Department at the World Bank. Tom Kellermann is Senior Data Risk Management Specialist in the same department. Valerie McNevin is Security Information Officer for the State of Colorado.

Library of Congress Cataloging-in-Publication Data has been requested.

TABLE OF CONTENTS

LIST OF BOXES:

LIST OF FIGURES:

LIST OF TABLES:

FOREWORD

Over the last decade technological advances have been revolutionizing the conduct of commerce and financial transactions. Technology has allowed financial services to be provided to a wider variety of institutional and retail clients at far lower transaction costs, with important implications for access to financial services. The advent of the Internet and advances in cellular, wireless, and satellite technology have multiplied the possibilities for moving digital information. Many emerging markets are aggressively adopting advanced technologies in efforts to bridge the "digital divide."

However, the increasing use of these technologies, especially in emerging markets, is not without risk. These systems, which rely on computers and the Internet technology backbone, are vulnerable to rapid, illegal intrusions that can disrupt, disable, or corrupt critical infrastructure such as power, telecommunications, government, education, hospitals, and financial services. Privacy, security, safety, and soundness are all at stake as service providers race to use these technologies to integrate functions and services at a higher speed and reduced cost.

In a series of papers starting over three years ago, World Bank staff have investigated the links between technology advances and financial sector development and access to financial services, with a particular emphasis on electronic security (e-security) concerns.[1] This monograph expands on this research to lay out a framework for policymakers and private market participants to use in developing a comprehensive, coherent approach to managing e-security risks.

As a starting point, the paper offers lessons learned from recent experience and lays out approaches that have been used by others. There are no cookie cutter or silver bullet solutions presented to solving the e-security challenges that companies and governments face in an open architecture environment. Instead, answers require the hard work of collaboration, discussion, debate, innovation, experimentation and the diligent exercise of continuous and layered e-security.

This monograph presents a four pillar framework for policymakers in emerging markets to use in designing responses to the challenge of assuring electronic safety and soundness of their financial systems. As such, this paper is focused in part on technological solutions, but more importantly on the incentives of the many parties involved in assuring the security of critical infrastructures—from telecommunications and financial sector service providers to the government and even to the many final consumers of financial or other services.

Securing the open network is first and foremost the responsibility of the service providers. Businesses need to understand the risks and responsibilities of providing services via these channels and seek continuous improvement in maintaining e-security. Technology is only a part of the solution; sound business principles such as responsibility, accountability, and trust are also essential to building infrastructure and a framework that can support e-business.

An effective legal, regulatory, and enforcement framework is essential for creating the right incentive structure for market participants. The legal and regulatory framework should focus on the improvement of internal monitoring of risks and vulnerabilities, greater information sharing about these risks and vulnerabilities, education and training on the care and use of these technologies and better reporting of risks and responses. Public/private partnerships and collaborations also are needed to create an electronic commerce (e-commerce) environment that is safe and sound.

---

1. These include: *E-Finance in Emerging Markets: Is Leapfrogging Possible?* (Claessens, Glaessner, and Klingebiel 2001), "Electronic Security: Risk Mitigation in Financial Transactions" (Glaessner, Kellerman, and McNevin, 2002), *Electronic Finance: A New Approach to Financial Sector Development?* (Claessens, Glaessner, and Klingebiel 2002), and *Mobile Risk Management: E-Finance in the Wireless Environment* (Kellerman 2002a).

Because of its rapid growth and technological complexity, e-security is often wrapped in myth. Most countries, including those that have greater experience dealing with e-security, still know little. As a result, the monograph focuses relatively more attention on lessons learned in the United States because it is considered the birthplace of the Internet and has had a longer time to experience its benefits and pitfalls, as well as to create some standards.[2] Just as important, this monograph looks at the experiences and efforts of certain advanced economies in Europe, as well as of countries in Asia and South America.

Clearly, however, much greater effort needs to be mounted to understand the specific problems of emerging markets in this area as well as to identify critical areas of legislation and relevant institutional arrangements needed to improve e-security worldwide. Without such efforts, the great potential offered by adopting e-finance and commerce can be significantly compromised, because the trust and confidence of market participants—so critical to transacting via the many different technologies now used—will be detrimentally affected.

The challenge for the World Bank in moving forward in this area is to assist countries to improve electronic safety and soundness in such essential financial system areas as payments systems, technology supervision, and most importantly within financial service providers, where investments in layered electronic security need to become standard business practice. This will help ensure that new technologies can be deployed safely in emerging markets and will deliver greater access to financial services to a wider proportion of the population. More broadly, the World Bank Group will need to examine how the generic issues in this complex area can be better incorporated in strategies for telecommunications and infrastructure, as well as for the financial sector and in country assistance strategies. The Bank Group looks forward to partnering with institutions throughout the world in raising awareness of and meeting this critical challenge

Cesare Calari
Vice President
Financial Sector Vice Presidency
The World Bank

---

2. Historically, the Internet was derived from ARPANET, which was designed in 1969 by the Advanced Research Projects Agency, Department of Defense.

ABSTRACT

This monograph and its technical annexes identify and discuss four key pillars that are necessary to foster a secure electronic environment and the safety and soundness of financial systems worldwide. Hence, it is intended for those formulating policies in the area of electronic security and those working with financial services providers (such as executives and management). The detailed annexes of this monograph are relevant for chief information and security officers and others who are responsible for securing network systems.

First, the monograph defines electronic finance (e-finance) and electronic security (e-security) and explains why these areas require attention. Next, it presents a picture of the emerging global security industry. Then, it develops a risk management framework to assist policymakers and practitioners in understanding the tradeoffs and risks inherent in using an open network infrastructure. It also provides examples of tradeoffs that may arise with respect to technological innovations, privacy, quality of service, and security in the design of an e-security policy framework. Finally, it outlines issues in four critical and interrelated areas that require attention in the building of an adequate e-security infrastructure. These are: (i) the legal, regulatory, and enforcement framework; (ii) external monitoring of e-security practices; (iii) public-private sector cooperation; and (iv) the business case for practicing layered e-security that will improve internal monitoring.

PREFACE

This monograph is the culmination of efforts over the past three years and builds upon a series of papers. These include: "Electronic Security: Risk Mitigation in Financial Transactions" (May 2002, June 2002, July 2002), *Electronic Finance: A New Approach to Financial Sector Development?* (2002), and *Mobile Risk Management: E-Finance in the Wireless Environment* (May 2002).

The authors wish to pay special thanks to James Nelms, Chief Information Security Officer in the Treasury Operations Department of the World Bank for his invaluable contributions, comments, and support. Special thanks as well to Tony Chew, Director, Technology Risk Supervision, Monetary Authority of Singapore, Hugh Kelly, Special Adviser for Global Banking for OCC and other members of the Basel Electronic Banking Group.

Beyond our special thanks to James Nelms and Yumi Nishiyama the authors would like also to thank the following individuals who have shared their time, background material, and provided valuable written and oral inputs: Julia Allen, Forrest Allison, Eric Bachman, Chris Bateman, Kenneth C. Brancik, Dan Caprio, Gerard Caprio, John Carlson, Tony Chew, Richard Clarke, Jerry Dixon, Dr. Dorothy Denning, Richard Downing, Ken Dunham, John Farber, Frank Fernandez, Rick Fleming, John Frazzini, John Frenkel, Jim Ferguson, Edward Gilbride, Sandra. E. Giuffre, Dr. Gary Jackson, Hugh Kelly, James H. Lau, Stephanie Lanz, Warren Lotzbire, Peter MacDoran, Michel Maechler, Linda McCarthy, Dr. Sarah McCue, Sallie McDonald, Joe McLeod, Shane Miller, Raj Nanavati, Kevin Nixon, Kari Oksanen, Brian Palma, Dr. Joseph Pelton, Peter Penfield, Richard Pethia, Larry Promisel, Bill Rogers, Ty Sagalow, James Savage, Phyllis Schneck, Troy Schumaker, Keith Schwalm, Don Skillman, Jack Smith, Mirion Sijtsema, Kurt Suhs, Gary Sullivan, Orson Swindle, Cornelius Tate, Dave Thomas, Tracey Vispoli, Mike Voorhees, Bob Weaver, Anne Wheeler, Lynn Wheeler, Bill Worley, Paul Zanker, and Richard Zechter.

In addition to these individuals, many private organizations and public agencies took time to share their ideas with the authors, both in person and in the annual Global Dialogues on Electronic Safety and Soundness held via the World Bank video conference facilities that included a discussion of e-security issues with officials from 15 countries in Latin America, Asia, and Africa. These 2002 Global Dialogues can be viewed at http://www.worldbank.org/wbi/B-SPAN/sub_e-security.htm. Proceedings from the third annual Global Dialogue held on September 10, 2003, can be accessed at: http://www.worldbank.org/wbi/B-SPAN/sub_electronic_safety.htm.

Finally special thanks are extended to Rose Vo who worked tirelessly to process this document and to Mark Feige for excellent editorial support.

EXECUTIVE SUMMARY

The Internet was designed as an open network distributed system to ensure the survival of information. It was not originally designed to handle commercial and financial transactions.[3] Yet, a mere decade after its widespread introduction into society, open network technology has increasingly become the primary tool by which governments, business and individuals all over the world are exchanging information. Ubiquitous access to the Internet is now expected by consumers, facilitated by readily accessible and affordable Internet connectivity and technologies such as wireless and cellular. Financial service providers in emerging economies are often finding it more advantageous to use technologies such as wireless or cellular for financial services, as opposed to landline telephone systems (Claessens, Glaessner, and Klingebiel, 2001). Over the past decade, financial services increasingly have moved their delivery channels from brick and mortar to these technologies because they are cheaper and provide better access, availability and quality of service.

Although the adoption of electronic finance (e-finance) and other electronic services offers emerging economies an opportunity to leapfrog, it also carries potential risk. Most of the crimes that exploit the vulnerabilities inherent in these technologies are not new—fraud, theft, impersonation, denial of service, and related extortion demands have plagued the financial services industry for years. However, the widespread use of these technologies exposes users to crimes of greater dimensions in terms of depth and scope. Open network technologies create a fertile environment for crimes of great magnitude and complexity to be committed very quickly. Countries need to understand the risks as well as the benefits that these technologies offer in order to protect themselves.

---

3. The Defense Advanced Research Projects Agency (DARPA) created the Internet in the 1960s to assure the United States that its communications system could survive a holocaust. Designed as an open network distributed system, it increased the chances of information surviving such an event. In the early 1990s, research and academic entities discovered it to be an effective, inexpensive means of communicating with colleagues.

Every day, governments, business, and consumers choose to use new technologies to build a global electronic economy. It is becoming apparent that the impacts of the use of these technologies on sustainable development deserve increased attention. This includes defining personal privacy and determining how to best protect it; deciding what levels of trust and confidence in service providers should be expected; determining how to measure these attributes; and deciding what protections should be provided by security measures. This monograph sets forth the proposition that e-security is crucial for e-finance to meet the expectations of business, government, and consumers and to deliver the potential benefits of leapfrogging through the use of these technologies. In essence, e-security protects the very heart of the new economy.

The objective of this publication is to lay out the framework for developing policies, procedures and processes for sustainable e-development. In doing so, the approach adopted does not rely solely on technology solutions, but views the issues relating to e-security as part of what should become "business process." This monograph has been developed in a multidisciplinary fashion precisely because knowledge of technology, business, law, economics, and finance must be brought together to develop a sensible and workable framework in this area. It is intended for policymakers working with financial services providers, especially executives and chief information and security officers. The publication is divided into two main parts, plus a glossary and six technical annexes. In the first part, the key issues associated with e-security are examined, which are then used to build a conceptual framework to highlight and analyze problem areas (chapters 1 and 2). In the second part, we present suggested policy responses, categorized into four pillars: regulation and enforcement; external and internal monitoring; certifications, policies, standards, and procedures; and public-private sector co-operation (chapters 3-6). The technical annexes reflect the views of many people who are active in the e-security industry; they should be of special use to those who administer e-security systems, bank examiners who evaluate the adequacy of e-security, and those who deal with the associated day-to-day risks inherent in both electronic transactions and data storage.

What is Electronic Security?

Speaking broadly, electronic security (e-security) is any tool, technique, or process used to protect a system's information assets. E-security enhances or adds value to an unprotected network, and is composed of soft and hard infrastructures. The soft infrastructure components are the policies, processes, protocols, and guidelines that protect the system and the data from compromise. The hard infrastructure consists of hardware and software needed to protect the system and data from threats to security from inside or outside the organization.

As a business principle, the appropriate degree of e-security used for any activity should be proportional to the activity's underlying value. E-security is a risk-management and risk-mitigation tool. Today's growing worldwide e-security industry provides a wide variety of targeted security services ranging from active content filtering, firewalls, intrusion detection, penetration testing, cryptographic tools to authentication mechanisms. Given that the Internet and other open network technologies basically are broadcasting mediums transmitting across an unprotected network, it is critical that security be added to assure that the information is sent only to the intended recipients, rather than accessible to the world at large.

E-Security is an increasingly important issue as technology plays an ever greater role in the delivery of financial services and promotion of e-commerce—and it would be worthwhile for policymakers to appreciate the urgency with which this issue should be addressed. By 2005, it is estimated that the share of banking done online will be close to 50 percent in industrial countries and will rise from one to almost ten percent in emerging markets (Claessens, Glaessner, Klingebiel, 2002). In both developed and emerging markets, the key sectors of the payment systems are migrating to an Internet based platform. There can be little doubt that in emerging markets it is even more critical that efforts be undertaken to ensure the trust and confidence of e-market participants. The safety and soundness of their electronic transactions is an essential infrastructure needed to support sustainable development and to realize the benefits of the new economy. Moreover, this is an issue with truly global implications—already thieves are taking advantage of weak regulatory environments to base their operations in one country, but attack institutions in others. As financial markets become increasingly integrated, the systemic risks of such attacks increase, and it will be emerging markets, with the least financial and institutional depth, that prove to be most vulnerable.

The Problems of Economic Incentives Posed by Electronic Security

In addition to providing e-security, a small number of vendors supply a multitude of interlinking services to e-finance providers (for example, financial service companies) in many countries. The cross-linking ownership raises many complex questions, such as the need to review the adequacy of competition policy, as well as the potential for, and ramifications of, multiple conflicts of interest. More important may be issues of the impact of ownership concentration on systemic risk, and the lack of incentives to report security breaches accurately. Convergence of the telecommunications industry and the financial services sector through the Internet heightens the importance of, and the necessity for, sound public policy and informed regulation to ensure that government, business, and people continue to have access to secure financial services.

Beyond the issues raised by cross-linked ownership of the e-security and telecommunications industries, there are even more basic issues to address in designing an e-security public policy framework.

First, telecommunications, energy, and financial services are crucial components of the critical infrastructures in every country. Disrupting these infrastructures for even a short period of time can cause significant economic and other damage to a country.[4] Each of these infrastructures relies heavily on electronics. Given the risks that electronic vulnerabilities pose to a country's critical infrastructures, e-security is an essential risk management tool, important in promoting and protecting the public interest and welfare. There is a fundamental public interest case for a government to regulate its financial services. The case has grown even stronger with these technologies so as to ensure that the financial system and its related components use the necessary level of e-security and access remains stable.

Second, a market failure is occurring because inadequate incentives exist within the workplace—as well as the regulatory and enforcement arenas—to require the timely and accurate reporting of e-security breaches. Clearly, regulators have a role to play in overcoming this dilemma. By requiring timely and accurate reporting with sufficiently strong penalties for failing to report, management and/or employees are given an incentive structure that encourages the reporting of breach incidents to appropriate authorities.[5]

Third, the reach of the Internet and open network technologies implies that access to financial services is global and its availability is no longer constrained by borders. The feared domino effect and contagion experienced so often in the financial services industries in the 1980s and 1990s serve to remind us of the dangers of an over-reliance on any given aspect of finance and the ensuing disproportionate concentration of risk. Hence mitigating e-security risks requires unprecedented efforts to promote collective action within countries (for example, interagency and public-private sector cooperation) as well as between countries by market participants, regulators and law enforcement.

---

4. The blackout that occurred on the East Coast of the United States in August 2003 is a prime example of the cascading effects that result from the exploitation or disruption of a critical infrastructure vulnerability by whatever means. In fact, the January 2003 Slammer worm disabled the proper functioning of the Ohio Davis-Besse nuclear power plant. For further information see Poulsen 2003.

5. However, even in this case the inherent reputation damage that can accompany the reporting of a breach inherently will make reporting of accurate information difficult if this is part of compliance versus part of good business practice and process.

Fourth, formulating e-security policy must balance a number of complex competing concerns; in the end, e-security cannot be seen as an end in itself, but rather as only one aspect of risk management. Given the interconnected nature of the global payments system it is a crucial fundamental component of global risk mitigation. The domino effect of a single e-bank failure could have significant ramifications. Tradeoffs exist between the costs of providing financial services, the size of a bank's transactions, and the sophistication of the e-security arrangements that may be required to mitigate the risks. In addition, it is necessary to carefully weigh essential tradeoffs between the paradox of using security to protect privacy versus a barrier to access. These tradeoffs cannot be decided in isolation. The public and private sectors must work through these issues on a collaborative basis.

A Proactive Policy Response

In light of these four complex public policy issues any approach to designing a public policy framework to improve electronic safety and soundness will need to rest on four fundamental pillars.

Pillar 1: Strengthening the overall legal, regulatory, and enforcement framework within and across countries.

Pillar 2: Improving external monitoring of e-security risks at a variety of levels that include: improvements in technology supervision (on and off-site); better monitoring by private insurance companies; and improving the education about these risks at the level of final users in companies and among consumers.

Pillar 3: Establishing public/private partnerships within and across countries in two critical areas: improving the basic database for e-security incident information worldwide; and improving and gradually harmonizing the certification processes and standards in e-security in a careful manner that allows for rapid dynamic technological change inherent in this area.

Pillar 4: Strengthening internal monitoring, by clearly identifying business objectives that link the costs of not securing a business to the potential and actual savings from e-security. Improve incentives for financial service providers and vendors to adopt e-security as a required element in any online business process and use, and to adopt better e-security practices such as the twelve layer approach advocated in this monograph.

CHAPTER 1

INTRODUCTION TO E-SECURITY

Is it a fact...that, by means of electricity, the world of matter has become a great nerve, vibrating thousands of miles in a breathless point of time? Rather, the globe is a vast head, a brain, instinct with intelligence! Or shall we say it is itself a thought, nothing but a thought...

—Nathaniel Hawthorne, 1851

Overview

The efficient delivery of financial and other services is an important and necessary step on the road to sustainable development, helping to promote economic growth and reduce poverty. However, the construction of an adequate and crisis resistant infrastructure is not an easy task, and a poorly-designed system can expose an economy to a multitude of problems (World Bank 2001). For example, unlike the industrialized economies most emerging markets suffer from an inadequate distribution network for financial services. However, the growth of new technologies—such as wireless telecommunications and the Internet—present the possibility for emerging markets to "leapfrog" this stage of development. In other words, by using these technologies, emerging markets can build an electronic infrastructure for services—as industrialized countries are now doing—without using scare resources as extensively to build and staff a physical infrastructure. However, while technology holds the potential to help support economic development, it can also allow criminals more efficient and quicker ways to commit old crimes, such as fraud and theft.

In the absence of proper safeguards, the increasing dependence on online systems can pose a serious threat to a country's economic viability. Online attacks are blind to national borders; foreign hackers can compromise a nation's financial infrastructure and pilfer millions of dollars, often effectively beyond the reach of domestic authorities. This type of compromise presents a grave threat to countries where financial institutions are already fragile and susceptible to large-scale ripple effects from any economic impact. In most emerging markets, there is a fairly high degree of concentration in both the financial sector and within telecommunications and Internet service providers (ISPs), making these economies particularly vulnerable to attack. Moreover, these threats and vulnerabilities cannot be contained within domestic borders.

One of the key principles of any financial system is trust—when two parties undertake a financial transaction, they need to be confident that it is valid and will be honored. If you write a check, or authorize a payment on your credit card, you are expecting to receive something—a new camera, some stocks, or reduced liability on a debt—in return. You are unlikely to put money in a bank unless you are confident that the money will still be there when you want to make a withdrawal. With brick and mortar institutions, confidence in the security of customer deposits was built with measures ranging from armed guards to deter bank robbers, to government regulations to ensure that funds were managed properly. Many of the same principles used to secure assets in a traditional financial infrastructure are still applicable in an electronic environment—but the techniques used may be so different that this is not readily apparent. For example, the function of the armed guard is now undertaken by sophisticated software that denies access to hackers—modern day thieves that prefer to use a mouse (maybe sitting comfortably in a foreign country), rather than a gun or acetylene torch, to get access to other peoples' money. The lock on a bank safe is, in effect, a mechanical puzzle, to which the key is the solution; e-finance uses complex mathematical puzzles as digital locks, and algorithms as keys. A manager at a small bank branch can rely on visual recognition to allow authorized employees access to confidential files, but a retinal scan may now be required to open these files across the Internet.

The provision of a sound and efficient financial infrastructure may be considered as a public good, but public and private incentives are unlikely to be fully aligned without some form of government intervention into market mechanisms. For example, are financial services providers given proper incentives to fully share timely and accurate information with law enforcement on security breaches? If not, is there a form of market failure taking place in this area within the financial services industry? What roles can the government, private market participants, and the e-security industry play in accurately measuring the extent of e-security risk within and across countries? We consider the appropriate role that the government should play in setting policies, standards, and guidelines for e-security, which also entails striking the proper balance between fostering technological innovation and establishing e-security standards.

As with bricks and mortar institutions, there are appropriate roles for both the government and the private sector in the provision of e-security, and we suggest actions that might be taken to facilitate public-private cooperation to remedy the situation. In particular, the private insurance industry appears to have an important role to play, especially in emerging markets, which often lack extensive human capital and capacity in regulatory agencies. Many developing countries lack the regulatory or supervisory agency necessary to assess vulnerabilities, make appropriate security recommendations, and enforce compliance at the local level. Furthermore, the lack of regulatory controls often serves as an obstacle for existing agencies to properly address the need for an e-security framework. One key issue that should not be underestimated is the scarcity of trained personnel to undertake such functions—both in the public and private sectors. This affects both industrialized and developing countries, but particularly the latter.

Objectives of the Monograph

This document examines the role of e-security in helping translate the potential of electronic finance into a positive and crisis-resistant force for development. We have three central objectives. The first is to define e-security and to discuss why this issue is becoming important worldwide. The second is to offer an economic incentive framework to use in addressing the problems posed by e-security, with particular attention to financial services provided by banks. The third is to identify four key policy pillars that every country should construct and maintain in order to develop a secure electronic environment. There are, of course, many other issues of e-finance—such as the impact on competition policy or the efficacy of monetary policy—which are outside the scope of this monograph. While most of the material in this report is of global relevance, inevitably most of the data and analysis reflects the state of play in the more advanced Asian economies (such as

Singapore and Hong Kong) or the OECD—especially some European countries and the United States—as many of these countries have had the most experience in e-finance and e-security. Clearly, more research is needed to understand the specific problems of emerging markets as well as to identify critical areas of legislation and relevant institutional arrangements needed to improve e-security standards worldwide.

Four Main Messages

- The Internet and new communications technologies offer emerging markets opportunities to boost economic growth. However, there are also considerable risks to exchanging digital information across these broadcast mediums, and governments need to develop effective policies to promote e-security.
- Businesses—whether providers and/or users or electronic services—are the first and best line of defense. We advocate a layered approach to e-security, but it is important to remember that e-security is primarily about techniques, not technology.
- E-security is a public good. The incentives facing businesses do not always align with the public interest, and some form of government regulation is warranted. However, governments will not be able implement effective policies without the active and positive support of companies.
- The Internet is global, and so is cyber crime. There can be no real e-security without intergovernmental cooperation on a global basis.

Outline of the Monograph

This monograph is divided into two main parts, followed by six technical annexes and a glossary. The first part (chapters 1 and 2) highlights the key structures and dynamics of e-security, while the second part (chapters 3-6) details four pillars to serve as the foundation on which public policy towards electronic security should be built.[6]

In Chapter 1, we define e-security and explain why it is important. There has been rapid growth in e-finance in recent years, reflecting convenience for users of services, and cost savings for their providers. However, the conduits through which these transactions are conducted—notably the Internet and wireless networks—are insecure, and electronic fraud is now growing even faster than electronic commerce (e-commerce). In many emerging markets there is often an extensive cross-linking ownership of the e-security and e-finance industries. This raises many complex questions, such as the need to review competition policy, as well as the potential for, and ramifications of, multiple conflicts of interest. More important may be issues that relate to the integrity of the services provided, as well as incentives to report security breaches accurately.

In Chapter 2, we address the policy implications of these structures and dynamics. We start by arguing the public interest case for public sector intervention into e-security. The financial services and payment systems are critical to the operation of other sectors of the economy, and hence e-security is considered to be a public good. E-security appears to suffer from classic market failure, particularly the asymmetric access to (and understanding of) information technology, and an incentive structure that does not prompt private sector operators to accurately report security breaches. Information technology is subject to large increasing returns to scale, and there is a tendency towards excessive concentration—particularly in hosting companies and Internet service providers—especially in emerging markets. Given the global reach of both the Internet and financial services, there is a strong case for collective action both within countries (for example, public-private cooperation, and interagency actions) and across borders.

However, while there is a case for public-sector involvement in e-finance and e-security, governments should not—indeed, probably could not—effectively regulate these sectors without the

---

6. These four pillars represent a consolidation of the eight pillars that some readers may associate with earlier iterations of our research.

active co-operation of interested private parties. Excessive government regulation would stifle innovation in this dynamic field, undermining much of the potential that these sectors have for economic growth. In addition, given the truly global basis of e-finance, a heavy regulatory burden would induce firms to move their activities offshore. Moreover, the huge volume of e-financial transactions suggests that determined private parties could hide illicit activities. Finally, given the complex and rapidly changing technology involved in e-security, governments may find it prohibitive to attract and retain the scarce and well-paid staff required for comprehensive oversight. In framing a public-policy response to the challenges posed by e-security, a government must determine when it is imperative to regulate, but also when it is more appropriate to act in concert with the private sector—for example, by providing information or assigning liability—to create an incentive structure that encourages private firms to act in the public good. From this perspective, we argue that there are four pillars on which public policy towards e-security should be built: government legislation and regulation; external monitoring; collective action; and internal or private monitoring.

The second part of the monograph gives a more detailed exposition of these four policy pillars, with one chapter accorded to each pillar. It is important to recognize that reforms in all four of these areas are needed in most emerging markets, and that reforms must be designed so as to ensure that they are mutually reinforcing. Work in design of reform must be multi-disciplinary to assure success, and will need to include the legal profession, finance and risk professionals, economists, actuaries, and persons with the requisite understanding of technology. There are many instances where lack of such an approach has resulted in less than adequate frameworks.

- *Pillar 1: Legal Framework and Enforcement.* Incorporate e-security concerns into laws, policies and practices. Notable areas of concern include: defining and recognizing the legal validity of electronic signatures; licensing, and regulating payment systems; and enacting privacy, money-laundering and cyber crime laws. Perhaps as important as the legal framework will be the need to enforce the provisions of e-security laws within, and across, national boundaries.
- *Pillar 2: External Monitoring of E-security Practices.* Improve the incentives for better e-security in financial service providers. In many emerging markets at least three parties have a role to play in monitoring and creating incentives for better e-security. The regulators and supervisors; the insurance companies, via the policies they can write and the related monitoring; and the public at large, including those that work in companies or financial service providers, and the final consumers of financial services.
- *Pillar 3: Public-Private Sector Cooperation.* Improve the nature and design of public-private partnerships within and across countries in two critical areas: improving the basic database for e-security incident information worldwide; and improving and gradually harmonizing the certification processes and dynamic standards established in the e-security area. Two categories that require particular attention in terms of certification are e-security service providers and the transaction elements in e-finance.
- *Pillar 4: Internal Monitoring: Layered E-Security.* Improve incentives at the level of the financial service providers and vendors for adoption of better e-security by adoption of an explicit twelve layer approach to e-security as part of day to day business process. This will not only need to include the processes to deal with Internet based technology but will also have to address areas such as wireless technologies. Specific layers range from the need to have a Chief Information Security Officer and an incident response plan, to finding the most appropriate type of firewall and encryptions systems.

What Is Electronic Security and Why Is It Needed?

E-security can be described on the one hand as those policies, guidelines, processes, and actions needed to enable electronic transactions to be carried out with a minimum risk of breach, intrusion, or theft. On the other hand, e-security is any tool, technique, or process used to protect a system's information assets. Information is a valuable strategic asset that must be managed and protected accordingly. Appropriate security means mitigation of the risk for the underlying transaction is in proportion to its value. Thus, security is a risk-management and risk-mitigation tool. E-security enhances or adds value to an unprotected network, and is composed of both a "soft" and a "hard" infrastructure. Soft infrastructure components are those policies, processes, protocols, and guidelines that create the protective environment to keep the system and the data from compromise. The hard infrastructure consists of the actual hardware and software needed to protect the system and its data from external and internal threats to security.

The Potential Growth of Electronic Transactions

The volume and variety of electronic financial services have increased significantly. The use of the electronic medium to do business, whether online or through remote mechanisms, has spread rapidly over the past decade. Countries, not just consumers, are becoming connected. As is evident in Figure 1.1, "these new technologies not only allow countries to leapfrog in connectivity, they also open new channels for delivering e-financial services" (Claessens, Glaessner, and Klingebiel, 2001). Since the mid-1990s, investment in financial services technology has focused on online banking and brokerage services to increase convenience and to reduce costs.

By 2005, the share of banking conducted online could rise from 8.5 percent to 50 percent in industrial countries, and grow from 1 percent to 10 percent in emerging markets (Claessens, Glaessner, and Klingebiel 2002). If better connectivity is available, online banking transactions in emerging markets could rise even further to 20 percent in 2005 (Glaessner, Claessens, and Klingebiel 2001). Some estimate that $6.3 trillion of bank-to-bank transactions will be conducted online by 2005 (Jupiter Communications 2001).

A parallel trend to the global use of e-finance is the adoption of new technologies that can act to expand the scope for electronic finance and access to financial services. Emerging markets increasingly find it more advantageous to use these "new" technologies, such as wireless or cellular technology, for e-finance as opposed to the Internet or a landline. Table 1.1 indicates that in a variety of emerging markets, wireless technology, as measured by cell phone penetration, is rapidly outstripping Internet penetration.

Electronic Risks

The access and availability that the Internet and new communications technologies provide are two way streets—interconnectedness allows us to reap mutual benefits, but also forces us to bear common risks to critical infrastructures. Reliance on computers for back-end operations, and integration with the Internet and other open network technologies as the front-end interface, allows anyone to enter a system and disrupt, disable or corrupt business, government, education, hospitals, financial services and any other sectors that rely on computers as their business engine. Privacy, security, safety and soundness are all at risk, as economic pressures to increase speed and reduce costs force business to use new technologies to integrate functions and services in order to compete.

These same technologies also facilitate more efficient and quicker ways to commit old crimes such as fraud and theft. Remote access, high-quality graphics and printing, and new multipurpose tools and platforms provide greater means to commit such crimes as theft and impersonation online (Jupiter Communications 2001). Disturbingly, as the technology becomes more complex, a perpetrator needs fewer skills to commit these crimes. While the art of online penetrations (that is, hacking) was once a highly sophisticated skill, now underground hacker websites provide multifaceted tools necessary to break into financial platforms. Perhaps the most frightening risk associated with the convergence of technology and crime is the speed and magnitude with which the crimes can be undertaken. For example, in the past it would have taken months or perhaps even years for highly organized criminals to steal 50,000 credit card numbers. Today, one criminal using tools that are freely available on the Web can hack into a database and steal that number of identities in seconds.

FIGURE 1.1: E-FINANCE PENETRATION: 2000 AND PROJECTED RATES FOR 2005 AND 2010

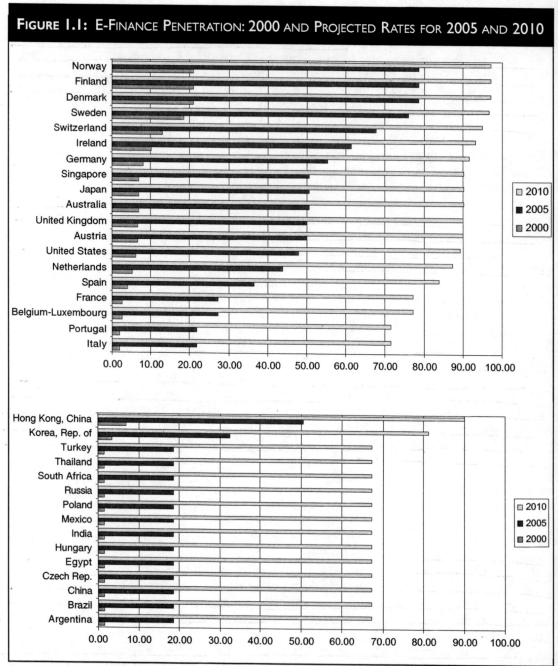

Note: The figures show projections based on takeoff years with better connectivity. The projections assume that all emerging markets have the same connectivity rating as in today's lowest-ranked industrial country, 6 (or better if their current rating is already higher); thus, the projections lead to the same minimum level of penetration in each emerging market.

Source: Authors' calculations. Claessens, Glaessner, and Klingebiel 2002.

TABLE 1.1: GLOBAL CONNECTIVITY TRENDS

Country	Number of mobile phone subscribers (Millions)	Percentage of population who are mobile or cellular subscribers	Percentage of population who are Internet users
Developed Countries[a]	45.0	64	39
Australia	11.2	58	34
Finland	4.0	78	43
France	35.9	61	26
United States	127.0	44	50
United Kingdom	47.0	78	40
Developing Countries[a]	21.6	15	7
Brazil	28.7	17	5
Bulgaria	1.6	19	8
Cambodia	.2	2	<1
China	144.8	11	3
Egypt	2.8	4	1
Guatemala	1.1	10	2
India	5.7	1	1
Indonesia	5.3	2	2
Mexico	20.1	20	3
Philippines	10.6	14	3
Republic of Korea	29.0	61	51
South Africa	9.2	21	7

a. These are averages for developed and developing countries respectively.
Source: International Telecommunications Union, *World Telecommunications Indicators Database 2001.*

Upward trends in cyber crime statistics reveal that criminals are in fact taking advantage of both the speed and capabilities which new technologies offer (see Annex A for a detailed listing of major e-security incidents made public). Attacks on servers doubled in 2001 from 2000. The 2002 CSI/FBI Computer Crime Survey[7] reported that 90 percent of organizations in the United States (including large companies, medical institutions, and government agencies) detected security breaches. Moreover, serious security breaches such as theft of proprietary information, financial fraud, denial of service attacks, and network compromises were reported by 70 percent of organizations in 2001. Eighty-four percent of the surveyed organizations cited the Internet connection as the critical point of attack (FBI and CSI 2003). The following CERT chart illustrates an upwards trend in reported cyber crime incidents.

In addition to Internet service interruption, cyber crime incidents can also put significant financial losses at stake. The 2003 CSI/FBI Computer Crime and Security Survey indicates that

---

7. For additional information, please see: http://www.gocsi.com/

FIGURE1.2: NUMBER OF INCIDENTS REPORTED BY CERT, WORLDWIDE

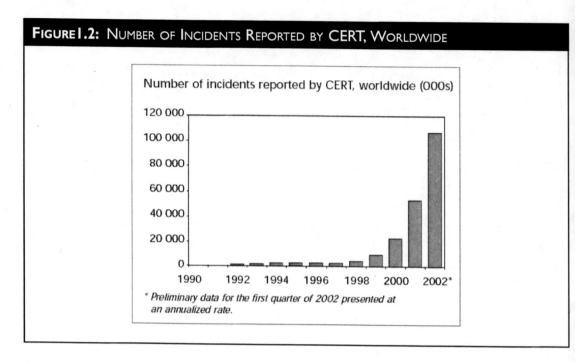

Number of incidents reported by CERT, worldwide (000s)

* Preliminary data for the first quarter of 2002 presented at
an annualized rate.

---

total annual losses reported by 251 organizations amounted to nearly $202 million. The Internet Data Corporation recently reported that more than 57 percent of all hack attacks last year were targeted towards the financial sector.[8] A Bank for International Settlements 2002 report on loss events surveyed 89 international banks and determined that those 89 banks sustained 47,000 loss events in 2002.[9] Sixty percent of those loss events occurred in retail banking and over 42 percent of losses were attributed to external fraud. In short, without strong security controls, banks risk the possibility of financial loss, legal liability, and harm to their reputation.[10]

Several pervasive venues for electronic attacks in the area of e-financial services have been publicly documented, but continue to be problematic. The most frequent problems in this arena are: (i) insider abuse, (ii) identity theft, (iii) fraud, and (iv) breaking and entering, often conducted by hackers. Though these areas must be addressed and risks mitigated, there continues to be a relative lack of accurate information about intrusions and associated losses. This deficiency in reporting intrusion to regulators and law enforcement is the fundamental reason why issues related to e-security are not recognized as an immediate priority. In the United States, a 2001 CSI/FBI Computer Crime Survey identified the following five major reasons organizations did not report electronic intrusions to law enforcement:

- Negative publicity;
- Negative information competitors would use to their advantage—for example, to steal customers;
- Lack of awareness that they could report events;
- Decision that a civil remedy seemed best;
- Fear among IT personnel of reporting incident because of job security.

---

8. www.idc.com. 2002 has been a worse year for hacking in the United States than 2001. Reported incidents in 2002 have surpassed 2001 totals to grow to over 83,359 (www.cert.org).

9. Bank of International Settlements, www.bis.org.

10. The United States Financial Intelligence Unit's (FINCEN) most recent report depicts a 300 percent surge in hacking upon US banks over the past eight months; 3,229 Suspicious Activity Reports (SARs) for computer intrusions were reported between September 15, 2002 to September 15, 2003. Please see Annex B of this monograph for additional information.

Box 1.1: MONEY LAUNDERING

Many governments acknowledge the large inherent difficulty in estimating the full magnitude of the money laundering (ML) problem. For example, former IMF Director Michel Camdessus estimated the global volume of ML at between two to five percent of global GDP, a range encompassing $600 billion to $1.8 trillion. One example of how this phenomenon is growing via the Internet are the operations of E-gold. This site provides users with an electronic currency, issued by E-gold Ltd., a Nevis corporation, 100 percent backed at all times by gold bullion in allocated storage. E-gold was created in response to a need for a global currency on the World Wide Web. E-gold operates in units of account by weight of metal, not US dollars or any other national currency unit. Weight units have a precise, invariable, internationally recognized definition. Additionally, precious metals, gold in particular, enjoy a long history of monetary use around the world. Thus, E-gold is being used for international transactions. Here a "non-financial institution is becoming a de facto money remitter or intermediary. No real records are stored, few diligence standards are followed, no specific reports on suspicious activity are filed, etc. E-gold sells the ability for people to exchange money, thus circumventing the financial institutions and their corresponding oversight/regulatory mechanisms. Intangible services like consulting are common facades for the disbursement of funds between organized criminal syndicates. These entities usually establish themselves in jurisdictions where secrecy laws prevent adequate disclosure. For example, E-Gold utilizes the Internet and nations like Luxemburg and other neutral regimes to base their servers.

Source: Bank staff. The E-gold website was used as reference, at http://www.e-gold.com/.

Public awareness is the critical first step. However, there are inherent reasons why it will be difficult to address these issues without some public sector role.

Decomposing the Risks Associated with Electronic Transactions
Technological advances have created a much more complex interrelationship between e-security and risks of different types. Attempts to systematically see how electronic transactions impact the old risk paradigm highlights some new sources of risk, although the basic categories of risk are not new, and financial service providers have always viewed them with concern.

Systemic Risk. One of the most important links between e-finance, e-security, and risk is the systemic impact that the associated risks can have on the related payment systems through interaction with compromised networks. Appropriate security should be proportional to the value of underlying transactions. For this reason, in the case of large-value clearinghouses, extensive e-security is or should be in place. Any intrusion or interruption in a payment system's electronic messaging could easily create significant system-wide exposure. Recent trends whereby major large-value payments networks are increasingly moving to voice over Internet protocol suggest that increasing care will be needed in the security of such systems as SWIFT[11] because it has moved from a closed legacy mainframe to an Internet technology backbone.[12] Another source of systemic risk that could become more important—especially in emerging markets—relates to the concentration or single point of failure associated with hosting services that are often provided by only one company to all the major banks (see Box 2.2 in the next chapter). Hence a compromising of this third party provider can cause extensive problems for the banks.

---

11. Society for Worldwide Interbank Financial Telecommunication (SWIFT). For additional information, please see: http://www.swift.com/.

12. Specifically it was moved from a X.25 legacy mainframe to an Internet protocol network. This means that Swift will be using digital lines rather than analog lines as well as an open network architecture in order to transmit messages relating to electronic fund transfers.

Operational Risk. Inadequate e-security can result in interruptions of service and—in some cases, depending on the nature and adequacy of backup systems—even the loss of critical information. As part of managing operational risk, financial services providers worldwide need to pay greater attention to the way they secure their IT systems. The risks involved in e-security often relate to extortion and reputation risk, which usually are not specifically taken into account in the allocations set aside to cover operational risk.

Risk of Identity Theft, Fraud, and Extortion. Penetration by hackers often leads to extortion demands. In addition, identity theft is a growing concern for e-finance service providers. Its growth has been rapid, but as in the case of hacking, it is not reported in a timely manner or accurately; thus, its growth may be considerably understated. This problem is not unique to financial services—it also affects the integrity and reliability of the credit information gathered and assessed by credit bureaus, downstream to credit decisions.

Risk of money laundering. Financial Action Task Force (FATF) principle XIII stipulates that knowledge of one's customers is critical in deterring money laundering, but unfortunately the very nature of the Internet and with the proliferation of e-finance, "know thy customer" has become extremely difficult in cyber space. The existence of special financial service providers like "E-gold" coupled with the anonymity provided by the Internet hamper efforts to curtail money laundering. Beyond the risks of identity theft or extortion, the use of the Internet and a large variety of casino websites along with other forms of quasi payment arrangements over the Internet can be shown to facilitate what amounts to the electronic laundering of money (Mussington, et al. 1998).

Risk of Credit Quality Deterioration for the Financial Services Provider. Although not often acknowledged, a substantial denial of service or long-term intrusion that results in fraud, impersonation, or corruption of data can effectively cripple a bank's operations for a period of time. If that time is sufficient, it can irreparably damage the bank's reputation and possibly compromise its credit standing. Because market participants' confidence is critical, such an event could have a pernicious impact in a relatively short time.

Risks in Failure Resolution. A final form of risk associated with the delivery of e-financial services and security relates to the risks introduced when a brick-and-clicks or wholly Internet-based bank fails. Here the process of closure itself is difficult to define and even more difficult to implement if the entity has its servers in offshore centers. Closure in this case would require extensive cross-border coordination among authorities in what could be numerous disparate jurisdictions. Cooperation, and thus closure, may not be feasible with the speed that can be applied in the case of a non-Internet-based bank. At the point of intervention, if the records and other essential information about digital assets are not preserved under well-defined guidelines, and if they are not secured or cannot be retrieved from servers, then, at the very least, claimants' rights may be compromised.

E-security in Emerging Markets

Increased worldwide connectivity to an open, networked infrastructure and the subsequent shift to online transactions creates new vulnerabilities and risks worldwide. Electronic risk is not only been present in developed economies it is also becoming prevalent in emerging markets (see Box 1.2). E-security issues are of particular importance in emerging markets where technological capabilities offer potential leapfrogging opportunities, but where concurrently, a lack of a technical workforce, education, and legal and regulatory infrastructure can thwart the safety and soundness of the IT environment. Because the sustainability of the digital infrastructure is determined by its level of security, including both the physical security of the Internet, and the enabling environment consisting of sufficient legal and regulatory frameworks, addressing security needs upon an infrastructure's development is of critical importance.

Barriers to Implementing E-Security in Emerging Markets

Through a number of case studies, the World Bank has identified several areas that can affect the extent to which emerging countries will effectively implement e-security measures. These are:

Box 1.2: SELECTED COUNTRY CASE STUDIES

The growing worldwide problems associated with e-security have impacted many emerging markets. Below are just a few selected examples.

In **Brazil**, where the information and telecom infrastructure is highly developed, and more widely accessible than in many other developing markets, electronic transactions have rapidly gained in popularity. The Brazilian Payment System (SPB) launched in 2002 operates over an Internet technology backbone and e-banking is offered over wireless devices. The Brazilian government is a major promoter of online technologies, as evident in the number of online services offered on the government portal, Redegoverno (http://www.redegoverno.gov.br). As an example of its widespread diffusion, an article from 2001 notes that 90 percent of all submitted income tax declarations were done online (International Trade Administration 2001). Brazil's increase in legitimate online activities came with its respective illegitimate, or malicious, activities. Cyber crime in Brazil leapt from 5,997 incidents in 1999 to 25,092 incidents a mere two years later, in 2002.[13] Recognizing the need for security, Brazil created the NBSO (the Brazilian Computer Emergency Response Team) in 1997 to raise public awareness and share information on cyber threats.

In **South Africa**, widespread technological diffusion is reflected in their high penetration rates, which are among the top in Africa. But, high connectivity rates and the diffusion of online capabilities creates a prime target for hackers. Recently, a hacker infiltrated ABSA Bank, one of South Africa's largest banks. Over 500,000 Rand was stolen from customer accounts. The country recently adopted regulatory initiatives, including the recent Electronic Communication and Transaction (ECT) Law. This law stipulates punishments for many forms of cyber crimes, including hacking. Additionally, many in the private sector are using Public Key Infrastructure (PKI) in an effort to assuage their growing numbers of security intrusions, electronic thefts, and denial of service attacks. However, similar to Brazil, which also set forth government-sanctioned provisions for a national PKI system, an over-reliance upon PKI can prove problematic if other critical layers of security are neglected.

The geographical landscape of the **Philippines** with its many islands and rugged terrain make this country an ideal place for cellular infrastructure growth. Difficult and costly to build a physical telecommunications network, the rapid and inexpensive cellular infrastructure creates leapfrogging opportunities to bring telecommunications and financial services to remote regions. However, increased connectivity does not come without risks. This country produced the creator of one of the most notorious worms and expensive viruses, the Love Bug, otherwise known as the I Love You virus. Ramifications of this virus were felt worldwide, and at a cost to the global community of several billion dollars. The types of vulnerabilities that can be introduced as Philippine citizens increasingly use cell phones as devices to not only obtain account information at banks but also confirm trades or purchases of government securities as now being planned will also present challenges.

Source: Authored by Yumi Nishiyama, World Bank Integrator Group. The statistics on Brazil were provided by the Comite Gestor de Internet Brazil. Additional information was garnered from International Trade Administration 2001. The information is based upon country case studies conducted by the Integrator Group, yet to be released.

■ Rapid technological growth without proper regard to security.
■ The lack of education on electronic risks to regulators and supervisors.
■ The lack of institutional infrastructure, including legal, regulatory and law enforcement.
■ The lack of social capital and technological "brain drain."
■ A high level of industry concentration in the telecommunications industry.

First, many developing countries are quick to embrace technologies, such as wireless, for the potential benefits they offer. These technologies are often adopted without proper consideration

---

13. These statistics were provided by Comite Gestor da Internet—Brazil.

to, or understanding of, the inherent risks (Kellermann 2002a). Or, countries adopt inherently risky technologies, relying on single silver bullet solutions such as Public Key Infrastructure (PKI) to mitigate all risks rather than adopting a multi-layered approach that secures each component of the technologies in play. Furthermore, due to limited access to information technology, a number of developing countries provide online services to deliver personal information and services through public kiosks, Internet cafes, or other public spaces where multiple persons use the same computer. Consumers use these computers without realizing that they are potentially bargaining away their privacy and as the confidentiality and integrity of their information for convenient access, speed, and reduced cost.

Second, a major problem is the lack of awareness of the dangers inherent in the digital environment. Many developing countries lack the educational materials to properly train citizens on risks and mitigation techniques. As a result, users do not take steps to mitigate threats in the online environment so that commerce can occur with minimal risk. Simultaneously, a lack of awareness proves to be a key limitation for e-finance; customers do not trust online transactions, which thus inhibits e-commercial activity. Without proper education, system administrators in emerging countries can face a critical handicap in their ongoing security efforts. This serves to weaken their technological infrastructures, making them vulnerable to cyber attacks, and ultimately affecting their chances of succeeding in the global marketplace.

Third, many developing countries lack the institutional structure to implement, monitor and enforce proper e-security measures. Laws, including cyber crime and e-commerce, must be restructured to create better incentives for proper e-security (see chapter 3). Furthermore, even if the regulation does exist, a deficiency in the enforcement capabilities for these laws can greatly hinder their effectiveness.

Fourth, many countries do not have a real e-security industry, which in part reflects the concentration in many emerging markets in the information and communication technology industry, especially in the telecommunications sector. Here, the hosting, service provision, and ownership of physical communications lines are often in the hands of one or a few entities. This concentration of risk results in an unacceptable level of systemic risk. In such a case, one cyber attack can ripple across a number of industries if there is only one critical point of failure (for example, all the banks and other companies use the same hosting services provided by a dominant telecom/cellular provider). Conflicts of interest also occur that hinder incentives for such a conglomerate telecom and e-security provider to provide adequate e-security in the services rendered.

Finally, deficiencies in the institutional structure for security include a basic lack of human capital in these technical areas of technology risk management. Many emerging countries in particular lack the human capital necessary to assess e-security vulnerabilities, to make recommendations to remediate, and to enforce compliance with cyber laws. Many well trained technical persons in emerging markets in such areas are lured to higher paying jobs in foreign countries. As a result, limited research and development occurs in e-security for many emerging countries.

CHAPTER 2

POLICY FRAMEWORK

C hapter 1 suggested that e-security considerations are a concern for the confidence of users in both developed and emerging market countries. Moreover, many emerging market economies are rapidly developing technology backbones in many areas of infrastructure. that are Internet based, and which are frequently using other technologies in conjunction with the Internet such as Voice Over Internet Protocol (VOIP), cellular, and even satellite technology. In the area of financial services, large value payments or electronic data interchange between companies, electronic benefit transfers, and electronic trade confirmations have been migrating to the use of the Internet, and even wireless technology—and these will gradually become the rule, not the exception. These applications will not only extend to various forms of payments services, but have also begun to be more prevalent in the areas of savings instruments and credit given online distribution and electronic data storage of digital information and assets. Under these circumstances ensuring trust becomes essential. This chapter outlines some of the reasons why public policy needs to address the issues raised by e-security, if the benefits of technology are to be obtained in a way that ensures the safety and soundness of the economic infrastructure.

The first section outlines a risk management framework that can aid policymakers in developing policy in this complex area and tries to provide some guidance regarding some of the more important tradeoffs that will need to be faced. Moreover, this section attempts to explain why the right form of regulation is needed in this entire area as there is a public interest in assuring e-security. The second section discusses some of the considerations that need to guide decisions regarding the appropriate roles of the public and private sectors and why some of the public policy issues in this area require cooperation. Finally, the third section outlines the policy response that is suggested by the framework outlined. It highlights the need for a multiple pillar approach that addresses the overall legal, regulatory, and enforcement framework, policies that can create incentives for monitoring e-security via the role of external agents (such as supervisory agencies, insurance companies and the public), public and private sector cooperative arrangements, and finally how to build incentives for proper layering of e-security and related internal monitoring at the level of specific financial service providers.

Risk Management Framework
The Public Interest and E-Security

Chapter 1 highlighted some of the key risks that the increasing use of technologies to exchange digital information poses to consumers, businesses, and the public interest. Technology may change the way services are delivered, but it has not changed the underlying basic principles of good business. Securing the open network is first and foremost a business issue, and is based upon basic principles of sound business such as responsibility, accountability, trust and duty. Technology is only a part of the business solution. However, what is in the best interests of businesses is not always in the best interests of consumers or the public good. In this section we identify the fundamental source of "public interest" and the case for regulation in this area. For several critical reasons, e-security warrants certain forms of public intervention.

First, financial services, particularly banking and the payment systems are integral parts of every country's critical economic infrastructure.[14] Compromising the payment system by illegal access and hacking can have broad ramifications for a country's entire economy. Given the level of integration between countries, it can evoke a detrimental impact on other economies as well,[15] as could similar impacts in other critical infrastructure areas, from transportation to energy, to telecommunications. Moreover, a problem in one area of critical infrastructure may compromise other critical infrastructures. For example an intrusion or breach in the case of a telecommunications company if the entity provides data storage or hosting services can have an impact on the banking system and risks of related intrusions. Hence, the public interest and welfare are potentially at risk when government, business, commerce, and consumers fail to meet certain minimum e-security standards. Recognizing the importance of the role of the public sector in maintaining and defending a country's critical infrastructure emphasizes the need for unprecedented cooperation between countries as set out by the Group of 8 (see Box 2.1).

Second, the role of government and law enforcement in e-security can be justified on familiar classic market-failure grounds.[16] Specifically, the existing base of information that supports projections about the extent of the e-security problem is substantially flawed. This is because financial services providers, hosting companies, and other enabling companies have inadequate incentives to report intrusion or penetration information accurately. Their legitimate concerns about the disclosure of such information and its potential damage to both their reputation and public confidence in their business logically create these incentives. In this case, insurance markets cannot price the insurance risk in an actuarially fair manner. Financial services providers react to incentives, and the pressure from stock analysts to cut costs and the related move to outsource key technology support functions has naturally led to much greater emphasis on connectivity and service reliability as opposed to e-security. More generally a fundamental asymmetric information problem exists in the area of technology services, whereby the sheer speed of advances and the complexity of some types of technologies have resulted in a situation where buyers of technology are often at an informational disadvantage vis-à-vis many types of vendors. This general problem also characterizes the entire area of e-security where evaluating the products being sold by e-security vendors and their proficiency is highly complex if not impossible and many forms of

---

14. The Policy on Critical Infrastructure Protection: Presidential Decision Directive 63 (PDD-63), issued by the Clinton Administration in 1998, provided a starting point for addressing cyber risks against the United States. This directive identified the critical sectors of an electronically dependent economy and assigned lead agencies to coordinate sector cyber security efforts. This directive identified eight sectors—finance, transportation, energy, water, government, aviation, telecommunications, and emergency—presenting the vision that "the United States will take all necessary measures to eliminate swiftly any significant vulnerability to both physical and cyber attacks on our critical infrastructures, including especially our cyber systems."

15. For example, the contagion associated with the 1997 financial crisis in Asia.

16. Classic reasons for a failure in a market are asymmetric information, increasing returns to scale, and network externalities. See Bator (1967), Varian et al. (1999), and Kahn (1970).

Box 2.1: G-8 Principles for Protecting Critical Information Infrastructures 2003

Information infrastructures form an essential part of critical infrastructures. In order to effectively protect critical infrastructures from damage and to secure them against attack, the G8 has developed 11 specific principles.

I. Countries should have emergency warning networks regarding cyber vulnerabilities, threats, and incidents.

II. Countries should raise awareness to facilitate stakeholders' understanding of the nature and extent of their critical information infrastructures, and the role each must play in protecting them.

III. Countries should examine their infrastructures and identify interdependencies among them, thereby enhancing protection of such infrastructures.

IV. Countries should promote partnerships among stakeholders, both public and private, to share and analyze critical infrastructure information in order to prevent, investigate, and respond to damage to or attacks on such infrastructures.

V. Countries should create and maintain crisis communication networks and test them to ensure that they will remain secure and stable in emergency situations.

VI. Countries should ensure that data availability policies take into account the need to protect critical information infrastructures.

VII. Countries should facilitate tracing attacks on critical information infrastructures and, where appropriate, the disclosure of tracing information to other countries.

VIII. Countries should conduct training and exercises to enhance their response capabilities and to test continuity and contingency plans in the event of an information infrastructure attack and should encourage stakeholders to engage in similar activities.

IX. Countries should ensure that they have adequate substantive and procedural laws, such as those outlined in the Council of Europe Cybercrime Convention of 23 November 2001, and trained personnel to enable them to investigate and prosecute attacks on critical information infrastructures, and to coordinate such investigations with other countries as appropriate.

X. Countries should engage in international cooperation, when appropriate, to secure critical information infrastructures, including by developing and coordinating emergency warning systems, sharing and analyzing information regarding vulnerabilities, threats, and incidents, and coordinating investigations of attacks on such infrastructures in accordance with domestic laws.

XI. Countries should promote national and international research and development and encourage the application of security technologies that are certified according to international standards.

Source: Group of 8 press release.

entities providing "certification" services are not really legally liable. Hence, as in most industries characterized by such informational problems there is a case for well designed regulation in the IT area and in the area of e-security specifically.

Third, information technology is subject to large increasing returns to scale on both the demand side and the supply side (Shapiro and Varian 1999). Market outcomes in such industries (including financial services, which is heavily dependent on IT) will tend to be somewhat concentrated and often will require industry standardization and coordination. In emerging markets that are not large, these effects are often magnified. For example, it is often the case that the same entity that provides telecommunications services also provides the only available hosting services to major banks. In addition, in many of these markets, the telecommunications provider is also an ISP and a provider of such services as digital data storage, and even e-security. Finally in many emerging markets the telecommunications provider may itself be government owned. Important

Box 2.2: THE ELECTRONIC SECURITY INDUSTRY: IMPERFECT COMPETITION

Today's e-security industry boasts an ever-growing array of companies. The types and numbers of choices can be confusing for the expert and overwhelming to the novice. These companies are involved in every facet of securing the networks used by financial services providers. They range from those that provide active content filtering and monitoring services to those that undertake intrusion detection tests, create firewalls, undertake penetration testing, develop encryption software and services, and offer authentication services (see below: Annex C). In scope, the e-security industry increasingly is becoming a worldwide presence as it grows parallel with the expanding connectivity to the Internet. The growing integration of technologies among the Internet, wireless, Internet provider (IP), telephone, and satellite will also present new challenges for e-security and the structure of the financial services industry and e-finance.

Because E-security companies are becoming increasingly global in nature, it is important when designing public policy to understand the links between such companies and the electronic finance industry. There is a high degree of cross-ownership and market concentration between and across various aspects of e-finance and e-security. One vendor may provide multiple services to several interlinked customers. For instance, a vendor may provide security to the financial services provider's online platform. This same vendor also may provide security services directly to the bank for its offline computer systems. In addition, it may supply security services to the hosting company. Telecommunications companies in many emerging markets provide hosting—or what many refer to as "e-enabling services"—to the banking community. By establishing a convenient online platform that customers can access through a variety of electronic devices, these hosting companies (ISPs) have become targets of organized crime.

In many emerging markets, the telecommunications company may have an interest in—or own outright—the ISP provider and the hosting company and may provide various forms of financial services as well. Moreover, many telecom companies also have multiple interests in many different forms of technology providers, from fixed-line telephony to wireless to satellites. This monopolistic industry structure should raise concern—it signifies the need to discuss and debate difficult public policy issues now, such as competition policy, and how these issues might be addressed in designing new legal and regulatory elements of the present frameworks (see Claessens, Glaessner, and Klingebiel 2002).

Along with a complex concentrated and cross-linked structure, convergence in technologies will present special challenges in the design of public policies relating to e-security. Specifically, increasing points of vulnerability will merge, and any well-designed e-security system must address them. These new points of vulnerability might include the potential interfaces between customer access devices, such as a PC with modems, land-line phones that can be linked with any Internet platform through voice recognition, wireless phones, or personal digital assistants (PDAs) with an online platform. The point at which the message leaps from one channel to another is the point at which it is most vulnerable. Hence, financial services providers will need to address a much wider array of risks and expend effort to define liability, and public policymakers will need to examine the impacts of potential weaknesses, given what is already a complex e-finance industrial structure.

Source: Bank staff.

public policy issues result from this industrial organization. The concentration of hosting services provided to banks can actually increase operational and related systemic risks related to cyber attacks, as there is inherently no built in redundancy and a problem that occurs in a hosting company serving multiple banks can create problems simultaneously in all banks. This may create a critical single point of failure. Concentration in the provision of these many types of services can also result in competition problems—and more insidiously, conflicts of interest—that can prevent adoption of implementation of proper e-security.

Fourth, the reach of the Internet and technologies imply that financial services are increasingly becoming more borderless and global. Hence mitigating e-security risks requires unprecedented efforts to promote collective action within countries (interagency and public-private sector cooperation) as well as between countries by market participants, regulators and law enforcement. Usually such collective action problems cannot be solved via simple cooperation among private parties so again the role of authorities in countries throughout the world and private market participants needs to be considered. Increasing efforts are being made to address these collective action problems.[17]

Compounding these problems is that collective action is needed even if one can solve the problem of market failure and create better incentives for timely and accurate reporting of e-security incidents. The integrated nature of these problems requires the private and public sectors (such as the law, regulatory and supervisory agencies within and across countries) to develop unprecedented approaches to cooperation. At its broadest level the problem of electronic safety and soundness is a risk management problem that is part of business process and needs to become much more a part of doing proper day-to-day commerce and risk management. Hence it is important to understand in some detail how to decompose the risks associated with electronic transactions in designing public policy.

These different arguments for a public interest role are not unrelated. They suggest that the way forward must take in to account the fact that e-security is a form of public good, reflecting the impact that it can have on key infrastructure and on other economic agents. A breach of e-security can compromise the identities of many un-knowing consumers of financial services. Paradoxically, financial service providers, ISPs, hosting companies, and other related companies do not operate under sufficient incentives to ensure that they secure their systems—rather, the emphasis is on providing fast and uninterrupted service. Even the contractual relationships between the many entities involved in the provision of the technology backbone have differing levels of actual liability and typical service level agreements do not address e-security breaches so incentives to secure computers or servers is often left to the ultimate user.

Tradeoffs: Security, Quality of Service, Privacy, Technological Innovation, and Costs

Designing public policy, creating legislation, and promoting regulation in this highly complex area requires balancing a number of essential tradeoffs. This even applies in designing standards and guidelines that might be used by a self-regulatory agency or by an official agency.

Security and Costs. Security should always be proportional to the real value of the underlying transaction. Given this proviso, it appears that when the transaction value is small, no clear economic or risk-management case can be made for employing the most sophisticated e-security regimes when a less expensive form of security will yield the same return. For example, a financial services provider would not want to use an expensive and cumbersome authentication process, such as PKI, for small-value transactions when tokens or other simpler forms of authentication will mitigate the risk of theft, and so on, to an acceptable level.

Security and Quality of Service. Similarly, tradeoffs exist between the convenience or quality of service, as computed in terms of speed and the extent and degree to which security is used. The more complex the security process used, such as PKI, the longer the transaction takes to be completed. Advances in these technologies are lessening this tradeoff. Over time, effective authentication or encryption systems will be available that do not slow the speed of transactions and do not disparage the quality of service. Moreover, one can argue that confidence in the security of services is an essential aspect of quality in providing financial services.

---

17. Two efforts to promote collective actions between countries stand out. In August of 2002 the OECD issued *Guidelines for the Security of Information Systems and Networks: Towards a Culture of Security.* These guidelines apply to all participants in the new information society and suggest the need for greater awareness and understanding of security issues and the need to develop a global culture of security. The G-8 recently released "Principles for Protecting Critical Information Infrastructures" (see Box 2.1).

Security and Technological Innovation. For e-security systems to be effective, it is important to ensure that private parties agree to certain standards and guidelines. But the proliferation of technologies that can be used to transmit information and their rapid rate of integration inherently creates a reluctance to adopt standards or guidelines. Technological innovation can be stifled and customer service can suffer if security standards are not sufficiently flexible and technology-neutral. As will be noted in later sections, even the definition of an electronic signature needs to be very carefully designed so as not to preempt the use of a number of alternative technologies. In other words, the concept of technology neutrality is an important one to adopt when formulating legislation and regulation (see Chapter 3).

Security and Privacy. Ironically, the need for more effective e-security may sometimes conflict with and negatively affect the user's privacy. Inadvertently, it may also affect the privacy of third parties who are identified in affected information. This tension is natural, and it is not new. On the one hand, certain types of e-security services may be consistent with protecting privacy (e.g., programs such as cyber patrol). On the other hand, security may be needed to track and verify the user's movements. In other cases, however, the person undertaking the transaction may want to remain anonymous as part of a trading strategy. Developing the proper balance between security and privacy is a delicate matter. It often is decided within a cultural paradigm. Sometimes this means that something considered private in one culture may not be deemed so in another. Moreover, the laws (for example, bank secrecy provisions) often compromise the ability of the authorities to investigate properly and take enforcement actions in complex electronic crime cases.

The Roles of the Private and Public Sectors

Any policy framework needs to try and delineate the roles of the public and private sector with some clarity. Technology and its rapid pace of change along with the informational and incentive problems outlined make it essential that both the private sector and the public sector play a role in improving e-security. The challenge is how to ensure that awareness of the issue and better transparency can become the norm as part of ordinary business process. The roles of the public and private sector must be designed to reinforce each other to the greatest extent possible. However, the design of such policies should put a premium on simplicity and assure that enforcement is a reality. Many of the approaches to be undertaken will need to be strongly conditioned by the underlying industrial organization of the telecommunications and financial services industries along with the e-security industry in specific emerging markets.[18]

Roles of the Private Sector

The private sector can play several important roles.

First, and most importantly as part of ordinary business practice, private companies should secure their electronic operations to avoid reputational and other actual losses. Hence, this source of operational risk needs to be much better assessed and dealt with in day to day operations. Internal monitoring is the first line of defense. However, despite the need for the private sector to take on this pro-active role, there are a variety of reasons why private companies often are pressured to underinvest in overall electronic safety and soundness. As noted above there is a classic market failure whereby there is a natural lack of incentives for "truthful disclosure" of e-security problems precisely due to possible reputation damage. Hence, a key aspect of the role of the public sector and other private market participants is to create more awareness of the risks being borne by the entire financial services industry due to lack of accurate information and cooperation. Internal monitoring and layered e-security should be a critical aspect of business practice,

---

18. For an example of how the framework and pillars noted in this paper have been practically applied see the forthcoming paper "The Small Investor Program in the Philippines: Electronic Distribution of Securities", forthcoming OPD working paper.

and e-security, but governments may need to provide incentives to ensure that such practices are rigorous enough.

Second, the private sector should seek means to cooperate with academic institutions and governments to greatly improve the education of the general population in this essential area of critical infrastructure. As noted the Internet can be viewed as a very large, semi self governing entity. Better governance overall of its common technology platform must become a much higher priority for the private sector not only the Government. To date systematic cooperation in educational efforts aimed at education of users as well as providers of financial or other services have been less than satisfactory even in some of the most advanced developed countries in the world.

Third, the private sector will need to make unprecedented efforts to cooperate with law enforcement agencies and with supervisory authorities within and across borders due to the very global nature of the Internet technology backbone. Here, law enforcement entities need to work with the private sector to develop ways of reporting and sharing information that guarantees that confidential information about a specific e-security breach will not be disclosed if it is shared with authorities. Establishing an infrastructure that can actually engender such incentives to report to authorities and even to properly report within specific financial services providers to the Chief Information Security Officer (CISO) is highly complex, but needs to be addressed.

Fourth, the private sector in many countries will need to couple improving awareness with a concerted approach to create governance and management structures inside financial service providers and banks that can greatly improve active internal monitoring of e-security and risks. Here although external supervisors can act to raise the standards, the need to establish much sounder policies, practices, and procedures is essential. In many emerging markets, financial service and non-financial entities do not even have a CISO; nor is an understanding of technology related risk management expertise a criterion for choosing Directors for appointment to Boards. Beyond actions at the level of individual financial service providers, private associations (including the bankers and securities markets associations or even self regulatory associations) have a key role to play in maintaining the reputation and trust that consumers have in their members. Hence, ways to self-monitor where banks are proactive in monitoring each other and setting certain minimum standards for management of such risks via such associations needs to be explored.

Roles of the Public Sector

Mitigating the risks of electronic transactions, as argued in the first section of this chapter, is an area of significant public interest. In designing policy there is a need for carefully structured interventions by the public sector, especially in emerging markets. The classic literature on competition and market failure suggests a number of roles that the public sector needs to play. As in the case of the private sector above, these key roles are neither well-established nor is an accountability framework in place for the agencies involved (for example, supervisory and enforcement) in most emerging markets.

Regulation

Given the public interest in this area and the importance of market structure combined with the rapid deployment of sophisticated technologies in many emerging markets and the increasing use of technology in delivery of financial services several areas of public sector legal and regulatory practice are especially important to define.

Defining Liability of Parties and Standards of Governance: Incentive problems often arise in the area of e-security, because governance and more broadly liability of multiple parties is ill-defined. In the case of e-security these problems arise at the level of the Board, the management, among the administrative and technology staff and vis-à-vis a whole host of different types of third party providers of enabling technologies. These third party providers run the gamut from hosting services or ISPs to e-security vendors as noted in Chapter 1. The legal and regulatory frameworks of most countries do not assign sufficient liability via representation and warranties in the case of these parties. In addition, corporate governance reform does not really address the need for companies to actually create a CISO or preferred arrangements with regard to the liability of the Board, the management, and the individuals or officers charged with undertaking the e-security function. As in most areas of corporate governance the issues to be addressed are complex and subtle because the degree of liability is not independent of the capacity to properly define the precise electronic related risks to which the provider of a service is liable. In addition assignment of liability between the provider of a service versus the financial institution purchasing the service is often complex. For example, many ISPs would argue that they are simply a pipe and should bear no liability for an e-security breach to a user of their service.

Defining legal concepts that are simple and are enforceable within and across countries: The governments of different countries need to pay special and increasing attention to how to define simple and enforceable legal concepts that will reduce incentives for e-security breaches. They must also assure enough harmonization to reduce the scope for new forms of regulatory arbitrage where hacking syndicates locate in countries with weak legal and enforcement frameworks.

Defining Standards and Certification Processes: Standards in an area like e-security cannot be static. It is apparent that the public and private sectors in many countries will need to work together to assure that standards are not in effect a means for entrenched providers of services to retain excessive market power. In many emerging markets certification is effectively used in this manner, and often self-regulatory associations have no effective legal liability, so that in the end the effectiveness of such entities to police providers of e-security services, certify such providers, or assure proper entry or security standards is suspect. More broadly the way in which certification processes are established in this area, as well as the setting of standards in many emerging markets is in need of review. Here the promulgation of certain international standards (such as the ISO standards) will require much more effort and cooperation.

The role of private companies that can act as monitoring agents of those offering services electronically is important to foster in many emerging markets with supervision and enforcement as well as human capital may be weak or underdeveloped. In this context the use of regulation in order to create incentives for financial service providers to have to insure against certain forms of e-security risks at the margin as part of an overall policy of prudence can be beneficial.

Monitoring

Beyond the role of the public sector in establishing the overall legal/regulatory and incentive framework in this highly complex area there is another role that the public sector plays via either direct or indirect monitoring of the e-security practices of financial service providers. This monitoring role is nothing new. Three key mechanisms are especially relevant: supervision as a means of prevention; supervision of third-party monitoring agents such as insurance companies, and supervision and monitoring of those entities claiming to provide various forms of certification services or developing "standards" for e-security such as certification authorities; self regulatory associations, etc.

Supervision of Electronic Financial Service Providers: This important function is now becoming more complex in the age of rapid advances in technology so that both examination and enforcement actions are becoming more complex. Regulatory supervision must work with the financial service industry and the e-security industry to develop new methods of examining, new concepts of monitoring, and new means of intervention. For example, it is now possible to remotely monitor banks on a continuous, automated basis. This enables supervisors to track risk, exposure, etc. on a real time basis.

Supervision of Private Monitoring Agents: Insurance companies writing cover need to be carefully supervised so that they properly insist on better overall e-security. In addition the establishing higher standards of security and due care by credit rating agencies and the insisting on better security processes by all companies and financial service providers in this key area (source) of operational risk are important. Securities regulators and insurance supervisors need to more carefully supervise private monitoring agents and insist on certain minimum standards in assessing their actions to monitor the e-security practices and operational risk of financial service providers.

Supervision of Certification Agents and the Technology Providers: Just as formal supervision entities have a role to play so too do other regulatory agencies such as the competition commission or trade commission, or the regulatory entity dealing with the telecommunications sector. In many emerging markets there are no real processes in place to supervise entities that certify providers of e-security services and in many emerging economies this e-security industry does not exist except for services provided by the local telecommunications provider.

Promoting Awareness and Education

Other essential roles for the public sector in this area are to promote awareness and to provide ongoing training and education. The importance of awareness and education among making persons in companies and consumers of electronically provided services cannot be underestimated in importance.

Global efforts to introduce the responsible adoption of technology will require unprecedented networking and coordination between Universities, governments and the corporate sector worldwide.

A New Role for Public Banks

The importance of e-security arrangements for the success of various e-commerce and e-finance initiatives is also going to revolutionize the role of public banks in emerging markets. Although these banks have been involved in extending credit in the past to other on-lending banks or to final borrowers their role vis-à-vis other banks may change in significant ways. In the Philippines, for example, the Development Bank of the Philippines will start to provide data storage services and also act as the front end hosting company to many banks participating in a Philippine Treasury sponsored electronic retail distribution of government debt. This will be a fundamentally new role for a Development Bank but such a role makes sense in the Philippines given the concentration of the telecommunications industry and of hosting services as well as the lack of e-security in such arrangements as designed in the private sector.

Policy Response: Overview of the Four Pillars

In light of these complex public policy issues, any approach to designing a public policy framework that improve electronic safety and soundness will need to rest on four fundamental pillars. This monograph is built on the concept that trust and confidence of market participants are fundamental component of a robust economy. It is important to recognize that to be most effective, reforms in all four pillars are needed in most emerging markets and the design of these reforms must reinforce each other. The balance between the public and private sectors and their roles is especially important in the first three pillars, and there is a real need for authorities to adopt simple and clear principles and legal reforms. Knowledge of the technology is essential in properly designing reforms in each area. At the same time, in many emerging markets, work in designing reform must be multi-disciplinary and must include at a minimum the legal profession, finance and risk professionals, economists, actuaries, and persons with the requisite understanding of technology. There are many instances where lack of such an approach has resulted in less than adequate frameworks.

Pillar I: Legal, Regulatory, and Enforcement Framework

Overall Framework: Countries adopting electronic banking or electronic delivery of other financial services (e.g., distribution and trading of securities) should incorporate e-security concerns into their laws, policies and practices. The framework must require business to be responsible for security, to use of security to protect back-end and front-end electronic operations, and to provide for appropriate punishment to combat cyber crime and cyber terrorism.

At a minimum, an e-finance legal framework should consist of the following:

- *Electronic Transactions Law:* This should define what is meant by an electronic signature, record, or transaction, and recognize the legal validity of each of these.
- *Payment Systems Security Law.* These statutes should identify, license, and regulate any payment system entities that directly affect the system. They should provide that all such entities must operate in a secure manner, and require timely and accurate reporting on all electronic-related money losses or suspected losses and intrusions. Finally, they should require that the financial institution and related providers have sufficient risk protection.
- *Privacy Law.* Privacy law should encompass data collection and use, consumer protection and business requirements, and notices about an entity's policy on information use. At a minimum, the privacy law should embrace the fair information practice principles of notice, choice, access, and minimum information necessary to complete the transaction.
- *Cyber Crime Law.* These laws should address abuses of a computer or network that result in loss or destruction to the computer or network, as well as associated losses. They should also provide the tools and resources needed to investigate, prosecute, and punish perpetrators of cyber crimes and, where needed, address the subject of adequate record retention to allow for electronic forensics and investigation.[19]
- *Anti-Money Laundering Laws.* These statutes should define money laundering and require international cooperation in the investigation, prosecution, and punishment of such crimes pursuant to the guidance provided by the Financial Action Task Force (FATF).
- *Enforcement.* Perhaps as important as the legal framework will be the need to enforce the provisions of e-security laws within and across national boundaries. The fact that so many different types of computer or system related intrusions actually originate through activities conducted in countries with weak legal and enforcement regimes for e-security, makes it essential that a broad international approach that relies on more homogeneous laws and enforcement actions across countries be put in place.

Pillar 2: Improving the Monitoring of E-security Practices

Designing incentives to improve the e-security practice of financial service providers is not independent of the various institutional arrangements and development of financial markets in countries or offshore. However, in many emerging markets at least three parties have a role to play in monitoring and creating incentives for better e-security. These parties are: regulators and supervisors; insurance companies through the policies they write and the related monitoring they provide; and the public at large, particularly those who work in companies or financial service providers and final consumers of financial services. Any framework must support actions in each of these areas.

Supervision and Prevention Challenges and Monitoring by the Regulatory Authorities

Beyond the monitoring of the payments system and the related supervision of money transmitters is the need to revisit the regulation, supervision, and prevention approaches to financial services providers that engage in electronic banking or provision of other financial services.

- *Capital Requirements.* The new Basel guidelines for capital, especially those dealing with operational risk, do not address the problem of measuring either the risk to reputation or the strategic risk associated with e-security breaches. A more productive approach might be to use the examination process to identify and remedy e-security breaches in coordination

---

19. See also: The Council of Europe, Convention on Cybercrime, "http://conventions.coe.int"

with better incentives for reporting such incidents.[20] In addition, authorities could encourage or even require financial services providers to insure against some aspects of e-risks (for example, denial of service, identity theft) that are not taken into account within the existing capital adequacy framework.[21]

- *Downstream Liability.* The interlinked nature of financial services providers, money transmitters, and ISPs implies that the traditional regulatory structure must change or expand beyond its present configuration. The legal or regulatory framework should create incentives for ISPs, hosting companies, application service providers, and software, hardware, and e-security providers to be accountable to the financial services industry.

- *Supervision and Examination Processes.* Further areas for the Basel Committee on Banking Supervision's Electronic Banking Group to evaluate include: the means used to examine the IT systems of banks or other financial services providers in order to modernize the examination approach; the institution's current documented security program; the current approaches to modeling operational risk in light of the growing importance of cyber-risks, and the procedures used to identify and assess entities that provide a data processing or money transmitter service to the institution[22].

- *Coordination of agencies within and across borders.* One important issue facing most countries is the need to improve the sharing of information across and among their regulatory and law enforcement agencies. Many countries have a number of entities for gathering critical information, but often it is not shared within a country or across nations (sometimes for legal reasons). Improvement in this area will require joint enforcement actions and much greater cross-border cooperation.

The Role of Private Insurance as a Complementary Monitoring System

The global insurance industry can increasingly act as an important force for change in e-security requirements. First, it can strive to improve the minimum standards for e-security in the financial services industry. Second, insurance companies can require that financial services entities use vendors that meet certified, industry-accepted standards to provide e-security services as a way of mitigating their risks of underwriting coverage. Third, insurance companies can encourage regulators to require that financial services entities both provide information and improve the quality of data and information on incidents so they can better actuarially measure e-risks and return on investment. Finally, the industry should promote solutions that require e-security vendors and other e-enabling companies (hosting, etc.) to engage in risk sharing and in carrying appropriate liability.

Education and Prevention of E-Security Incidents

In many countries, more than half of all e-security intrusions are still carried out by insiders. An uneducated or undereducated workforce is inherently more vulnerable to this type of incident or attack. Educational initiatives will have to be targeted to financial services providers (both systems administrators and management), to various agencies involved in law enforcement and supervision, and to actual online users[23] of financial services. Initiatives in this area must not only be undertaken with countries but worldwide. This is likely to be one of the most important

---

20. See the discussion of Pillar VI in this executive summary.

21. In many emerging markets, the insurance industry itself may need to be restructured and be stable; however, cross-border provision of such coverage may be an option.

22. The EBG and certain regulatory/supervisory agencies (OCC, MAS, FSA, HKMA) are already taking a proactive approach to e-security.

23. The Internet Security Alliance issued "Common Sense Guidelines for Computer Users" that identify best practices necessary for home users to secure their own PCs. (See http://wbln0018.worldbank.org/html/FinancialSectorWeb.nsf/(attachmentweb)/CommonSenseGuideforHomeUsers/$FILE/Common+Sense+Guide+for+Home+Users.pdf)

initiatives that multilateral and bilateral lenders can support over the next decade to support the timely and proper development of proper e-security infrastructure in emerging markets. Due to the dynamic nature of both technology and the cyber-threat, recurrent security training is essential for all IT personnel and management. Education regarding the institution's policies and proper procedure in protecting open architecture systems will ensure that each participant is an important actor in the provisioning of security. Use of innovative techniques for training including distance learning and use of other technology in educational initiatives will also make this effort more economical.[24]

Pillar 3: Public-Private Sector Cooperation and the Need for Collective Action

Two highly important areas that must be a focal point of public policy in the area of e-security relate to the accuracy of the basic information about such incidents and standards and certification processes in a number of dimensions. These critical areas are not only impacted by the legal regime in place and the degree of monitoring and reporting, but also by the nature of institutional arrangements in place to encourage collective action within and across countries.

Accuracy of Information and Public-Private Sector Cooperation

The lack of accurate information on e-security incidents is the result of the lack of incentives to capture the data, measure it, and inform users. E-security would improve worldwide through the creation of a set of national and cross-border incentive arrangements to encourage financial services providers to share accurate information on actual denial-of-service intrusions, thefts, hacks, and so on. Greater public-private sector cooperation is needed in this area. Critical to any global solution will be for a universally trusted third party to administer a global base of information relating to e-security incidents. In this area, the role of multilateral agencies to facilitate cooperation deserves examination as well as the potential for use of self-regulatory organizations with very wide global ownership under a wholly separate technical management (such as Carnegie Mellon CERT) that might act to assure the absolute privacy and non-identification of parties contributing the information. Such arrangements and relevant non-disclosure provisions and potential liability for any third party that would store such information could be highly complex to organize but does merit investigation as well.

Certification, Standards, and the Roles of the Public and Private Sectors

Both public and private entities must work cooperatively to develop standards and to harmonize certification and licensing schemes in order to mitigate risk even if such standards are essentially sufficiently dynamic to allow for rapid technological advances. Two categories that require particular attention in terms of certification deal with e-security service providers themselves and the transaction elements in e-finance. A necessary first step in securing e-finance is to require licensing by financial regulators of vendors that directly affect the payment system, such as money transmitters or ISPs. A further step could be to require the financial services and e-security industry to jointly certify vendors that provide e-security services. Incentives to undertake this responsibility carefully will not be unrelated to the underlying legal framework and relative liability borne by these parties (for example, financial service providers and third party vendors). Obtaining collective action across members of diverse industries will require a definite joint public private partnership in support of the public interest role of the electronic safety and soundness of financial services.

---

24. Multilateral organizations and agencies (e.g., the FTC) have a very important role to play. IN the case of emerging markets the World Bank has created a web-site dedicated to acting as a clearing house for educating end users, regulatory officials, market participants and others about electronic security issues. See ww1.worldbank.org/finance and click on E-Security.

A second area to address is certification of such transaction elements as electronic signatures. The value certification brings to a transaction in part depends on who or what provides the certification and on the elements that are being certified. Certification structures located in different jurisdictions must consistently provide the same attributes to the transaction and that a certifier's scope of authority and liability must remain consistent across jurisdictional borders.

Pillar 4: Business Process and Incentives for Layered Electronic Security

Security is a business issue, not a technical issue. Risk of being hacked deals with probabilities not possibilities. Understanding the business is critical when attempting to be proactive in cyber space.

One of the most important efforts needed to improve e-security is to clearly link business objectives to processes that link the costs of not securing a business to the potential and actual savings from layering security in a world where open architecture systems prevail. Three general axioms to remember in building a security program include:

- Attacks and losses are inevitable.
- Security buys time.
- The network is only as secure as its weakest link.

Twelve core layers of proper e-security are fundamental in maintaining the integrity of data or digital assets and mitigating the risks associated with open architecture environments.

Twelve layers of electronic security

These twelve layers of e-security are recommended as a required component of best business practice, and should the remit of a CISO with designated roles and responsibilities:

- Risk management frameworks that are broader based than those often associated with operational risk and business continuity;
- Cybernetic intelligence to provide antecedent analysis of threats and vulnerabilities;
- Carefully designed access controls and authentication on a multilevel basis that relies on more than one authentication technology;
- Firewalls that allow for the implementing of boundaries between networks;
- Active content filtering at the application level;
- Implementation of adequate intrusion detection systems;
- Use of virus scanner to limit the entry of malicious codes and worms;
- Use of strong encryption so that messaging can proceed with integrity;
- Vulnerability and penetration testing to see where key points of vulnerability exist, with required remediation and reporting;
- Implementation of proper systems administration,
- Adoption of policy management software to ensure control of bank policies regarding such issues as employee computer usage; and
- Development of an explicit business continuity or incident response plan to assure a rapid recovery after any significant computer security incident.

CHAPTER 3

LEGAL AND REGULATORY FRAMEWORK (PILLAR I)

A s argued in Chapter 2, it is in the public interest for governments to actively develop the legal, regulatory, and enforcement framework for e-security. As countries adopt open network technologies to deliver financial services, they should develop public policy, laws, regulations, and enforcement mechanisms that focus on the security, privacy and structural concerns discussed in this monograph. Governments should work with other governments, and with the private sector, to develop as much coherence in these areas as possible. In this way, they can build a cohesive global security framework that will support the safe and sound operation of their institutions, combat crime and cyber terrorism and protect consumers. At a minimum this should include protection against unsolicited communications, adhesion contracts, and should provide access to an adequate dispute resolution mechanism.[25] These areas of law address the *basic relationship transactional activities and risks* that flow through any e-payments system.[26] Since risks are greater and more concentrated in e-finance, these laws are the minimum necessary to protect the public's interest and welfare, to uphold the public's trust and confidence and to assure that the financial service provider is meeting its fiduciary duty and is using basic principles to maintain a safe and sound environment for e-transactions.

■ *Electronic Transactions and Commerce Law*: At a minimum, it should define what is meant by an electronic signature, record or transaction, and recognize the legal validity of each.

---

25. See also, the EU e-commerce directive (nr.2000/31/EC), which requires that commercial communications should be clearly identifiable by a recipient, and that senders must abide by opt-out registers.

26. The scope and objectives of this paper do not permit a full analysis of these laws or suggest that enactment of these laws provide a sufficient framework. Each country must analyze its existing framework to determine whether additional laws are necessary. It does, however, provide a guideline against which a gap analysis may be initiated.

It should identify the stakeholders in such transactions, the roles and responsibilities of these parties and the potential risks associated with e-transactions.

■ *Payment Systems Security Law*: This law should identify, license and regulate any payment entities or affiliates that directly affect the system. It should require all such entities to operate in a secure manner, and require timely and accurate reporting on all electronic-related money losses or suspected losses and intrusions. Finally, it should require that the financial institution and related providers have sufficient protection against cyber risk. It also should provide for adequate enforcement powers.

■ *Privacy Law*: This law should encompass data collection and use, consumer protection, business requirements, and notices about an entity's policy on information use. At a minimum, this law should embrace the Fair Information Practice Principles of notice, choice, access, and capture only the minimum information necessary to complete the transaction. It should provide for redress by the aggrieved party when that person's privacy is violated as well as a means by which incorrect information can be corrected.

■ *Cyber Crime*: These laws should assign responsibility and liability for abuse of a computer or network that results in loss or destruction to either, as well as associated losses. It should also provide the tools and resources needed to investigate, prosecute, and punish perpetrators of cyber crimes and, where needed, address the subject of adequate record retention to allow for cyber forensics and investigation.

■ *Anti-Money Laundering Laws*: These statutes should define money laundering and commit a country to cooperate on an international basis in investigations, prosecutions, and punishment of such crimes pursuant to the guidance provided by the Financial Action Task Force (FATF).

It is important to note that each of these major areas of legislation and attendant regulation should address the key risks noted in Chapter 2. For example, both the anti-money laundering and cyber crime laws need to specifically contain provisions that treat the specific and particular issues associated with electronic money laundering. The payments systems act will need to define what agencies have the responsibility for supervising online payment and quasi retail payment systems such as money transmitters, and the legal liability and supervisory responsibilities of the Central Bank or other supervisory agencies over E-gold, Pay-Pal and other entities that use the Internet technology backbone as "money transmitters." The legal and regulatory framework can and should play a significant role in mitigating payments system risks. Given the continuing integration of economies, designing laws must acknowledge and identify impacts on other existing laws and the full impact implementing such laws may have on the system as a whole.

The cornerstone of an e-finance legal framework is the recognition of the legal validity of electronic signatures, transactions, or records. These laws should prefer technology-neutral solutions, provide basic consumer protections for electronically based transactions, promote interoperability, and address records retention. Two basic models exist: the act developed by the United Nations Commission on International Trade Law (UNCITRAL), titled 2001 UNCITRAL Model Law on Electronic signatures; and the Uniform Electronic Transactions Act (UETA), a Model Act promulgated in the United States by the National Conference of Commissioners on Uniform State Laws (NCCUSL). An electronic commerce law might address all consumer-related financial transactions and records, while a payment systems law should govern conduct with consumers and on basic financial payment mechanisms such as EDI, EBT, EFT, and ETC. Specifically, the latter would define what constitutes a secure financial services system in an open network architecture and would require entities to practice due diligence.

The ability to enforce the laws and regulations within and across one's boundaries is as important as providing an adequate legal and regulatory framework within which to prosecute perpetrators and penalize those entities operating in an unsafe and unsound manner. To achieve enforcement, many countries need to take a number of critical steps. Regulatory enforcement reforms should address, at a minimum, varying degrees of cease-and-desist orders and compliance actions. Cease-and-desist orders could range from removal of the entity from the online system until it comes into compliance to closing the entity down. While a financial services provider may not have access to online activity, it still may be conducting unsafe and unsound operations to such an extent that it is jeopardizing other entities. Without a concerted international cooperative effort, e-finance hackers will commonly move to jurisdictions with the most lax legal and enforcement frameworks.

Access, availability, and interoperability should be the mantra to guide financial supervision and enforcement efforts. The traditional regulatory structure must expand to include all entities directly related to the delivery of financial services. This entails everything from ISPs to application service providers (ASP), software and hardware vendors, and security providers. Legislation needs to incorporate these providers into the regulatory and enforcement net. Moreover, professional liability needs to attach to these providers, to the directors who contract with them, and to the lawyers and accountants who provide services to them because, in the new paradigm, all are indispensable to the institution's ability to provide financial services. One approach might require that these providers be bonded, licensed, and subject to periodic audits and examination under the appropriate regulatory scheme. This would create a relevant basis from which to undertake enforcement actions.

Electronic Transactions and Commerce Law

The past seven years have produced tremendous worldwide growth in electronic-commerce-related legislation. In 1995, only a handful of countries had basic computer or intellectual property laws. Today, almost every country has enacted an electronic signature or electronic transaction act. The basic elements of these laws are the same, with minor variations. Most of the laws use UETA or UNCITRAL's Law on Electronic Signatures as the model.

Significant differences exist in the provisions of UETA and UNCITRAL's Law on Electronic Signatures, but the objectives of both are the same: to promote electronic commerce and to ensure that electronic signatures, however they may be defined, have the same effect under the law as manual signatures. For example, UETA defines an electronic signature as "an electronic sound, symbol, or process attached to or logically associated with a record and executed or adopted by a person with the intent to sign the record." UNCITRAL Law on Electronic Signatures defines an electronic signature as "data in electronic form in, affixed to, or logically associated with a data message, which may be used to identify the signatory in relation to the data message and indicate the signatory's approval of the information contained in the data message." [27] Each provides a different perspective on timing and intent. UETA presumes that by signing the document, the signer intends to be legally bound. Its wording creates a presumption in favor of the validity of the contract. UNCITRAL's Law on Electronic Signatures, in contrast, uses permissive language, creating no presumption in favor of the contract. Further it should address the issues of record management and record retention.

With the proliferation of electronic signature and electronic transaction legislation over the past decade, e-commerce has come into its own legally. In general, an electronic signature has the same force and effect as a manual signature in most of the world. While the legal framework can often be slow to adapt to changing circumstances, in this instance the law appears to be trying to adapt to electronic commerce needs as quickly as the world is coming online. This is a major phenomenon that raises issues of importance beyond the scope of this monograph.

Security of Payment Systems

Though most countries have laws in place to regulate different components of the payments system, no country has yet addressed payments systems issues comprehensively. Payment systems legislation should identify, license, and regulate any directly related payment system entities, such

---

27. Article (II) Subsection A of the 2001 UNCITRAL Model Law on Electronic Signatures.

Box 3.1: MONEY TRANSMITTERS AND INTERNET SERVICE PROVIDERS

The convergence of the telecommunications, computer, and financial services industries is changing the fundamentals of the industrial organization of the financial services sector. It also is redefining traditional boundaries and jurisdictional limits of responsibility because of shifting legal, regulatory, and financial concepts. Money transmitters and Internet service providers (ISPs) have become a critical sector of this new economic structure, and can have a direct impact on the security of a financial service provider, and potentially on the wider financial sector and economy as a whole. However, as a result of the lack of standardization in regulation and oversight, many money transmitters and ISPs insert significant risk into the payments system. Yet they are not required to post bond for their services and they carry no liability. In fact, legislation in some countries holds that ISPs are not liable for transmission failures or losses. Also, because money transmitters and ISPs are not subject to reporting requirements, little information is available on the extent of the vulnerability—though frequent losses are known about informally.

The ability to define a function or service is a crucial first step in determining whether it should be regulated or not, and who or what should regulate it. Money transmitters may perform a variety of services, including money order issuance, wire transfers, currency exchanges, check-cashing, and check-presentment. More recently, money transmitters have been providing electronic check-presentment services and point-of-sale money payment order information to the accepting bank. Money transmitters operate outside the depository institution but often are associated in some way with one or more depository institutions in a downstream relationship. An ISP is often referred to in the law as a "common carrier". This is the same term that is used to define the basic utility service provided by telephone companies. The term implies that the provider holds itself out to the public as willing and able to move information from one point to another. Whether or not an entity is an ISP is difficult to determine under existing laws. ISPs are not regulated in most countries. Because the primary focus of legislative initiatives targeting money transmitters has been to deter money laundering, most of the activity affecting this industry is derived from anti–money laundering sources (see Money Laundering section below).

Developing appropriate regulatory schemes includes developing an approach to mitigate or manage risk. Here, the concern is that money transmitters and ISPs are not legally liable for the services they provide. With the escalation of Internet-related commercial activities and the requisite need to provide ubiquitous payment system conduits, money transmitters are increasing the disintermediation of the traditional payments systems and have a higher profile in the eyes of law enforcement. The open, universal access architecture of the Internet places greater emphasis on identifying and analyzing systemic risks and vulnerabilities, eliminating risks where feasible, and continually monitoring both risks and security. Few emerging markets appear to have dealt with these issues explicitly thus far. This poses the question of how to do more with less and yet still increase security and privacy.

The first recommendation is to enact legislation regulating all money transmitters and any ISPs that provide service to the financial services sector, requiring them to be secure. The Uniform Money Services Business Act would be a good basis for regulating these providers. Another approach would be to build in a service-level agreement with appropriate refund mechanisms, liability, and warranties to the terms and conditions. Another avenue of defense is self-regulation through the automated clearinghouse process or, more broadly, via specific arrangements outlining security standards in the case of wholesale or retail payment networks. Building clearinghouse rules requiring all entities to use vendors that provide an appropriate level of security and to post sufficient money or bond to cover losses would create an incentive for the parties to establish a proper e-security standard. Insurance coverage is yet another means of protection. Financial services entities should use insurance to protect themselves from gap loss, whereby e-risk is realized even after insurance companies have required a financial services provider to meet specific security standards. The next chapter (Pillar 2) will examine this issue in more detail.

Source: Compiled by Bank staff from a variety of sources.

as money transmitters and ISPs.[28] It should require such elements to operate in a safe and sound manner so as to protect the integrity and reliability of the system. It should require the timely and accurate reporting of all security incidents, including all electronically related money losses. Finally, it should require all payment system entities to adhere to a documented security program and should encourage some form of shared risk protection.

In particular, money transmitters and ISPs that provide services to the financial sector should be required by regulation or legislation to provide liability for their services. Sharing risk is a proven model in the financial services arena, and there is as yet no evidence that this would increase the basic service cost. In fact, only when service entities are required to report losses or suspected losses can sufficient information be garnered to improve pricing for e-security performance bonds and e-commerce liability insurance.

As a result of the lack of a comprehensive law regulating payment systems coupled with the lack of standardization in regulation and oversight, many money transmitters insert significant risk into the payments system. Typically, they are undercapitalized, use little or no risk-management analysis, and are extremely susceptible to bankruptcy and failure. With the escalation of Internet-related commercial activities and the requisite need to provide ubiquitous payment system conduits, money transmitters are increasing the disintermediation of the traditional payments systems and have a higher profile in the eyes of law enforcement.

Privacy

Clearly, privacy is an area of the law that is undergoing considerable scrutiny throughout the world. It is an issue of fundamental importance, reflecting the very substance of our cultural identities, values, and mores, and it must be handled with the utmost care. Poorly considered decisions made in this arena may haunt us for years to come.

On the issue of privacy protection, some countries have chosen to legislate on a functional or piecemeal basis, while others have taken a more encompassing, process-oriented approach. Two approaches are also being used on the issue of consent. The first is to assume consent unless the party affirmatively chooses not to have the information sold or used for other purposes. The second is to assume that the party has not consented to any use of the information unless the party gives that consent. The United States follows the first approach in financial activity and the second in medical information. The European Union (EU) exemplifies the second in each area and continues to be the leader in providing privacy protection to its citizens with its 1990 EU Directive on Data Collection.

No matter which approach is used, at a minimum, privacy laws should embrace the Fair Information Practice Principles set out in the European Union Directive on Data Protection and adopted by the Federal Trade Commission.[29] These principles consist of notice, choice, access, and consent. They should address privacy rights concerning any data collected, stored, or used by an entity for different purposes, in particular those uses that could affect a person's basic human rights, such as criminal, financial, business, or medical uses. In practice, privacy laws would require entities to do the following: advise persons about how data will be used; collect only the minimum data needed to complete the transaction or record at issue; use the data only for those purposes that it advised the person it would be used for; and permit persons to view any information collected and dispute the validity of any such information with timely corrections. Finally,

---

28. One partial exception is the case of the European Union, where Directive 2000/46/EG applies to so-called electronic money providers, and is therefore, an attempt to regulate them.

29. The term, Fair Information Practice Principles, generally refers to practices adopted by organizations that seek to protect consumer's rights concerning data privacy, accuracy, collection and use. Several countries have examined this issue of Fair Information Practices, including the United States, Canada, United Kingdom, and countries in the European Union. For more information see: http://www3.ftc.gov/reports/privacy3/fairinfo.htm.

the law should impose restrictions on any entity collecting, holding, or disclosing information in a form that would allow identification of the person it relates to, however that may be defined.

Cyber Crime

Significant debate is transpiring in legal communities worldwide over the impact of cyber crime on fundamental concepts of law, such as jurisdiction, and in particular on how the electronic culture is changing traditional legal paradigms. Financial cyber crime is a top priority in this dialogue because, more often than not, it requires intense international cooperation among what can be an overwhelming number of law enforcement agencies and regulators from different countries. Because no country is immune, every country should benefit from pooling resources to address this problem. But, more than any other aspect of computer law, financial cyber crime tests the continuing validity of the industrial regulatory and law enforcement model. For example, as a result of their lack of cyber crime legislation the Ukraine and Belarus have become major staging grounds for organized hacker syndicates. Because of the underlying complexity of such cases and the overlapping jurisdictions of authority within a country, one of the first things the laws should address is who or what has authority and responsibility for these cases. A significant cost avoidance could result from such reform, and money saved could be invested in training resource experts and the tools needed to investigate, prosecute, and punish cyber crime perpetrators. Substantively, the laws should address abuses of a computer or network that result in loss or destruction to the computer, the network, or people, and should include provisions for restitution for associated losses.[30]

A December 2000 McConnell International survey provides a snapshot of the state of computer crime legislation worldwide. It examined the legal frameworks of 52 countries to determine each one's ability to prosecute perpetrators of ten types of computer crime. The survey showed that a patchwork of outdated and inconsistent laws effectively functions as a shield from prosecution for cyber criminals who attack electronic systems and information.[31]

In April 2002, an unauthorized user accessed over 260,000 California state personnel files. It took the state six weeks to discover that the system had been hacked. In response, that same year California enacted Senate Bill 1386. This law, effective July 1, 2003 mandates every state agency and every person or business that conducts business in California, that owns or licenses computerized data that includes personal information as defined in the Act, to provide notice in specified ways to any resident of California that the security of the data had been breached and that the entity's personal information was or is reasonably believed to have been taken by the unauthorized user. California is the first state to require mandatory reporting of security breaches. It acknowledges the exponential growth of identity theft and the need for reforms to address the market failure. Although the Act is a giant step forward for consumers, it contains certain exemptions from the notice requirement. Nevertheless, other states now are responding to California's lead and are introducing mandatory reporting legislation.

For countries looking to develop cyber crime legislation, the Council of Europe provides some guidance. In 2001, it developed the first international treaty on crimes committed via the Internet and other computer networks, dealing particularly with infringements of copyright, computer-related fraud, child pornography, and violations of network security. The treaty also provides for a series of powers and procedures, such as the search of computer networks and interception.[32]

---

30. The United States has enacted various computer intrusion laws that treat identity theft and computer-initiated fraud as criminal offenses with severe penalties. Recent legislation grants individual banks the power to freeze customer accounts if criminal activity is suspected. Penalties for fraud and related activities perpetrated in connection with computers can include imprisonment of up to 25 years (see http://www.cybercrime.gov/cclaws.html).

31. See http://www.mcconnellinternational.com/services/securitylawproject.cfm

32. See http://conventions.coe.int/Treaty/en/Treaties/Html/185.htm).

Money Laundering

Since 1990, the Financial Action Task Force (FATF) has spearheaded the adoption and implementation of measures designed to counter the use of the financial system by criminals (see http://www1.oecd.org/fatf/). It established 40 recommendations that set out the basic framework for anti–money laundering efforts and are intended to be of universal application. In 1996, the FATF recognized the link between cyber vulnerabilities and money laundering when it modified its 40 recommendations in 1996 to include number 13, which states, "Countries should pay special attention to money laundering threats inherent in new or developing technologies that might favor anonymity, and take measures, if needed, to prevent their use in money laundering schemes." The points addressed in cyber crime laws also apply here. Substantively, at a minimum, these laws should define money laundering and should commit to international cooperation in the investigation, prosecution, and punishment of such crimes pursuant to the guidance provided by the FATF. The FATF regularly reviews its members for compliance with the 40 recommendations, with the result that the recommendations are now the principal standard in this field.

In its 1998-99 annual report, the FATF noted a growing trend to use non-financial professional service providers as conduits for money laundering and other nefarious activities. The convergence of the telecommunications, computer, and financial services industries has highlighted the role—and associated risks—of money transmitters in the financial infrastructure. Money transmitters may perform a variety of services, including money order issuance, wire transfers, currency exchanges, check-cashing, and check-presentment. More recently, money transmitters have been providing electronic check-presentment services and point-of-sale money payment order information to the accepting bank. Money transmitters operate outside the depository institution but often are associated in some way with one or more depository institutions in a downstream relationship. Money transmitters do not operate alone. They require access to telecommunications to transport information from point to point. Usually a money transmitter contracts with an ISP to transport the information across network lines.[33]

Until January 2002, money transmitters in the United States were not regulated at the federal level. However, they are coming under increased scrutiny, because there are now an estimated 200,000 money transmitters operating in the United States and the evidence is mounting that some are being used to launder money. Because the primary focus of legislative initiatives targeting money transmitters has been to deter money laundering, most of the activity affecting this industry is derived from anti–money laundering sources.[34] There are two main approaches to this in the US:

1. **The Uniform Money Services Act**, adopted by the NCCUSL in 2000 and known as the Money Transmitters Act.[35] The act requires a money transmitter to obtain a license to operate; sets forth certain licensing criteria, enforcement, and compliance provisions; makes a statement on jurisdiction; and includes provisions on the scope of the act and audit and examination authority. It also contains bond provisions, minimum net worth criteria, provisions on management experience, and requirements that the money transmitter disclose prior litigation and criminal prosecution of management. Only seven states have adopted the act.

2. **The MRTA Act**, created by the Money Transmitters Regulators Association (MRTA), formed in 1989 as a state regulators organization. Though not as comprehensive as NCCUSL's Money Transmitters Act, it is still a model for dealing with the licensing and regulation of money transmitters. Only five states have adopted it.

---

33. A more detailed analysis of the regulatory issues associated with money transmitters and ISPs is provided in Annex C.

34. See Section V for additional information on money laundering.

35. See www.law.upenn.edu/bll/ulc/moneyserv/UMSA2001Final.htm

CHAPTER 4

EXTERNAL MONITORING OF E-SECURITY PRACTICES (PILLAR 2)

O ne of the most important ways to provide incentives to bank managers, CISOs, CTOs, employees, and the general public to report e-security incidents and to improve e-security practice—and thereby reduce this source of potential operational risk—is by making reporting mandatory and by rewarding rather than punishing people for reporting. The first and best line of defense in monitoring is to educate the user population and reward them for reporting any anomalies in the system. The second pillar of public policy focuses on the *external monitoring* of e-security practices. Note as well that incentives for monitoring at the level of individual financial service providers (or banks) and their internal e-security arrangements and governance is also an essential form of effective monitoring. External monitoring and internal monitoring need to reinforce each other and the use of external monitoring to set a minimum dynamic standard for e-security practices in financial service providers is highly important. Pillar Four (Chapter 6) of this monograph focuses greater attention on internal monitoring. This can be defined as those specific processes, policies, and governance arrangements that will need to be in place as part of business process that create incentives for users to monitor, report or provide remediation in an accurate and timely fashion and to adopt adequate e-security practices such as layered e-security.

Three forms of complementary and reinforcing types of external monitoring will often need to be further developed in emerging markets to ensure better e-security practices. These include supervision and prevention, insurance of cyber-risk and related monitoring, and finally education of consumers, management, employees, and investors all of which can play a more active role in monitoring e-security practices.

Supervision and Prevention Challenges

In 1999, the Basel Committee on Banking Supervision established the Electronic Banking Group (EBG) to focus on developing risk management and bank supervision guidance for e-banking as necessary. The EBG is now addressing specific supervisory issues related to e-banking security.

Box 4.1: PRINCIPLES FOR MANAGING RISK IN ONLINE BANKING

The Electronic Banking Group of the Basel Committee on Banking Supervision released their "Risk Management Principles for Electronic Banking" in July 2003. This Report identifies fourteen "principles" for banking policies and processes that seek to manage the risks associated with electronic banking. These 14 principles fall under three distinct categories: Board and Management Oversight, Security Controls, and Legal and Reputational Risk Management.

Of particular importance is principle 3 under the category of "Board and Management Oversight," which acknowledges risks resulting from the complex, interdependent relationship between banks, e-banking capabilities, and networked technology. To mitigate systemic risks inherent in these types of interdependent relationships, this report establishes the notion that there be proper contractual accountability, due diligence, organizational risk mitigation policies, and audits. Specifically third-party contractors used to support e-banking services should be closely monitored and audited, and administrative access to sensitive e-banking databases and applications should be segregated. This is a critical step towards creating a stronger culture of security tailored for the complex, interdependent, and increasingly inter-connected world where Internet technology serves as the backbone.[36]

The fourteen principles are as follows:[37]

A. Board and Management Oversight
  1. Effective management oversight of e-banking activities.
  2. Establishment of a comprehensive security control process.
  3. Comprehensive due diligence and management oversight process for outsourcing relationships and other third-party dependencies.

B. Security Controls
  4. Authentication of e-banking customers.
  5. Non-repudiation and accountability for e-banking transactions.
  6. Appropriate measures to ensure segregation of duties.
  7. Proper authorization controls within e-banking systems, databases and applications.
  8. Data integrity of e-banking transactions, records, and information.
  9. Establishment of clear audit trails for e-banking transactions.
  10. Confidentiality of key bank information.

C. Legal and Reputational Risk Management
  11. Appropriate disclosures for e-banking services.
  12. Privacy of customer information.
  13. Capacity, business continuity and contingency planning to ensure availability of e-banking systems and services.
  14. Incident response planning.

Source: Bank for International Settlements.

They recently established cyber-risk as a source of operational risk, and identified it as an essential area to address in modernizing technology supervision. The EBG report released in July 2003, is titled "Risk Management Principles for Electronic Banking" and elaborates on the 14 principles introduced in their initial May 2001 report. These principles are summarized in Box 4.1 above.

---

36. See also the World Bank, Integrator Group, "Technology Risk Supervision Guidelines", September 2003.
37. Taken from the text of Basel Committee, "Risk Management Principles for Electronic Banking", July 2003, pgs. 7-8.

Additionally, the Financial Stability Forum (FSF) has established a special contact group on e-finance that is in the process of reviewing opportunities for cross-sector information sharing and coordination on e-finance trends, developments and supervisory issues (including risk management) between various financial services supervisory groups.

Because e-banking is based on technology designed to expand the "virtual" geographic reach of banks and customers without necessarily requiring a physical expansion, market expansion beyond national borders significantly increases cross-border supervision challenges for bank supervisors. Although such supervisors agree that the supervisory principles of traditional banking are applicable to e-banking, changes in technology and dependence by banks on service providers magnify the level of risk. The 14 principles for risk management of e-banking issued by the EBG fall into three fundamental categories: (1) effective board and management oversight, (2) security control related risk issues, and (3) legal and reputation risk issues.

The ability of regulatory agencies to regulate and supervise e-banking entities effectively in today's virtual banking environment must be strengthened to handle the special challenges of e-security. Authentication, security control, integrity, and even incident response planning figure prominently in the 14 EBG principles. In particular, the EBG emphasizes the need for a bank's effective internal controls. Moreover, the EBG principles place liability on the bank in the event of e-security problems with vendors. Despite this emphasis, there is still a need to make the chain of vendors involved in the delivery of e-security services or other e-enabling services secure and to impose better downstream liability on these entities within and across borders. For example, the Office of the Comptroller of the Currency in the United States (OCC) has done extensive work to draft e-security guidance for U.S. banks and vendors, on risk management and supervision of cross-border e-banking. This issue has been further highlighted in special annexes in a recent EBG report and is also of concern to the banking community more broadly in the United States and elsewhere.[38]

Challenges to Modernizing Financial and Technology Supervision

In many countries, a bank is subject to examination on a periodic basis. In the past, traditional examinations were done on-site and based on safety and soundness through the CAMEL rating system.[39] In addition, banks in most countries throughout the world are subject to some variant (where weights may differ) of the Basel I capital adequacy guidelines. The challenges presented by e-security breaches are not explicitly accounted for in this framework and, as noted below, even the present capital standards do not really explicitly address this form of risk. Changes envisioned under Basel II, that will make further modifications to the treatment of operational risk also do not actually address mitigation of this source of operational risk explicitly.

Bank Capital Standards and E-Security

In May 2001, the Basel Committee on Banking Supervision issued a consultative document relating to capital adequacy regulations. This document defines operational risk as the "risk of direct or indirect loss resulting from inadequate or failed internal processes, people, systems, and external events."[40] It identifies three ways to measure operational risk: (1) the basic indicator approach, (2) the standardized approach, and (3) the internal management approach. Under the basic indicator approach, banks have to hold capital for operational risk that is equal to a fixed percentage of gross income. In the case of the standardized approach, a more complex process is used whereby the financial services provider breaks up its overall operations into distinct business

---

38. See the recent work of the Banking and information technology group (BITS)—cite

39. Capital Assets Management Equity and Liquidity (CAMEL) is a system that is based on a ranking of one to five, with one being the best that was initially developed by U.S. Banking Supervision Agencies.

40. See Basel Committee on Banking Supervision Consultative Document: The New Basel Accord, January 2001.

lines and uses different indicators for each and then computes the capital charge via the use of a capital factor provided by supervisors. Finally, the most advanced approach is the internal measurement approach, which relies on calculations that result in expected losses and which often employ advanced statistical techniques that often are heavily reliant on the robustness of key assumptions.[41]

None of these frameworks allows for extortion-related risks caused by penetration of a bank's systems that can result when e-security breaches occur. Moreover, the concept of operational risk that is now used addresses only legal risk, not the problems of strategic and reputation risks. Since incentives to report losses or compromises of the system accurately are often lacking, taking proper account of e-security risks in any concept of operational risk will be highly subjective and complex. Even measurement of losses will be highly complex, although metrics are in the development stage via the use of methods to try and simulate possible areas of weakness and then estimate potential losses from various forms of specific e-security breaches. A complex issue here also relates to whether the inter-relation between different areas of layered security imply that improvements are not simply additive as each layer of security is added.

E-Security and IT Examination Processes

What, then, is the best way forward if capital regulations cannot be adjusted sufficiently? One of the most fruitful avenues is to publicize the actions that can be taken to measure and manage the risk of e-security breaches and for regulators to be pro-active in providing guidance as well as modernizing the approaches to on-and off-sight supervision of such electronic transactions as is occurring in some countries.[42] Implementing new guidelines and risk-management processes that can be monitored by bank examiners via continuous modification of technology risk supervision guidelines would impose a minimum standard for dealing with e-security on the financial services industry because it could reduce the prospect of security breaches. Here, adoption of some form of layered e-security risk protocol might also be worthy of consideration (See Chapter 6). A number of these actions are not costly to implement for any financial services provider, yet they are often lacking. Technology risk supervision guidelines could increasingly ensure that all these layers are reviewed in the context of on-site examinations.[43]

Finally, the process of monitoring, auditing, and examining should be modernized. Technology exists to enable supervisory entities to monitor, audit, and examine on a continuous and remote basis via automated software. Utilizing real-time information to analyze the health of a financial institution could result in significant benefits by identifying and stopping unacceptable risk behaviors before it brings down an institution or results in extensive collateral damage to the payment system.

In recent years, IT examinations have been performed on banks that possess online transactional banking systems. One approach to suggested supervisory processes of IT can be found in OCC Bulletin 98-3, "Technology Risk Management," as well as in the 1996 Federal Financial Institutions Examination Council (FFIEC) IS Handbook, Chapters 2-4. Among its key points, these documents stress the importance for bank management to engage in a rigorous, analytical

---

41. Many statisticians working on the so-called internal or advanced modeling approach have employed "extreme distribution theory" which is subject to significant error unless the underlying quality of loss information is very strong and in the case of cyber–risk the base of information is likely deficient in reality to support well defined quantitative modeling and estimation along such lines. Even measurement of the impact of undertaking different e-security measures is a complex undertaking.

42. Recent actions taken in the United States, Hong Kong, United Kingdom, Singapore, and the European Union are all of interest.

43. See the forthcoming "Technology Risk Supervision Guidelines" (2003). More specifically forthcoming joint work between the World Bank and the EBG will be intended to develop some new technology risk supervision guidelines that do embody the 12 layers of e-security discussed in greater detail in Chapter 6 (Pillar 4).

process when planning and implementing uses of technology systems. This process should identify and quantify risks, to the extent possible, and establish risk controls to manage risk exposure(s).

More specifically, more proactive approaches deployed in the United States and parts of Europe and Asia recognize that the use of technology-related products, services, and delivery channels exposes a bank to transaction, strategic, reputation, and compliance risks. Hence, certain Asian regulators increasingly expect banks to have an "integrated" and layered approach to address e-security risk. Increasingly, a bank's core competency will be the ability of its management to engage in a rigorous analytic process to identify, quantify, and mitigate not just e-security risks but also blended risks.

Recently, a number of countries, including the United States, have passed legislation stipulating the need for financial services providers to strengthen their information security. For example, the GLBA, also known as the Financial Services Modernization Act or Title V 12 CFR 573, applies to "financial institutions." These are defined very broadly in Section 509(3) of the act to mean "any institution the business of which is engaging in financial activities described in section 4(k) of the Bank Holding Act of 1956." In Section 501(b) of the Act, the law stipulates that regulators must "establish appropriate standards for the financial institutions...relating to administrative, technical, and physical safeguards" for customer records data. Specifically, these safeguards include: "(1) to ensure the security and confidentiality of customer records and information; (2) to protect against any anticipated threats or hazards to the security or integrity of such records; and (3) to protect against unauthorized access to or use of such records or information that could result in substantial harm or inconvenience to any customer."[44]

GLBA guidelines suggest that these institutions must adhere to the following actions:

- Identify and assess the risks that may threaten customer information.
- Develop a written plan containing policies and procedures to manage and control these risks.
- Implement and test the plan.
- Adjust the plan on a continuing basis to account for changes in technology, the sensitivity of customer information, and internal or external threats to information security.

Essentially the GLBA identified a pivotal question as it relates to safeguarding a customer's private information by asking, "What is being done to secure customer data, both physical and electronic in origin?" As in the case of payment system security this is a step in the right direction. However, the effectiveness of the law and its enforcement will require improvement vis-à-vis the specifics as to how banks should protect their electronic information assets. The 1996 Federal Financial Institutions Examination Council's IT examination manual has been the U.S. banking industry norm, and it is currently undergoing an important update in an effort to address e-security practices.

In December of 2002 the FFIEC issued its *Information Security: IT Examination Handbook*. U.S. bank examiners use this booklet when evaluating a financial institution's IT risk management process, including the duties, obligations and responsibilities of the service provider from information security to the oversight exercised by the financial institution. Despite being deemed among the best guides issued by the regulatory communities to date, the handbook does contain areas that demand further fortification if it is intended to thoroughly assess IT risks. First, the handbook could provide timetables or schedules for patching software vulnerabilities. Second, operational risks posed by WLANs, as well as best practices for securing WLANs, would be vital additions to the current FFIEC manual. Third, risks inherent in the use of satellite systems—particularly GPS

---

44. For greater detail on guidelines related to these safeguards, see also OCC 2001c.

which is used heavily for the time stamping and tagging of transactions—should be included. Fourth, mitigating the operational risks inherent in IP telephony is another important, but currently overlooked, topic. Finally, systemic risks posed by unsecure third-party systems, such as hosting providers and data warehouses, is a key issue that should certainly could be given more prominence in these examinations.

Until recently, IT examiners had followed guidelines that were in effect, a modified version of the old FFIEC IT examination manual. Under those processes, IT examiners performed "risk scoping," a practice wherein they only check new systems or software installations that have been implemented since the last examination. If the examiner has checked an institution in the past and given it a good score, he or she will not recheck any of the older systems and configurations. This approach, however, can be problematic. Systems change, and new vulnerabilities in software and configuration appear daily. Examiners cannot assume systems checked in earlier audits are secure or even adequate.[45] Today it is no longer appropriate to react, but instead the government is expected to be proactive to anticipate, plan and be prepared.

In the United States, hosting companies (third party service providers) are examined by joint examination teams from the Office of the Comptroller of the Currency (OCC), the Federal Reserve, the Office of Thrift Supervision (OTS), and the Federal Deposit Insurance Corporation (FDIC). The Bank Service Corporation Act states that if an entity provides a data processing service to a bank, then it, too, can be examined. These entities, however, cannot fail the exams. The examiners note deficiencies, and then the entity and examiners agree to a plan of action. If negotiation fails, the enforcement action calls for implementation of a cease-and-desist order. Yet again there is a loophole. Because no real reporting requirements are in place for these hosting providers for losses or rates of intrusions, the cease-and-desist "stick" is negated because there is no information on which to base it. Hence, no standard exists for the evaluation and subsequent regulation of e-security in banking institutions. It should be noted that preliminary investigations suggest that such issues are arising in many emerging markets, where often even organized supervision of third party service providers is not undertaken and where the existing human capital in technology risk assessment is limited as is overall development of the e-security industry.

Supervision will also need to be proactive, given the potentially hostile nature of the Internet and open network environment. As far back as 1995, the ISO/IEC 13335, better known as the Guidelines for the Management of IT Security (GMITS), recognized that the Internet was a precarious environment that would require the use of proper e-security.[45] Box 4.2 outlines the processes that were advocated. Note that the layered e-security risk analysis advocated in this monograph (see Chapter 6 below) has many similarities to this ISO standard, which has not been well implemented in many types of institutions, including banks.

Toward a New Approach to Regulation and Supervision

Redefining Regulatory Authority and Legal Liability of Downstream Vendors. Regulatory agencies need improved powers and the appropriate authority to regulate fully all third-party money transmitters and ISPs. Their budgets and legislative tools will need to increase. There also will be a need to rely on auditing companies (if properly reformed) and the insurance sectors of emerging markets to play a role in the oversight process. The following regulatory and compliance actions might help mitigate the threat of system compromise yet not overzealously extend the safety net. In addition, processes to monitor the extent to which financial services providers adopt and employ better layered e-security risk-management practices will be essential as part of any enhanced regulatory and compliance regime.

---

45. Nor should they assume that the snapshot provided by onsite examinations is an accurate picture of real time activity.

Box 4.2: ISO/IEC 13335 INFORMATION TECHNOLOGY—SECURITY TECHNIQUES—GUIDELINES FOR THE MANAGEMENT OF IT SECURITY (GMITS)

This ISO/IEC technical report, published in 1995, is generally known by the acronym GMITS. It is made up of five parts, designed to address different aspects of Internet security.

Part 1. Concepts and Models for IT Security
Part 2. Managing and Planning IT Security
Part 3. Techniques for the Management of IT Security
Part 4. Selection of Safeguards
Part 5. Management Guidance on Network Security

GMITS was written to be usable and useful in the worst-case environment; that is, a hostile environment, such as the Internet. The properties of assets (information) that need to be taken into account and protected are extended from the classical confidentiality, integrity, and availability to include accountability, authenticity, and reliability.

Vulnerability is refined to include any property of the asset that can be exploited for purposes other than intended. Thus, a firewall represents a single point of failure and is susceptible to a denial-of-service attack, which does not detract from its value as a protections mechanism but does mean that this vulnerability needs to be considered and addressed.

Likelihood is refined to be associated with use of the data to perform risk analysis, risk assessment, and risk management.

Part 3 focuses on the topics of risk analysis, risk assessment, and risk management. GMITS recommends that the organization establish a baseline minimum set of controls that will be applied to all aspects of the organization. This baseline will be maintained through the use of a median level risk analysis. Policy is used to ensure the enforcement of the baseline throughout the organization, so that all areas can rely on it.

There are never sufficient funds to implement the ideal set of safeguards, and thus safeguards that provide multiple functions are to be preferred, provided the compromise does not reduce effectiveness. The most important situation to guard against is a false sense of security, which is actually worse than having less security or no security at all. A modicum of paranoia is a good thing.

Having been developed as a generalized document, GMITS does not address in detail particular aspects or subtopics of IT security, such as network, cryptographic, or emanations security.

Source: International Standards Organization (ISO) and International Electrotechnical Commission (IEC).

Regulatory
- Expand the circle of regulated entities to include those elements that traffic in or assist in money transmission and directly connect to any payment system.
- Review regulatory goals and needs in an electronic environment.
- Train special audit and examination teams in risk analysis, risk management, and IT issues.
- Revisit capital adequacy requirements and the definition of operational risk to evaluate how best to accommodate e-risks noted in this monograph.
- Provide report cards to the public on how well the financial services industry is doing to attain the new security objectives in this area.
- Require clearer management responsibility and accountability to create and sustain safety and soundness.
- Define the regulatory paradigm for the new market.

Compliance
- Develop analytical teams to assess and monitor e-risk management.
- Disconnect any entity from the system that is not in compliance.
- Require warranties, indemnification, and liability from service providers that connect to the payments system.
- Require insurance coverage to accommodate additional risk.
- Institute well-developed reporting requirements for all electronic money or electronic data losses from all service providers and financial services entities.
- Require information sharing between the regulator and the financial services entity concerning losses.
- Require artificial intelligence software, and make affirmative the duty to report all irregular activity from or through any service provider.
- Ensure that in management letters and other correspondence between examiners and management of financial services providers adequate attention focuses on communication between the systems administrator, chief information officer, security officer, etc. and senior management (including the CFO, CEO) and even the board of directors.[46]

Access, availability, and interoperability should also be key objectives of supervision and enforcement. The very interlinked nature of e-security providers and e-enabling companies or money transmitters implies that the traditional regulatory structure must expand. It does not imply that a greater number of entities be under the safety net, but rather that the regulatory framework create incentives for accountability in such entities as ISPs to application service, software, hardware, monitoring detection, and penetration assessment providers. Liability must attach to these providers just as to the directors of those financial institutions that contract with them. These providers are as indispensable to the institution's ability to provide electronic financial services with integrity as lawyers and accountants. They should be bonded, licensed, and subject to periodic audit and examination.

In summary, traditional regulatory and supervisory schemes in developing countries as well as in many emerging markets are outdated and need to be revised in order to determine whether an online financial institution is operating in a safe and sound manner.

Coordination in Supervision and Information Sharing Across Agencies and Borders

In many countries throughout the world, supervision and enforcement in the area of e-security is complicated by unclear jurisdictional lines across relevant agencies. In practice, often the central bank, the securities or banking regulator (if separate from the central bank), law enforcement agencies, and many other entities must be in a position to share information and reports. In many cases, this can be problematic from a legal point of view (for example, provisions of bank secrecy), or a general lack of incentives may result in no established forum or process for undertaking coordinated action.

This coordination problem is magnified when we consider the extent to which banks outsource to third-party service providers from offshore jurisdictions. In light of these cross-border coordination issues, it is important to seek and promote cooperation between law enforcement agencies and regulatory authorities for financial services providers to develop a global registry and better quality information about such "third party service providers." Such arrangements will have to go beyond the pursuit of those engaged in money laundering activities; it will require the

---

46. During the Y2K effort, systems administrators were given more attention, but in many financial services conglomerates, very little communication goes on between management and the systems people until after the fact. As technology budgets and related security issues grow in importance, this is likely to change—but the regulatory authorities can make management more sensitive to these issues in the course of the examination process.

development of a more accurate and timely system for reporting all incidents of e-security breaches, and not just loss-related information. This is an important area, in which worldwide cooperation will be needed on an increasing scale.[47] To achieve such cooperation may also require greater harmonization across countries in fundamental areas of legislation, including bank secrecy statutes, privacy statutes, etc.

The Role of Private Insurance

While technology and good monitoring mechanisms are essential to proper cyber risk management, it is clear that these activities will not alone fully mitigate financial loss. Hence, cyber insurance programs can play a role. As a complement to network security products and services, financial service providers will increasingly have this relatively new option in rounding out their e-risk management programs. The development of e-risk insurance started in the mid-1990s when insurers recognized that traditional insurance policies left insurees exposed to the new perils associated with doing business via the Internet and computer networks. These exposures include third party risks stemming from Internet media liability, professional services liability and network security, cyber extortion as well as direct losses, or first party risks, such as theft and damage to information assets, and Internet business interruption.

Today, even cyber terrorism would have to be included as a form of cyber risk—so one can ask if present political risk policies can deal with this new form of cross-border, quasi-political risk. In response to these new risks, insurers initially attempted to retrofit traditional insurance such as the comprehensive general liability and errors and omissions policies, tacking on insuring agreements and developing new definitions and exclusions. This method has generally been abandoned because both the insurance industry and the insured community realized that in order to offer comprehensive coverage for e-risks, new standalone policies needed to be drafted that provided express coverage for liability and loss arising out of cyber risks. Market participants sought guidance from the actuarial data and claims history of professional liability, property and crime policies to build pricing and underwriting methodologies for this new insurance. This was always the most basic starting point since reliable network security offering must also include loss prevention services and thus began to undertake individual security assessments. These assessments had a dual purpose: One, to assist the prospective insured in understanding its security vulnerabilities, if any; and two, to assist the underwriter in his risk analysis. Together with the insurance application, the prospective insured provided extensive information about its network security profile. In turn, they received feedback on the quality of their security.

Traditional Insurance Policies

Typical insurance policies have not dealt with e-security risks or, more broadly, the types of risks emanating from such security breaches. For example, so-called first-party coverage in the context of commercial property policies usually requires physical loss or damage to property via fire but not denial-of-service attacks via computer hackers or other types of e-risk. Also, an employee theft exclusion is usually included in such policies; in many cases of e-security breaches, an insider or former employee may be involved. In fact, in the fall of 2001, one insurance service office explicitly excluded software- and computer-related losses in commercial policies so that coverage would need to be sought via other specialized policies or arrangements. Commercial and crime policies generally cover theft of money and securities, not theft of information, as do many forms of fidelity bonds. Finally, kidnap and ransom policies often limit coverage for extortion to threat of bodily injury, they do not extend to the possibility of severe reputation damage associated with making public penetration into a bank's systems or theft of other critical or private information.

---

47. See Chapter 5 which includes a few examples of such cooperative ventures such as Computer Emergency Response Teams (CERTs) or the New York Electronic Crimes Task Force.

Recently, insurance carriers have been offering e-risk policies that do provide coverage for cyber risk. Here there is the broader question of how to characterize the specific risks to reputation entailed in e-security breaches and—because reputation risk is highly complex—the kinds of loss payouts for which insurance carriers would be liable. One could just as easily view these risks as similar to catastrophic risk, or perhaps even to kidnapping risk. The latter is relevant not only in the case of electronic identity theft, in which a ransom may be sought from the financial services provider, but also in the case of a pure hack where the hacker threatens to go public and may demand what amounts to a form of extortion payments. Defining the nature of the risk in the case of first-party coverage deserves more thought in light of how industry participants are now writing such e-risk policies.

Another form of insurance that is generally not adequate is third-party coverage. Here there have been gaps in the narrow provisions for advertising injury coverage in which claims can be sought only if the injury occurs in the coverage territory during the policy period-thereby excluding many possible e-security events. Despite refinements made to the definition of advertising on the Internet via the electronic data liability amendment in the fall of 2001, this is an area that remains unresolved. Also, because electronic data is not defined as tangible property, these forms of coverage have limited effectiveness.

Cyber Risk Insurance Today

Today in spite of formidable reportage problems inherent in establishing a benchmark to actuarially measure the risk of hack attacks, electronic identity theft, and other forms of related e-risk, insurance companies are writing coverage for such risk. The development of e-risk policies first occurred in the mid-1990s. Insurers developed stand-alone e-risk policies rather than adding coverage to existing property and liability insurance. Market participants have also used employee liability coverage as a model for pricing and issuing this insurance.

In underwriting this risk, insurers combined information security standards, such as the BS7799, with principles of risk management that included analysis, avoidance, control, and risk transfer. Today, insurers recognize the ISO 17799 information security standard, which addresses these issues in the following ten major sections:

1. Business continuity planning
2. System access control
3. System development and maintenance
4. Physical and environmental security
5. Statutory, regulatory, or contractual obligation compliance
6. Personnel security
7. Security management for third-party access or outsourcing to a third-party service provider
8. Computer and network management to safeguard information assets
9. Asset classification and control
10. Security policy management support

As part of the e-risk application process, several major insurers, including AIG, Zurich, Chubb, St. Paul, Progressive, and Lloyd's, have incorporated the ISO 17799 standards into a baseline security questionnaire that becomes part of the insurance application in e-risk policies they underwrite. In order to bind coverage, the insured must meet a certain security threshold for insurability, but precise nature of such thresholds has not been completely standardized within and across countries. In part, this reflects the very dynamic impact of technology in this area. Despite these developments, the use of e-risk policies is still nascent.

In the case of first-party coverage, such policies are being explicitly designed to provide coverage against network extortion, computer theft, damage to digital assets and information as intellectual property, and business or dependent business losses. In the case of third-party coverage, such policies are designed to cover network security or loss event liability and electronic publishing and multimedia liability.

In underwriting these special e-risk policies, insurers are increasingly assessing the extent to which specific providers of financial or other services are in compliance with appropriate standards in each of the 10 areas specified under ISO 17799. These areas are also relevant in the design of appropriate layered security systems, such as the recommendations in Chapter 6 of this monograph. These types of considerations still do not make it possible to actuarially calculate proper premiums for these forms of first- and third-party e-risk coverage. The underlying defects in the information about intrusions and extortion make the pricing of such policies very difficult.

Among the earliest adopters of cyber insurance were financial institutions. In underwriting e-risk policies for financial institutions, insurers review the network security profile of the bank itself, as well as the third party service providers that provide services to the bank, such as Web hosting and online banking services. In addition, insurers can provide credits to financial institutions that demonstrate strong risk management programs with trusted vendors or products and services. While this underwriting methodology provides a quality assessment of a financial institution's security profile, the banking industries reluctance to share data regarding losses due to hacking, denial of service attacks and malicious code make for a difficult underwriting and pricing process. Clearly, carriers who are attempting to get into this field face a number of challenges even when using ISO 17799 as a method of assessing risk.

Given the lack of significant loss history and unknown potential for loss, carriers are understandably proceeding cautiously. Proper underwriting requires not only a detailed application and security assessment but preferably the vulnerability assessment should be done more than once a year given the potential rapid change in security technology. Financial Institutions, however, who are more apt to take a proactive approach to their network security may want to look for underwriters with the following characteristics:

- Dedicated unit of underwriters who do nothing other than cyber-risks with dedicated claims, legal and technology professionals' assistance
- High financial strength
- Worldwide operations
- Specific cyber-risk expertise
- Loss Prevention services such as affordable on-site security assessments
- Capable third party vulnerability assessment corporations

Shortcomings of ISO 17799

There are four inherent weaknesses within the approach laid out by ISO 17799 standard. The first relates to the lack of good information to underwrite these policies. Due to lack of significant loss history and unknown potential for loss, carriers are proceeding cautiously, thereby making premiums prohibitively costly for some types of financial service providers. This may help to explain the lack of growth in this line of insurance.

The second weakness relates to static third party assessments. If a carrier does require a third party assessment; it is done once a year and is "static" based upon the standards recommendation. Vulnerability assessments need to be reoccurring. Due to the rapid pace of technological change, there is great potential for carriers to be insuring companies with significantly different profiles than what was found in the original assessment.

The third weakness corresponds to the loss of control by banks and corporations. These entities are paying substantial premiums and receiving a negligible amount of education on new vulnerabilities and subsequent proactive risk exposure procedures. Although certain carriers have been more proactive than others in this regard, the ISO standard should stipulate that good policies, procedures and budgets to deal with new vulnerabilities should be enacted. If not, then they should be deemed non-insurable.

Finally, the weakest aspect of ISO 17799 is the static nature of policies. The rigidity of policies and the subsequent inability of consumers and underwriters to edit policies to specific to risks/legislation associated to a specific enterprise or bank can undermine the coverage entirely. For example, ISO 17799 does not take into account the vulnerabilities associated with new technologies such as wireless, IP telephony, satellite-based systems like GPS and GPRS and Public Key Infrastructures. The static nature of this standard compounds the risks associated with e-commerce. Many of the actual e-risk policies reviewed in preparing this report pay no attention to the special risks that wireless technologies are creating in the delivery of financial services. As documented in Kellermann (2002a), insurance providers should clearly identify the standards for financial services providers to meet for wireless risk mitigation before they underwrite an e-risk policy. The ISO technical committee has been revising the current Banking Information Security Standard and will be releasing a revised, more robust, Banking Information Security Standard 13569 by the Spring of 2004.

In thinking about the future coverage under this standard, one must consider:

- How identified vulnerabilities will be linked to potential subsequent losses and applicable coverage grants.
- How uniformity of vulnerabilities under review by auditors will be addressed.
- How financial industry specific vulnerabilities will be assessed.

Insurance Companies as a Force for Change
Over time, the growth in e-commerce liability insurance and, specifically, e-risk insurance is likely to be quite substantial. Estimates by AIG suggest that the market for this insurance may be as much as $2.5 billion. The viability of providing this type of insurance coverage is related to more systemic approaches to improving the base of information for pricing[48] and the e-security risks to be covered. Although vendors of e-security services are working with insurance companies on this issue, government, industry, and law enforcement officials clearly need to find ways to improve the reporting of such information (see Chapter 5). Current efforts to develop public-private partnerships to solve this problem should therefore be a high priority.

The global insurance industry can and should act as an important force for change in e-security arrangements worldwide. First, it should strive to improve the minimum standards for e-security and should strongly advocate enhanced layered e-security systems (see Chapter 6 and Annex A). Second, it should work to improve certification standards for vendors of e-security services described in Chapter 5 as a way of mitigating covered risks and of curtailing the spread of risk. Third, it should be concerned with improvements in worldwide cooperation and efforts to improve the data and information available with which to actuarially measure e-risks in companies and financial services providers. Finally, it should require vendors of e-security and other related services (e.g., hosting) to bear some liability, in contrast to some of the outsourcing arrangements that do not create adequate incentives to obtain or maintain e-security.

Education and Prevention
The OECD has recognized that the global nature of the Internet can cause systemic risks that we all share as a global community. Principle I of the OECD Guidelines on a Culture of Security stress the importance of building awareness and education about e-security. In many countries, half of e-security intrusions are still carried out by insiders. An uneducated or undereducated

---

48. QUAID (Questions Used to Access the Information Database) is an active database storing past, present and ongoing assessments along with known vulnerabilities dating back to 1985. Specifically developed for the transfer of risk through the creation of new pricing models for E-risk.

workforce is inherently more vulnerable to this type of incident or attack. In contrast, a well-trained workforce, conscious of security issues, can add a layer of protection. Hence, the safety and efficiency of technology is directly related to the training and technical education of the persons using the technology.

Educational initiatives will have to be targeted to financial services providers (both systems administrators and management), to various agencies involved in law enforcement and supervision, and to actual online users[49] of financial services. Initiatives in this area must be undertaken worldwide. This is likely to be one of the most important initiatives that multilateral and bilateral lenders can support over the next decade.

Due to the dynamic nature of both technology and the cyber-threat, recurrent security training is essential for all IT personnel and management. Education regarding the institutions policies and proper procedure in protecting open architecture systems will ensure that each participant is an important actor for ensuring security. Realistically educational initiatives will only become effective when senior management recognizes that their technological assets present operational risk that must be dealt with through a combination of policy, procedure and technology. Cyber crime does not discriminate between the technologically savvy and the laymen. E-security educational programs will need to be tailored for all from children to adults, from IT personnel to senior management. Virtual reality does come with externalities that can be mitigated through education. Use of innovative techniques for training including distance learning and use of other technology in educational initiatives will also make this effort more economical.[50] In order to be successful at preventing electronic fraud education must be a priority. Awareness of the risks posed by the Internet will be the first step towards a more safe and sound global marketplace.

More specifically, any plan of action to improve education will need to involve a number of important actions, such as the following:

- Improve awareness and education of financial sector participants about cyber ethics and appropriate user behavior on networked systems. Ensure that employees (and also management), especially those involved in payment system transactions and systems administrators, special chief information officers or security officers, are aware of the risks and proper approaches to layered security.
- Create institution-wide e-security policies on appropriate behavior and the corresponding channels for reporting intrusions or incidents in close coordination with any effort to improve worldwide information in intrusions (see Chapter 5).
- Develop awareness in emerging markets' banking communities about the need to formulate "incident response plans." In many countries, this will involve efforts to improve capacity; to teach risk assessment, risk management, and prevention; and to develop the essential components of a good security program, and most importantly, implementation of proper processes in such financial service providers.
- Facilitate cooperation and transfer of know-how among law enforcement entities, financial intelligence units (FIUs), and supervisory agencies in developed and emerging markets through such methods as more active exchange programs between personnel. This kind of cooperation can facilitate better education of law enforcement officials, supervisors, and others in emerging market economies about how to deal with e-security.

---

49. The Internet Security Alliance issued "Common Sense Guidelines for Computer Users" that identify best practices necessary for home users to secure their own PCs. (See http://wbln0018.worldbank.org/html/FinancialSectorWeb.nsf/(attachmentweb)/CommonSenseGuideforHomeUsers/$FILE/Common+Sense+Guide+for+Home+Users.pdf)

50. Multilateral organizations and agencies (e.g., the FTC) have a very important role to play. In the case of emerging markets the World Bank has created a web-site dedicated to acting as a clearing house for educating end users, regulatory officials, market participants and others about e-security issues. See ww1.worldbank.org/finance and click on E-Security.

- Launch some education initiatives in this area targeted to bank examiners,[51] via the Toronto Institute, the Federal Reserve courses for bank examiners, or the Financial Stability Institute. The focus of the education should be on techniques for determining whether the layered e-security systems of brick-and-click banks can be better assessed and evaluated.
- Consider developing a cross-border university outreach program (for example, involving such entities as Carnegie Mellon's CERT) to promote the training of future e-security professionals, and develop innovative approaches to sharing of information in e-security incidents. Some private entities (for example, Cisco) provide training at reduced costs for government.
- Develop online programs[52] to improve education of users of e-financial services; develop processes and incentives to have customers report suspicious activities in the use of their accounts. Users and the information they provide are critical to any overall approach to e-security and risk sharing.

---

51. The World Bank Financial Sector has launched such a campaign. Please refer to http://www1.worldbank.org/finance (click on e-security).

52. Consumers and businesses should visit "http://www.ftc.gov/infosecurity" for tips pertaining to the securing of personal information online, and links to free FTC publications on security, e-commerce, spam, privacy, and identity theft.

CHAPTER 5

CERTIFICATIONS, POLICIES, STANDARDS, AND PROCEDURES (PILLAR 3)

In the previous chapters pillars one and two set up the legal, regulatory and public policy foundations that are required for sustainable e-development in any country and also discussed the key areas where external monitoring will need to be strengthened (for example, external supervision, insurance as a monitoring devices, and education). Pillar 3 explains the framework that must exist within an organization to effectively run an open network system from an industry perspective. In addition, it looks at setting industry policy, standards and procedures and the role that these can play in influencing the law and assisting corporations to develop their internal structures and improve their own internal monitoring processes and procedures. This chapter explores the potential roles of the government, industry and academia in evaluating the effectiveness of security vendors and their products. Four areas of certification to address in the electronic environment are: software; hardware products; IT security vendors; and electronic transactions. This chapter drills down into the purpose of developing corporate policy, standards, processes and procedures and how they must be evaluated to determine whether the company has the requisite knowledge and commitment to engage in e-finance in a safe and sound manner.[53]

---

53. For example, a financial institution must comply with the legal, regulatory and monetary policies of a country. Its internal policies, standards, processes, and procedures should reflect the company's commitment to comply and should set forth the means by which the institution can show the government that it is complying with the law. Here, a company must create policy that states that the company is committed to practicing good e-security and then show how it is committed by documenting what needs to happen when an incident occurs. In the end organizations must be committed to operating in a safe and sound manner and this commitment must be documented and part of the everyday culture in the institution. E-security is a continuous improvement process and an ongoing cross-disciplinary program. It is not a one-time event.

The Internet is a massive system of distributed but connected hosts.[54] No one "owns" the Internet. As a result, no one can claim the right to govern it. In fact, it is a self-regulating entity. Although standards have been written on the proper use of the Internet and securing operations on the Internet, there is no entity with recognized legitimate authority to enforce these standards. To compound this problem open network technologies also are distributed but connected, resulting in all of these technologies being interconnected at some level. As a result standards, processes and procedures cannot be developed in isolation but must take into consideration how a standard for one technology will affect its interface with other technologies. In order to meet the overarching goals of access, availability and interoperability standards often must forego security or a higher level of security to retain these three features.

Certification, policies, standards, procedures, training and education translate the system's values and beliefs into actions. However, if the processes leading to these outcomes must be flexible and dynamic as the system is constantly evolving. Continuous deployment of new technologies means that users must continually review and update policies, standards, procedures and certifications and train customers and employees on these changes. Since people are the most resistant to change, policies, standards and procedures must be clearly and concisely written to reflect and enhance the culture of the entity using the system.

The area of certification, standard setting, processes and overall policies relating to e-security usually requires cooperation between the public sector and the private sector. In fact it will be essential in ensuring that such a framework can work. What makes these issues so challenging given the internet is its global nature. Hence there is the collective action problem noted in Chapter 2 whereby not only must cooperation be sought between industries, academia, and the Government within a country but also across countries. Hence, developing this critical pillar in any country to deter e-security breaches is highly challenging.

Certifications
Certifying Software and Hardware Vendors
Software and hardware vendors were discussed earlier in this monograph. Here, the main concern is that these vendors often sell products to financial entities knowing that they contain vulnerabilities and that they should not be used for financial transactions. Yet, they sell these products to banks without advising them of the vulnerabilities and then refuse to provide warranties or liabilities to the banks for losses sustained as a result of these vulnerabilities. One approach is to require products to be certified for specific uses. Industry, government or a certification board composed of academia, industry and government could be used to certify products for use in the financial services sector. Another approach that can be used in concert with product certification or as a stand alone hurdle is to require vendors to warrant their products and provide either liability coverage or a notice and disclaimer that a product is not suitable for certain uses to the buyer. Additionally, one could employ a mix of these approaches. No matter what approach is used the certifying entity must be a recognized, trusted authority.

Certifying Security Vendors
The second area of certification involves IT security vendors and IT security personnel. What is the role of government or the private sector in licensing or certifying IT security vendors or IT security personnel? Licensing is a governmental function that indicates an entity has successfully mastered certain entry criteria and is in good standing with the licensing authority. Certification is an industry action attesting to an individual's level of knowledge or expertise. These functions are

---

54. When the Defense Advanced Research Projects Agency (DARPA) created the Internet in the 1960s, it was to assure that the United States communications system would survive a physical assault. Its original purpose was to devise a communications medium that could route messages to large numbers of researchers in a variety of ways and that could survive if part of the system were destroyed or attacked.

not stand-alone approaches. Often certification is one of the entry criteria required to obtain a license. The first question is whether there is a case to require IT security vendors or personnel to the financial sector to obtain a license. Since such vendors and personnel play a critical role in maintaining and protecting the integrity of one of the thirteen critical infrastructures of the electronic economy, it is a matter of great public interest. Some would argue that licensing vendors or personnel would widen the regulatory safety net. This is a possibility, depending on how the licensing system is designed and enforced. Another alternative might be to require vendors and security personnel to provide assurance without unduly burdening the regulatory structure. For example, such vendors or personnel might post a performance bond or obtain industry certification. This would allow them to provide services to the level of certification they have achieved. The question then is who or what should determine the certification levels and decide what criteria shall be included in each level of mastery and who or what will enforce the certifications?

Approaches to Certifying Security Vendors

Licensing would provide the simplest and most agreeable approach to regulation of e-security vendors, as governments tend to have greater longevity than companies. However, it is possible that industry could self-regulate by using an industry approved certification process. This could possibly yield the most consistent results, particularly if insurance companies provide incentives to certified vendors by sharing in the risk through professional liability coverage. Whether security vendors are regulated by the government or by industry, only those parties that are absolutely essential to the delivery of the financial services should be included in the regulatory net. To make this approach viable, e-security would be accepted as a prerequisite for a vendor to provide services to the financial sector, and all could share proportionately in the attendant risks. Thus the scope of regulation could be contained to those entities, such as money transmitters and ISPs that hold themselves out as being able to provide hosting to the financial services industry. The steps in brief are for government to regulate security vendors through the licensing process or for industry to certify vendors to levels of professional ability, which then would allow the vendor to obtain insurance coverage or post performance bonds, and have risk appropriately shared.

Understanding the Value of the E-transaction to be Certified

Certifying electronic transactions or elements of that transaction is fraught with controversy. This is due partly to significant philosophical differences about the life cycle of data and the roles and responsibilities of those who "own" each part of that cycle. It is important to know what the value of the transaction is to determine whether it warrants the cost of certifying it. Once the institution knows what the transaction's value is it can analyze from a cost-benefit perspective, the benefits that each technology solution brings to the table and weigh that against the costs or concerns associated with each.[55] In other words, the expected value should outweigh the projected costs including risks of the transaction.

---

55. Then it should implement a data security classification system through the business rules engine that automatically attaches a level of security to each type of transaction. The business criteria used to make these decisions should include, at a minimum, the following value matrix: integrity, reliability, authentication, verification, authority and non-repudiation. The value of a transaction should then be equal to the sum of the total risks associated with the transaction. Using a value matrix could also assist the insurance industry in evaluating coverage, risks, and pricing. Also, it could help the financial entity to self-monitor risk by pinpointing where and why particular risks are greater. The value matrix would also help to enrich the information that is reported. The institution could use a mix of security solutions, fitting the solution to the value and risks of the underlying transaction. Although insurance companies could play a role in encouraging the security industry to set standards and to endorse the best practices in terms of authorizing and verifying transaction elements, setting harmonized standards for authenticating documents and other related issues goes beyond the role of any private entity and requires significant cooperation between governments.

Certifying Authorities

Another area of considerable controversy is the question of how to transmit information securely over the Internet. Traditionally encryption has been used as a means of protecting information transferred over the Internet, together with other types of protocols (for example, secure socket layer and others) designed to provide security to naked or "open" wide area network systems. Although effective, these mechanisms are meant only to provide protection against certain kinds of vulnerabilities for specific technologies. Of these possibilities, PKI has received the most acceptance and controversy.

Because all of these elements are interrelated, together with certification, and certification authorities (CA), government needs to address the issues of authentication, confidentiality, and non-repudiation in designing valid electronic transactions, since these form the backbone of transactional activity. Chapter 6 discusses these issues in detail and compares the benefits and drawbacks of potential technologies, such as biometrics and digital time-stamping. More generally, government needs to encourage the development of technologies that can be used to authenticate without certifying. To preserve confidentiality, the government can require the double signing of a key or the use of certain encryption. Again, government should encourage the private development of solutions that maintain confidentiality and privacy for business and consumers. In fact, a global industry has already developed, and many U.S. companies provide privacy and security solutions to companies and consumers worldwide as noted in the Standards section below.[56]

Finally, it is important to consider how to ensure an appropriate level of trust in any given transaction. The legal or regulatory transactional framework must be technology-neutral. In reality, a variety of technologies can certify or authenticate transactional elements and can protect against non-repudiation. The major strengths and weaknesses of the technologies in use today are examined below.

Trust and Confidence in Certification and Authentication Technologies

"Trust and confidence" translates into the following: Party A is able to access online services and transfers funds from one account to another. Party A then checks his account balances, and the correct amount has moved from one account to the other. At the end of the month, he goes online again and confirms that all activity for that month has been properly posted and that the account balances match his figures. As a result, he has a high level of trust and confidence in the system. Or Party B receives certain monies from the government on a monthly basis. Or Party C sets up automatic bill paying for all her utilities. Each month, her account is debited for the correct amount of the utilities. Studies have shown that when someone uses a new technology, that party will bond with the use of the technology if it works favorably with no complications the first three times of use. Conversely, assume that Party D approaches an ATM and attempts to take money from his account. He inputs his personal identification number (PIN), and the transaction is refused. He tries again, and it is refused. The third time, the ATM machine eats his card. Studies show that the opportunity to create trust in technology has been lost. This person will not willingly use this technology again unless no other delivery channel is available.

PKI Technology. An extraordinary amount of research and development money has been spent on developing PKI and certification authorities over the past decade. As a result, PKI is the best-known electronic signature verification technology. Clearly, it has its strengths. Yet, easier and simpler technologies perform just as well. Again, it is important to understand the business drivers and the consequential risks in choosing an appropriate technology. Moreover, there is no accepted standard legislation, and record retention requirements for certification authorities are often undefined.

PKI refers to the Infrastructure built to enable use of Public Key or asymmetric key cryptography. PKI is based on asymmetric key cryptography. Although PKI can operate through individual

---

56. These solutions include systems providing safety in browsing to detect cookies or manage cookies; e-mail security; and even personal firewalls for retail consumers.

agreements between parties, legislation is required for it to have large-scale operational efficiency. It needs a sophisticated infrastructure to achieve operational credibility. This infrastructure requires programs, management policies, procedures, communication protocols, and processes that govern the life cycle of the key pairs. PKI is an intensely process-oriented technology. Each step of the process must be handled correctly for it to be effective.

Asymmetric key encryption occurs when the key used to encrypt is not the key to decrypt. In a PKI system each person involved in the transaction is given a private key that is mathematically related to a public key. The private key is used to decrypt everything that is encrypted with the public key. The public key is published and used by anyone who is transacting business with the publishing entity. The private key must remain a secret for the system to work. The public key is used to encrypt the message and the private key is used to decrypt it. Thus, the intended recipient is the only one who should be able to decrypt the message.

Certification Authorities. PKI is composed of three processes: certification, registration, and verification. In simplistic terms, certification occurs when the public key is associated with a person, entity, access authority, or credential that results in a digital certificate. The digital certificate is the heart of PKI. Typically, digital certificates are issued by a central CA or a trusted third-party. Ownership of a digital certificate issued by such an entity evidences that the entity has validated the identity of the party requesting the public key. Validation implies that the CA has "vetted" the requesting party. Vetting typically means the requesting party has proven his identity through some process, often by showing a birth certificate or driver's license. Sometimes the CA also requires a face-to-face interview or other documentation to assure the CA that the person or entity is who or what it claims to be. If the party passes scrutiny, the CA issues a certificate with the public key embedded in it along with other identification information, credentials or permissions. The CA signs the certificate and depending on the legal structure of the CA's authority, the CA typically assumes some measure of responsibility for the vetting process. Arguably when an entity accepts the certificate the entity is doing so because he has placed trust in the CA and the process used by the CA to verify the requestor's identity.

A great deal of confusion and controversy surrounds PKI. This is due partly to the significant costs and degree of sophistication associated with managing it correctly. It is also attributable to "hype" promulgated by companies that have invested a significant amount of research and development into PKI, and need to recoup their investments. Mainly, it has to do with the lack of common legislative standards to govern the PKI industry, its processes, and its obligations. For example, in the United States there are at least four models of legislation governing CAs. Each of these differ in who or what can be a CA, what their obligations are, how they are governed, and what CAs legally provide when issuing a certificate. The first law to be passed in the United States, which can also be considered the most comprehensive, is the Utah Digital Signature Act. It has since fallen out of favor.

In every system the CA registers, verifies, manages, and revokes or destroys certificates. Each of these elements may be handled differently in any given jurisdiction. So if Party A is in one jurisdiction, Party B is in another jurisdiction, and Party C is in a third jurisdiction. CAs are used in each jurisdiction it is imperative that the parties know what the law requires the CA to do for each of these elements to know what the parties are relying on for the certificates issued. For example, in jurisdiction A, a party may only need to provide a government issued photo ID, whereas identification requirements might be much stricter in the other jurisdictions. Also, in jurisdiction A, the CA may only be liable if the validity of the photo ID is in question and the CA was negligent in failing to take further action to verify the ID's authenticity. Another concern is the CAs responsibility to revoke and publish the revocations of certificates. Without going into further detail it is important to understand the rights, obligations, and responsibilities of any CA that you rely on.

Today, a proliferation of public and private key providers and related CAs are available through government agencies, such as postal authorities; by technology providers such as GTE and Verisign, by telecommunication providers such as Entrust, and by financial service providers.

Currently, seven global financial institutions are such providers.[57] Some countries have opted to endorse only one recognized public CA (such as the postal service). In other countries, both public and private authorities provide this function. Although one could claim that certification is a "public good" and therefore should be kept under the control of a public entity, such as the post office, private companies can act as certification agents as long as the government has a viable means of cross-certifying in order to check on the competence of the service being provided. In all likelihood, the desire to maintain the institution's reputation will act as a significant incentive to resolve the moral hazard problem.

Notaries. One alternative to PKI is to provide a new type of notary license. In this scenario, a notary could apply for a Class A license. This authorizes a notary to accept and to certify digital signatures, as well as to time-stamp documents and to notarize manual signatures. Or a notary could apply for a Class B license. This authorizes the notary to time-stamp and to notarize manual signatures only. Finally the notary could apply for a Class C license. Under this licensing scheme the notary could only notarize manual signatures.

This Multi-license notary scenario is a tempting resolution to the issue of non-repudiation for a number of reasons. First, it utilizes an existing and accepted regulated service for verifying signatures. It assesses a greater fee to a Class A license than the others, which in turn, acts as a user's fee. This, then can be used by governments to pay for the necessary personnel and equipment it needs to provide online assistance to users and to the expanded notary industry.

The negatives of such a solution are also fairly clear. In emerging markets, notaries may not be well trained to undertake this role, and they would need to receive certifications to perform this function. Another concern is that the licensing system, or in many cases the notaries themselves, may be subjected to corruption; this concern emphasizes the need for sufficient oversight. Moreover, in the context of many transactional arrangements, notaries often increase the costs of transactions.

Digital Time-Stamps. Another alternative to certification authorities is a digital time stamp provider (DTS). A DTS issues a time stamp. A time-stamp associates a certain date and time with a digital document. The time stamp can be referenced to prove that the document was recorded at a specific date and time. For example, Party A signs a document and wants it time-stamped. He computes a message digest of the document using a secure one-way hash function and sends it to a time-stamping service. In return, the DTS service sends back a digital time-stamped document. This includes the message digest, the date and time it was received by the time-stamping service, and the digital signature of the time-stamping service. Later, Party A presents the document to verify its creation date, a verifier re-computes the message digest and determines whether it matches the digest in the original time stamped document. It then verifies the digital signature of the time-stamping service. The strengths of this are that a message digest does not reveal the contents of the document, it simply verifies that the underlying message was received on a certain date and time. As stated above a DTS could be an added dimension to a Notary's license. In addition, or separately, the DTS could be provided by the post office for set fees. Again this would utilize an already existing entity that is familiar to the consumer.[58]

Biometrics and Certification. Biometric technology is another alternative to the verification process. Biometric authentication techniques can be used to verify the identity of people online

---

57. The CA authenticates the public key by distributing it with a certificate (digitally signed by the certification authority). Both the potential liability of the certification authority, as well as the implication of security-related breaches to reputation, have been used as an argument for the outsourcing of the public key infrastructure to private providers. The seven banks that are CA are ABN, Bank of America, Deutsche Bank, Barclays, Chase, Citigroup, and Hypoverensbank.

58. Increasingly, technology will offer unique ways of authenticating. Such digital time stamps that utilize satellite technology and global positioning systems (GPS) will identify the location where a DTS was created or executed, adding value to the document for evidentiary and other purposes. Companies such as Cyber-locator can provide this service.

automatically through their distinctive physical or behavioral traits. A biometric identifier represents a physical characteristic of the user. The global recognition of this authentication technology will assist in the non-repudiation of financial transactions and subsequent documentation. These technologies facilitate the process by which entities can transact on a medium that facilitates anonymity. In this case, the two issues to address would be: (1) certifying the specific biometric technology and its accuracy, and (2) defining a digital signature in a broad enough manner to allow certification of the parties to a transaction through whatever authentication technology makes sense.

In summary, government should let the private sector lead where possible but should temper this approach by adopting open standards, endorsing technology-neutral solutions, encouraging the industry to self-regulate and certify, and helping insurance and other industries use incentives to share risk and responsibility in identifying and correcting vulnerabilities. Such objectives can be difficult to achieve in emerging markets where oversight of self-regulating entities can be defective (Glaessner 1992, Bossone and Promisel 1999).

Policy

Policies perform numerous vital functions. First they are communication vehicles that inform all individuals operating in the system as to how they should behave given a particular issue or topic. A well-written policy provides a framework within which executive management tells the organization how it feels about a given subject and what steps it is prepared to take in relation to that topic. It sets out the specific objectives that management is trying to achieve together with the scope of the policy, identifying who is responsible for meeting these objectives, and management's intentions to implement it.

Security policies cover a wide range of topics including access controls, authorization, conducting investigations, audits and reporting requirements and disciplining workers for security violations. Second it provides a legal function. It establishes the intent of the entity to live up to certain behaviors and establishes the management's level of awareness concerning issues. For example, a policy might state that management expects employees to report security breaches in a timely and accurate fashion. By setting such a policy, employees are assured that they will not suffer harm for reporting an incident. It also establishes with the world that management supports the proper reporting of incidents. However, if management acts contrary to policy or fails to implement the appropriate procedures to support the policy, this "failure to act" can be used against the entity in a court of law. Third, policies affect how the entity is managed, especially how the budget is determined. A matter of high importance should be a high budget priority. If policy states that security is a high priority but fails to budget appropriately this too can be used as evidence against the entity.

For policies to be effective, they must accurately reflect the entity's culture and behavior, especially its values and ethics. Policies should drive behavior. Security policies in particular must "work" within that culture or management must be prepared to exert the necessary pressure to change the culture. For example, the policy of the US government is that security is management's responsibility and is a business prerequisite. This policy makes it clear that management must ensure that there is sufficient money budgeted for security and it has appropriate security for its line of business. Failure to implement appropriate security is management's fault. By setting this policy, the federal government made its priorities clear. Each department head now understands the role he plays, the expectations of his management and the need to prioritize money for this important issue in developing his budget.

Standards

Industry Standards

At the global level, standards are agreements reached on products, practices, or operations that are formally approved by nationally or internationally recognized industrial, professional, trade, or governmental bodies. Standards are an effective trade mechanism. In the global market, the dominant standards maker is the dominant market shareholder. Governments use standards as a gatekeeper or deciding factor in setting project requirements and awarding contracts. In addition they use standards as one of the primary tools in choosing trading partners. In many ways standards have created the framework within which we live today. For example, the standards are the governing means by which we order our lives through time zones and navigate our lives through longitude and latitude. At a more specific or local level, standards are a specific set of rules, procedures or conventions that are agreed upon by parties in order to assure more uniform effective and therefore efficient operations and communications.

Standard Setting Bodies

Industry standards evolve from numerous sources; government-related entities, international organizations, private sector industry and trade associations. The number of standard setting bodies is growing almost as fast as connections to the Internet.[59]

The current major thrust for standardizing and evaluating system security is based on the Common Criteria (CC); short for "Common Criteria for Information Technology Security Evaluation" ISO standard 15408.[60] The Common Criteria grew out of a February 1993 European Commission sponsored workshop in Brussels on the US Federal Criteria presented by NIST. Alignment of criteria between Europe and North America was determined to be important. Both U.S. and Canadian officials already had agreed to harmonize their criteria (Federal Criteria and CTCPEC, respectively). Six nations are represented on the project by the following sponsoring organizations:

- Canada: Communications Security Establishment
- France: Service Central de la Securite des Systemes d'Information
- Germany: German Information Security Agency (GISA)
- Netherlands: Netherlands National Communications Security Agency (NLNCSA)
- United Kingdom: Communications and Electronics Security Group (CESG)
- United States: National Institute for Standards and Technology (NIST) and the National Security Agency (NSA)

---

59. There are numerous standard setting organizations around the world. The following represent the most influential international standards setting bodies. It is not intended to be an exhaustive list, but rather is a guideline on where to go for the most up to date information on standards.

- Institute of Electrical and Electronics Engineer (IEEE) is a non-profit professional technical association composed of approximately 400,000 members in 150 countries. It is a leading authority in areas ranging from computer engineering to telecommunications to electric power. (http://www.ieee.org)
- International Standards Organization (ISO) is a network of national standards institutes from 140 countries. It works with international organizations, governments, industry and consumer organizations. (http://www.iso.org)
- International Telecommunications Union (ITU) is an organization in the United Nations system. Its primary objective is to help governments and the private sector coordinate global telecommunication networks and services. (http://www.itu.org)
- ISOC: Internet Society. ISOC represents the Internet Engineering Steering Group and the Internet Research Task Force. These are the standards setting and research organizations of the Internet community. (http://www.isoc org/standards).

60. The majority of standard setting bodies emerged in the late 1990s. Prior to that the main certification process for secure systems. In December 1985, the National Computer Security Center, a branch of the NSA published the document DOD 5200.28-STD entitled the "Department of Defense Trusted Computer System Evaluation Criteria." This became known as the "Orange Book." It attempted to define security requirements and to guide computer as to what to build into their systems in order to provide a trusted system. This system was designed for systems that predate the Internet.

The CC defines two types of security requirements: Functional and Assurance. The former defines the security behavior of the IT product or system; the latter are employed to establish confidence in the security functions, their correct implementations and their effectiveness. Generic Protection Profiles, including threat models are defined to specify what customers require. Product specific security targets specify the threat capabilities offered by a product, are defined for products or systems submitted for evaluation. Security evaluations are recognized internationally and result in one of seven defined assurance levels:

- EAL1   Functionally tested
- EAL2   Structurally tested
- EAL3   Methodically tested and checked
- EAL4   Methodically designed, tested and reviewed
- EAL5   Semi-formally verified design and tested
- EAL6   Semi-formally verified design and tested
- EAL7   Formally verified design and tested

Late last year a group composed of US government and leading technology companies released new certification standards for security professionals. This certification is known as Security+. It is intended to provide a standard method for training and evaluating the abilities of IT security professionals. Participating organizations include Microsoft, IBM, Sun Microsystems Inc., RSA Security Inc., Entrust Inc., and Verisign Inc. Government entities included the FBI, the U.S. Secret Service and NIST. Security+ is targeted at professionals with at least two years of computer networking experience. It is an objective measure that companies and organizations can use to assess the security training needs of employees and job applicants.

The CC shows the best promise of being able to move forward and instill some discipline into the system. In the end it will depend on how seriously the country leaders adhere to the criteria in developing and maintaining their systems, since this will drive the smaller countries towards action that is aligned with the CC.

Corporate Standards

Internal corporate standards translate policy into action. They set a level of expectations that must be reached or complied with in order to fulfill one's obligations or responsibilities. Standards impact a system's security. Poor standards or non-existent standards can eat up an entity's energy, inflate the support needs of the system, drive up costs and increase risk. Standards require significant energy and social organization to develop. Once standards are implemented they affect the individual and collective behavior of the organization. They then become the means used to judge performance or assign responsibility, accountability and liability.

Procedures

Procedures are plans, processes, protocols or operations that describe how to perform certain actions. Procedures are the documented intimacies of how the system(s) works. It is the knowledge transfer tool between people that do the same job. A procedure typically answers the questions of where, when, and how. Policies and standards are of no use if someone is not schooled on "how" to perform security functions. Each system is different since each system is composed of different technologies that must be configured in a particular way in order to function efficiently. Procedures explain what to do and when to do it in order to achieve optimal performance. Significant resources can be expended to achieve a functional set of working security procedures.

For example, the timely and accurate reporting of security incidents is crucial to creating a safe, sound and sustainable electronic economy. Here documenting reporting procedures are extremely important and can mean the difference between catching the culprit or sustaining a significant loss with a cold trail. One reporting procedure is to provide a checklist that identifies each step that a party must take to preserve the evidence and report the suspected breach. It should identify who to call, what to look for, and how to maintain the crime scene. By outlining this procedure companies could save significant sums of money each year alone. Training exercises also help to develop the quick decision making ability that is needed when confronted with a crisis.

Financial institutions in particular resist mandatory reporting requirements arguing that if they report break-ins the institutions will suffer reputation and value losses. This is a self-serving argument for the following reasons. First, financial institutions have a fiduciary duty to their customers. Failing to disclose this kind of information violates that fiduciary duty as well as the public trust, particularly where the deposit fund could be affected. Second, these institutions have a duty to their shareholders and Board to disclose such incidents. The Board can be held liable for losses resulting from a security incident whether it had actual knowledge or not. So in reality failing to disclose will cause more harm to the institution in the end than reporting it to the appropriate authority. Third, most countries want the incidents reported only to the appropriate authority. These authorities also have a duty not to disclose the information. Rather than fighting so hard against reporting requirements financial institutions should realize that reporting such incidents actually helps them. By reporting an incident the institution may realize that other institutions were involved or if it is an isolated incident they may be able to quickly determine who the culprit is, usually an insider. By sharing this information, they bring to bear greater resources to address the problem rather than bearing the entire cost. Fourth, every institution is in the same position and consumers will quickly realize this and act appropriately.

Public-Private Cooperation

Another action that would improve e-security worldwide is to create a set of national and cross-border incentive arrangements that encourages financial service providers to share accurate information on denial-of-service intrusions, thefts, hacks, and so on. Ample evidence shows, as noted in Chapter 2, that no accurate base of information exists either within or across countries. This information deficit limits both awareness and the scope of private sector solutions that can be provided and may even increase the cost of insuring against such risks.

Prompted by law enforcement, industry participants, and the academic community, greater public-private cooperation is starting to become a reality in the United States and, increasingly, in many other countries as well. Some innovative examples of such efforts, but by no means the only ones, are described below.

The Financial Services ISAC (FS-ISAC) is exclusively for, and designed by, professionals in the banking, securities and insurance industries.[61] An Information Sharing and Analysis Center (ISAC) is composed of a secure database, analytic tools, and information gathering and distribution facilities designed to allow authorized individuals to submit either anonymous or attributed reports about information security threats, vulnerabilities, incidents and solutions. ISAC members also have access to information and analysis relating to information provided by other members and obtained from other sources, such as US Government and law enforcement agencies, technology providers and security associations, such as CERT.

The Internet Security Alliance (ISA) and the Computer Emergency Response Team (CERT).[62] The ISA is a collaborative effort between Carnegie Mellon University's CERT Coordination Center and a cross-section of private international companies that include NASDAQ and Mellon Financial, TRW, and AIG. This alliance is an industry-led, global, cross-sector network focused

---

61. For additional information on Financial Sector ISACs, please see: http://fsisac.com/
62. For additional information on Internet Security Alliance, see: www.isalliance.org. For additional information on CERT, see www.cert.org.

on advancing the security of the Internet. CERT (see Glossary for detail) is expanding its operations and now has counterparts in more than 140 countries. It is beginning to implement its methods for extracting this information from users on a global basis.

The Forum of Incident Response and Security Teams (FIRST).[63] FIRST brings together a variety of computer security incident response teams from government, commercial, and academic organizations. FIRST aims to foster cooperation and coordination in incident prevention, prompt rapid reaction to incidents, and promote information sharing among members and the community at large. When FIRST was founded in 1990, it had 11 members. By the end of 2001, FIRST consisted of more than 100 response and security teams, which spanned the major global regions.

The Electronic Crimes Task Force (ECTF).[64] The six-year-old ECTF focuses primarily on the New York area, but its network is expanding to include the rest of the United States. The ECTF, a sort of central cyber crime clearinghouse for all arms of local, state, and national law enforcement, is headed by the New York office of the Secret Service and has a membership of 180 top federal and local law enforcement agencies and prosecutors. The ECTF is careful to guard its top secret data, but it welcomes new members to its network, which consists of about 200 companies from the private sector, mostly from the telecommunications, banking-finance, and vendor-services communities. With the passage of the Patriot Act in 2002, this task force model has been expanded to include the cities of Washington, Boston, Chicago, San Francisco, Miami, and Las Vegas.

InfraGard.[65] InfraGard is a partnership between private industry and the U.S. government, represented by the Federal Bureau of Investigations (FBI). The InfraGard initiative was developed to encourage the exchange of information by the government and the private sector. Private sector members and an FBI field representative form local area chapters, which set up their own boards to govern and share information within the membership. Each chapter is also part of the larger InfraGard organization. The National Infrastructure Protection Center (NIPC)[66] in conjunction with representatives from private industry, the academic community, and the public sector, further developed the InfraGard initiative to expand direct contacts with private sector infrastructure owners and operators and to share information about cyber intrusions, exploited vulnerabilities, and infrastructure threats. The initiative, encouraging the exchange of information by government and private sector members, has continued to expand through the formation of additional InfraGard chapters within the jurisdiction of each FBI field office. It is possible that InfraGard could expand to a more international presence.

All of these alliances and cooperative arrangements rely on trust, because each declares it will not divulge the respondents' identities. In some cases, such as with the New York ECTF, partnerships have gone so far as to allow private market participants and law enforcement agencies involved to sign explicit nondisclosure statements as a form of legal safeguard against disclosure of the information being provided. A universally trusted third party collects the information, scrubs it of any identifying information and disseminates it in a generic format. This provides value to the entire financial community.

A fruitful exercise might include further study of existing arrangements to share information about e-security breaches among industry participants, law enforcement, and possibly academic entities with expertise in the technology issues involved. Multilateral lenders such as the World Bank might play a more active role in facilitating such cooperation. In addition, the initiatives of the World Bank and the International Monetary Fund in such areas as initiatives against money

---

63. For additional information on FIRST, please see: www.first.org

64. For additional information on the Electronic Crimes Task Force, please see: http://www.ectaskforce.org/

65. For additional information on InfraGard, please see: http://www.infragard.net/.

66. For additional information on the National Infrastructure Protection Center, please see: www.nipc.org.

laundering and the establishment of financial intelligence units (FIUs) need to be properly integrated into a well-defined information-sharing framework. For example, suspicious activity reports often can lead to investigations that relate to e-security breaches and related crimes (for example, identification thefts). As institutions provide reports, the information can be analyzed to reveal patterns of activity, methods of operation and to establish threshold criteria for reporting so that institutions will not need to report every incident.

Trust and confidence are the bedrock of a free-market economy. Trust is built by providing structure to the marketplace. Confidence is secured by showing that the structure will be enforced without preference or discrimination. In designing this structure certifications, policies, standards and procedures are critical building blocks. Public-private sector cooperation is essential. The marketplace, regulators, and law enforcement are on a steep learning curve in trying to understand the open network environment much less create a safe and sound e-financial system. Cooperative efforts should be undertaken at every level of government and business to identify and distill best practices. The changing nature of the Internet and the networked environment requires continuous monitoring and assessment which in turn requires continuous updating and revising of policies, standards and procedures. These building blocks provide the means by which we can build trust in one another and the technology we are so dependent on. Taking the time to develop and implement them is well worth the effort as it increases the efficiency, security, and privacy while lowering risk and costs, and assuring that the institution behaves consistently.

CHAPTER 6

TWELVE LAYERS OF SECURITY (PILLAR 4)

As was noted in Chapter 2, an especially important pillar to develop to reduce e-security risk, particularly in emerging markets, is the enhancement of day-to-day e-security internal monitoring and processes as part of good business practice. This is the topic of this chapter.[67] While the previous three pillars have identified areas where the government takes an active role—either as a regulator, or in conjunction with the private sector—this final pillar identifies a set of precautions that can be taken at the operational level. While these actions will be significantly less effective without the supporting framework of the other three pillars, it is also worth stressing that without active security programs and related internal monitoring and proper governance undertaken at the firm level, the goals of the other pillars can not be achieved. Here as opposed to the previous chapter the emphasis is not on the policies, practices, standards, and certification at the industry level, but rather the actual implementation of e-security in financial service providers.

One of the most important efforts needed to improve e-security is to clearly link business objectives to processes that link the costs of not securing a business to the potential and actual savings from layering security in a world where open architecture systems prevail. Senior management should view e-security not as an overhead expense, but as essential to business survivability. This philosophy should be reflected in all documented policies. Management of e-security risks can be thought of as a twofold process. The first part is risk analysis, which has three major components: identify and inventory assets for a baseline, analyze and assign values to the assets, and establish how critical each asset is, in priority order. The second part of security is development of an approach to risk management. The major elements of risk management are to develop and implement policies and procedures, educate users (employees and customers), and audit and

---

67. A more comprehensive and technical exposition of this material can be found in Annex D.

monitor for quality assurance.[68] A prudent approach might reflect the following thesis: "Expect to be hit—prepare to survive." There are three general axioms to remember in building a security program:

- Attacks and losses are inevitable.
- Security buys time.
- The network is only as secure as its weakest link.

Twelve core layers of proper security are essential for maintaining the integrity of data and mitigating the risks associated with open architecture environments, and in many instances, actual implementation of a specific layer need not entail large capital investments or outlays. The creation of the position of Chief Information Security Officer (CISO), who oversees that the 12 layers are carried out and implemented in accordance with the best practices laid out in greater detail in the Annex D, is essential in order to preserve the survivability of the network.

1. **Risk Management**—A broad-based framework based upon CERT's OCTAVE paradigm for managing assets and relevant risks to those assets.
2. **Cybernetic Intelligence**—Experienced threat and technical intelligence analysis regarding threats, vulnerabilities, incidents, and countermeasure should provide timely and customized reporting to prevent a security incident *before* it occurs.
3. **Access Controls/Authentication**—Establish the legitimacy of a node or user before allowing access to requested information. The first line of defense is access controls; these can be divided into passwords, tokens, biometrics, and public key infrastructure (PKI).
4. **Firewalls**—Create a system or combination of systems that enforces a boundary between two or more networks.
5. **Active Content Filtering**—At the browser level, it is prudent to filter all material that is not appropriate for the workplace or that is contrary to established workplace policies.
6. **Intrusion Detection System (IDS)**—This is a system dedicated to the detection of break-ins or break-in attempts, either manually or via software expert systems that operate on logs or other information available on the network. Monitoring approaches vary widely, depending on the types of attacks against which the system is expected to defend, the origins of the attacks, the types of assets, and the level of concern for various types of threats.
7. **Virus Scanners**—Worms, Trojans, and viruses are methods for deploying an attack. Virus scanners hunt malicious codes, but require frequent updating and monitoring.
8. **Encryption**—Encryption algorithms are used to protect information while it is in transit or whenever it is exposed to theft of the storage device (for example, removable backup media or notebook computer).
9. **Proper Systems Administration**—This should be complete with a list of administrative failures that typically exist within financial institutions and corporations and a list of best practices.
10. **Vulnerability Testing**—Vulnerability testing entails obtaining knowledge of vulnerabilities that exist on a computer system or network and using that knowledge to gain access to resources on the computer or network while bypassing normal authentication barriers.
11. **Policy Management Software**—A software program should control Bank policy and procedural guidelines vis-à-vis employee computer usage.

---

68. Proper "Risk Management" is achieved through a comprehensive checklist per the cyber-risks that affect the network as a whole. The Integrator Unit, in collaboration with the World Bank Treasury Security Team, is refining a "Technology Risk Checklist" for Financial Institutions that intends to build upon standards set by ISO 17799.

FIGURE 6.1: FIVE LAYERS OF DATA FLOW

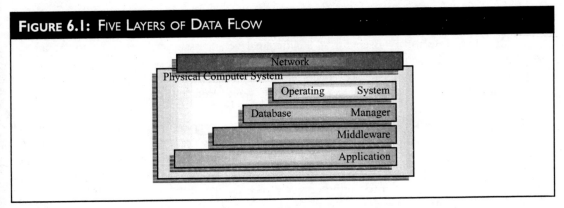

Source: Provided by James Nelms, CISO, World Bank Treasury.

12. **Business Continuity/Incident Response Plan (IRP)**—This is the primary document used by a corporation to define how it will identify, respond to, correct, and recover from a computer security incident. The main necessity is to have an IRP and to test it periodically.

Security is a dynamic process, and the 12-layer matrix crystallizes the virtual boundaries of an organization's critical assets, or the cyber castle. The process of implementing and carrying out the various layers is overseen by the CISO, who serves as the critical leader of the information security team, and who is responsible for the oversight of all electronic assets. Establishing the position of a CISO is essential for bringing the issues of e-risk to the proper attention of senior management and the Board of Directors. Having a CISO brings accountability into the matrix of the sustainable development of technology. A CISO must understand the business, understand what makes it successful, identify factors that can put that success at risk, and then find ways of managing that risk through technical, operational or procedural safeguards. He or she should create policies that address key security topic areas such as security risk management, critical asset identification, physical security, system and network management, authentication and authorization, access control, vulnerability management, incident management, awareness and training, and privacy. This entails ensuring that the intent of each policy is reflected in standards, procedures, practices, training, and security architectures that implement it. A CISO's security awareness is heavily dependent upon his or her last vulnerability/penetration test (security audit) and the quality of cyber intelligence he or she receives.

In outlining this compendium of best practices, it is important to note that these are necessary, but not sufficient, to assure e-security. The implementation of actual e-risk management processes, as well as related, standard business risk controls are equally important practices.

Risk Management

Security is a business issue, not a technical issue: understanding the business is critical when attempting to be proactive in cyber space.

As illustrated in Figure 6.1, systems are built in software layers. Each of these layers of data flow are mutually inclusive of the layer below it. "Compromising security at the lower level places the levels above at risk. Within this business process data flows horizontally, whereas the supporting technology flows vertically. Where the data intersects the technology choke points for risk can exist."[69]

---

69. James Nelms, CISO, World Bank Treasury, Speech to the United Nations Global E-Commerce Summit, held May 17, 2003, New York.

Good business and good regulation require that financial institutions manage risk appropriately. Security is a twofold process. The first part is risk analysis, which has three major components: identify and inventory assets for a baseline, analyze and assign values to the assets, and establish how critical each asset is, in priority order. The second part of security is development of an approach to risk management. The major elements of risk management are to develop and implement policies and procedures, to educate users (employees and customers), and to audit and monitor for quality assurance.

Phase I:[70] Build asset-based threat profiles. An analysis team consisting of management and technical staff must identify and inventory the institution's mission-critical assets, set priorities among them, and determine what is being done to protect these assets. The creation of a CISO is critical to the management of risk within banks network. It is essential that this position be filled so as to bring accountability into the process of e-security. The Information Security Officer should be responsible for carrying out each layer of the risk management framework. Trained in OCTAVE[71] he or she will be the focal point for proactive e-risk mitigation.

Phase II: Identify infrastructure vulnerabilities and interdependencies. A multidisciplinary team analyzes key system vulnerabilities, exploits interdependencies, and identifies potential points of entry and workflow processes. An outside contractor then should initiate a formal assessment and design a secure architecture. The architecture should include, at a minimum, appropriate policies, procedures, protocols, and tools to evaluate the current software and hardware and to audit and monitor against the workflow processes and procedures.

Phase III: Develop a business continuity plan. A multidisciplinary team should identify potential attack scenarios and develop contingency plans to eliminate/mitigate risk if any of the mission-critical assets identified in Phase II are compromised. Appropriate policies and procedures should be in place company-wide, and periodic testing and surprise attacks should be mounted to assure management that safeguards are in place, up-to-date, and in use.

Cyber Intelligence

The "caffeine crazed" hacker out to prove his or her technical prowess is no longer a proper characterization of the information security threat. Instead, today's threat is rapidly evolving to include—if not feature—well-organized criminal syndicates employing sophisticated and structured attack techniques. Just who are these threat "actors," what motivates them, what capabilities do they possess, what are our vulnerabilities and, most importantly, where might they strike next? Answering these questions is the objective of security intelligence services companies. Experienced threat and technical intelligence analysts collect and analyze data from global sources on threats, vulnerabilities, incidents, and countermeasure and provide timely and customized reporting to prevent a security incident *before* it occurs.

Access Controls/Authentication

The value of e-finance is defined, in part, by technology's ability to move information and to affect markets quickly. The underlying assumption is that the movement of information is reliable and secure. Access allows those who should be able to get onto the system access for the purpose for which they are authorized. Authentication is assuring the system that the person trying to gain access or engage in a certain activity is, in fact, the person he or she claims to be and that the person is authorized to engage in the act. Used together and diligently, these processes are the most cost-effective security devices available.

---

70. OCTAVE Method Implementation Guide v2.0, Computer Emergency Response Team, Carnegie Mellon University.

71. Operationally Critical Threat, Asset, and Vulnerability Evaluation, and its acronym OCTAVE, are service marks of Carnegie Mellon University. www.cert.org

Financial institutions can use a variety of access and authentication tools and methodologies to authenticate customers. Existing access control techniques and authentication methodologies involve three basic factors:

Two-Factor

- Something the user *knows* (for example, password or PIN)
- Something the user *possesses* (for example, ATM card, smart card, or token)
- Something the user *is* (for example, biometric characteristic, such as fingerprint or retinal pattern)

An effective access and authentication program should be implemented across the organizational structure, including affiliate entities, which requires the appropriate use of controls and authentication tools. Authentication processes should also maximize interoperability and offer consistency with the financial institution's assessment of the e-finance system risks.

Firewalls

A packet filter firewall works by looking at each packet of network information and determining, based on the contents of the headers of that packet, whether it is allowed to traverse the network. There are three types of firewalls: packet filter, "stateful" inspection,[72] and application proxy. A stateful inspection firewall also looks at the packets, but instead of looking at just the addressing information, it looks at how the connection has been set up between the computers to determine if the packet of information is in a valid state. For instance, after the connection is set up in a stateful inspection firewall, and a packet of network traffic shows up destined to a particular host, the firewall can look to see if that connection has been established. If not, the packet may contain spoofed information and it should be discarded. An application proxy firewall is a process-based control device that stands guard in front of the application to permit only authorized parties to access to all or parts of an application.

Firewalls have one basic goal: to keep network traffic from passing a given point that does not meet certain connection criteria. For instance, it is very common for firewalls to only allow traffic into servers connected on ports 80 (http) and 443 (https). While this may stop much unwanted traffic, additional steps are needed to protect the resources. It is very important to remember that the firewall *does not* stop traffic on the ports that *are* allowed. A firewall cannot prevent what is already allowed through the system.

When using a firewall, an organization should consider the type of technology used and determine whether that technology is sufficient, given the new demands and uses on it. For example, an organization that is simply accessing the Internet, but is not providing any Internet-accessible services, might be adequately protected through the use of network address translation and filtering. Another organization might require a firewall that supports application proxies for additional protection. In many cases, the best firewall to select is one that combines multiple forms of firewall technology. For example, both the Cisco PIX and Watchguard Firebox systems effectively combine stateful inspection with application level proxies for protection.

The cost-effectiveness of a firewall for an institution depends on four factors: the type of connectivity, the amount of bandwidth, the number of gateways, and the skills set of the firewall and systems administrator. The firewall should be able to support the type of connection the institution has, and the staff needs to be able to administer it effectively. Generally, the best option is a good hardware-based firewall that is dedicated to firewall functionality and is a true stateful firewall. Which firewall the institution uses depends greatly on the institution's needs, and in particular the scale of its operations. Implementing a $10,000 firewall such as Secure Computing's Sidewinder or Cisco's PIX into an organization with only 50 employees will not provide a good return on investment. At the same time, a smaller class of firewall would be insufficient for an organization with more than 1,000 employees.

---

72. Stateful inspection is a specific method of firewall packet analysis (for further information, see http://www.webopedia.com/TERM/s/stateful_inspection.html).

Active Content Filtering

Once connected to the Internet, an individual or an organization undertakes a degree of risk from malicious code. The impact of allowing malicious content to enter a banking network unchallenged is far-reaching. A well-defined policy and procedure detailing proper network usage should be implemented institution-wide, and implementation should include active content filtering.

At the browser level, it is necessary and prudent to filter all material that is defined by policy to be inappropriate for the workplace or that is contrary to the institution's established workplace policies. Active content filtering can be accomplished by filtering Internet sites that would otherwise be accessible to employees and through the use of e-mail filters that are designed to detect references to a company's proprietary data.[73] All content that does not promote the functioning of an organization should be filtered. Technology can be deployed to detect references to the company's proprietary data in e-mail messages and their attachments.

Intrusion Detection Systems

An intrusion is a suspicious pattern that may indicate a network or system attack from someone attempting to break into or compromise a system. An intrusion should be defined as any system/network activity that cannot be justifiably explained or activity that results in the disruption of services or loss of data."

Intrusion detection systems (IDS) need to be monitored 24 hours a day to obtain the best return on investment. This work schedule positions the institution to respond to suspected intrusions in a timely manner and prevents the inadvertent loss of resources resulting from a misconfigured IDS.[74] In addition, an IDS should be installed inside the firewall and should operate only on traffic that is not allowed within the firewall's perimeter. An IDS installed inside the firewall is critical for assisting the administrator to determine if the attack was successful in breaching the firewall.

Approaches to monitoring vary widely. Effectiveness depends on the anticipated types of attacks the system is expected to defend against, the origins of the attacks, the types of assets, and the level of concern for various types of threats (inability to conduct business, damage to reputation, loss of trust, defacement, theft of IP address, dissemination of critical information, unauthorized access, insider policy violations, etc.). In addition, company policy, individual responsibilities, and the purpose/use of the monitored systems/segment determine how threats are identified and categorized and how priorities are established. By addressing these concerns, the institution can determine where the monitoring needs to be performed, what needs to be monitored, and how to interpret events.

Monitors are categorized based on their placement (network-based or host-based) and the types of sensors they employ (traffic monitors, log file analyzers, system call tracers, integrity checkers, policy monitors, etc.). Regardless of the placement, all monitoring systems are based on three basic detection technologies for identifying security events: signature-based detection, statistical anomaly detection, and protocol anomaly detection.

No matter what method is employed, network systems should be monitored at least daily, depending on the amount of traffic allowed into the network by the firewall. It should be pointed out that an IDS is usually considered a post-event security device. Depending on how it is configured, it may be able to notify you that someone has compromised your systems, but it may not be able to stop the compromise. By far the most effective means to stop intruders is to routinely scan your systems for vulnerabilities and to repair them before they can be exploited.

---

73. Input provided by Galaxy Computer Services Inc.
74. Input contributed by Galaxy Computer Services Inc.

Virus Scanners

Worms, Trojans (the analogy is to the Trojan horse), and viruses are vehicles for deploying an attack. A virus is a program that can replicate itself by infecting other programs on the same system with copies of itself. Trojans do not replicate or attach themselves to other files. Instead, they are malicious programs that are hidden within another program or file. Once the Trojan file is executed, it can perform malicious activity at will. Virus scanners are critical in the mitigation of these attacks.

Worms, which are a relatively new phenomenon,[75] use existing security vulnerabilities to gain access to the device. Worms replicate themselves onto other systems via a network connection.[76] Typically, viruses and worms become malicious only when the infected files are accessed or deployed. Most of the time, these vulnerabilities can be eliminated by simply applying patches. The irony here is that someone who is not keeping up-to-date with patches most likely is not keeping up-to-date with virus software either. This human "system" failure can have catastrophic implications for an institution's e-financial network.

Virus scanners should be updated every night. Beginning with an institution's e-mail gateway, every inbound attachment should be scanned for viruses. Fileservers should be set to active scanning mode where they scan every file copied onto them. Desktop scanners that protect the user's PC should also be updated. Data should be tested against standard loads if updates catch anything.

Any reliable anti-virus software can be set up to check with the manufacturer and to receive pattern and scan engine updates automatically. However, as a general rule, IT staff should check for updates at least weekly. Most virus scanners can detect and effectively eliminate worms and Trojans found in e-mail and downloaded files. Still, some worms may propagate by exploiting vulnerabilities that are not being monitored by the scanning system. The good news is that most of these are discovered once the scanner is updated and a complete rescan is accomplished.

Encryption[77]

Cryptography and cryptographic tools sound complex and mysterious. The details of how these tools are constructed and work are intricate, laced both with mathematics and with properties that are provable and not provable. The security of some tools can be based firmly upon some intractably difficult mathematical problem. The security of other tools cannot be proven formally, but is trusted as a result of the inability of experts to find and demonstrate any weaknesses in the tools over periods of years. However, what cryptographic tools do and how they are used are very easy to understand. There are only six basic types of cryptographic tools. They are:

- Symmetric (secret) Key Encryption.
- Asymmetric (public/private) Key Encryption.
- One Way Hash Functions.
- Message Authentication Codes.
- Digital Signatures.
- Random Number Generators.

By careful use of these cryptographic tools one seeks to design systems that can provide system security in the face of any of the attacks defined in an associated threat model.

---

75. Worms manipulate networks to spread from computer to computer. This form of malicious code has the ability to enter a network through an open browser. This characteristic is a result of worms' concentrated attacks on servers. In some instances—Code Red, for example—worms have been used to set up back doors into financial networks.

76. Interview with Linda McCarthy, Vice President of Systems Engineering for Recourse Technologies.

77. Bill Worley, HP fellow, Chief Scientist for Hewlett Packard, Inc. contributed inputs for this section.

Proper Systems Administration

Proper e-security is a combination of policy, processes, and technology. Systems administrators are the front lines of policy implementation. Systems administrators throughout the organization should consider information security a normal part of their responsibility and the responsibility of every employee. System administrators should have clearly defined responsibilities and ensure adequate resources are allocated to fulfill these. Systems administrators enforce, and regularly review security policy. One example is Instant Messaging (IM) should be used with caution. Box 6.1 depicts the dangers posed by IM.

Box 6.1: INSTANT MESSAGING

Instant Messenger, or IM, is a real-time chat session, which International Data Corporation (IDC) estimates will reach over 500 million combined corporate and personal users by the year 2005. Generally, instant messaging software is free and downloadable to any user. The network architecture of IM systems comprise of either client-server or peer-to-peer structures. In a client-server model, a user subscribes to an IM provider, and is then able to send text messages from his/her local client (including computers, PDA, wireless devices), through the provider's server, to another subscriber/user's client. In a peer-to-peer model, a user will first connect to the IM provider's server to locate other users, at which point, a direct connection between two or more users is established.

Possibly the biggest threat posed by IM is the false public perception of security, and the behaviors to which this leads. For example, users will transmit sensitive information, such as critical corporate information, user names and passwords via IM. And, in addition to believing transmissions are secure, users will conduct this type of behavior under the misconception that data from messaging sessions cannot be stored long-term.

Technically, the dangers posed by IM systems are founded on the basic fact that it opens a TCP/IP tunnel to a user's computer through which any hacker on the Internet can access. More than just simple chat sessions, IM technology enables full file transfer capability, including audio and video. Within these transmitted files, malicious users can embed viruses, worms, and other forms of harmful code. This code can not only spread using the Internet as its conduit, but do so in a matter of seconds to millions of users by accessing users' address books, or buddy list. Further, a user's IM connection can also make an entire network vulnerable to denial-of-service attacks.

In addition to risks posed by a connection to the Internet, the IM technology carries vulnerabilities of its own. Many of the IM connections are configured to bypass corporate firewalls. Moreover, digital data usually travels in unencrypted form over the Internet, thereby exposing it to multiple points of attack. Hackers can intercept data, steal a user's identity, or spoof an IM session. Inherent vulnerabilities in wireless devices and transmission compound this problem, especially considering the growing use of IM capabilities over wireless. Finally, a user's trust greatly contributes to the ease with which malicious action can be conducted in an IM session. Users trust they have connected to a legitimate user just by seeing a buddy's name on-screen. In fact, the end user can be anybody.

Some basic risk mitigation techniques for IM include using encrypted transmission, employing proper firewall configurations, using desktop firewalls and anti-virus software, filtering content for key words, and blocking file transfers over IM. Be wary of user spoofing and eavesdropping by packet sniffers. Finally, adopt a policy of ongoing awareness; remain up-to-date on IM bugs and vulnerabilities and install patches when they are released.

Source: Authored by Yumi Nishiyama, World Bank Integrator Group. The data was compiled from a variety of sources. The Symantec White Paper, "Securing Instant Messaging," describes in further depth the vulnerabilities inherent in instant messaging. This paper can be accessed at: http://securityresponse.symantec.com/avcenter/reference/secure.instant.messaging.pdf.

Mary Brandel of Computerworld addressed risk mitigation methods in "Plug IM's Security Gaps," 14 Jul 2003, (http://www.computerworld.com/securitytopics/security/story/0,10801,82943,00.html).

The recent release of Security Assertion Markup Language (SAML) is supposed to "secure" all Windows 2000 operating systems. Security can never be guaranteed. In reality SAML is merely a "box full of patches" that will likely give users the illusion of safety. Systems administrators should remain vigilant per outbreaks of malicious code. Improper user behavior can contribute to externalities associated with such outbreaks. Systems administrators should update anti-virus software nightly and remain cognizant of employee terminations. Virus scanning and authentication revocation are two critical roles of systems administrators.

Vulnerability Testing and Penetration Testing

Vulnerability is a set of conditions in a software system that allows an intruder to violate an implicit or explicit security policy. Blended threats (for example, worms) exploit vulnerabilities in software code, allowing them to circumvent perimeter defenses like firewalls, intrusion detection systems, virus scanners, and encryption.[78] According to CERT, over 4,000 such vulnerabilities were discovered last year. A recent Internet Security Systems report depicted a precarious trend in malicious code. The ISS *X-force International Risk Impact Summary* discovered that blended threats rose by over 700 percent between Q4 of 2002 and Q2 of 2003 up from 101 in Q4 2002 to over 752 in Q1 2003.[79]

Box 6.2: BLENDED THREATS

Blended threats exploit vulnerabilities in software code. Also known as worms, their danger lies in their ability to circumvent perimeter defenses like firewalls and IDS. To get an idea of just how great a risk these blended threats can be, currently blended threats are exploiting only a fraction of documented vulnerabilities. Over 4,000 new vulnerabilities were discovered last year alone.

Examples of blended threats include the Slammer and Code Red worms. The Slammer worm, also known as Sapphire, was unleashed in January 2003. Attacking a buffer overload vulnerability in Microsoft's SQL Server, the worm spread around the world within a mere ten minutes, wreaking havoc and crippling countless websites as it infected network systems in telecommunications, airline, and financial systems. Among the estimated 150,000+ computers infected, South Korea had the highest number of infected systems. In the financial sector, 13,000 of Bank of America's ATMs were disabled and the Australian AMEX website had to be temporarily taken down on account of Slammer.[80]

Code Red is another blended threat worm launched in 2001. This particular worm attacked a buffer overload vulnerability in the Microsoft IIS software. Though debilitating effects of Code Red included DOS and heavy traffic congestion, its most egregious characteristic was its ability to leave back doors wide open for future attacks.[81] According to Computer Economics, CodeRed was responsible for an estimated $1.2 billion dollars in damages. It spread to approximately 250,000 network computers within a nine-hour period, even forcing the government to take down its website for a period of time.[82]

Source: Authored by Tom Kellermann and Yumi Nishiyama, World Bank Integrator Group. For further information see Kellermann and Nishiyama 2003a. Information was garnered from a variety of sources. The Internet Security System's white paper titled "Case Study: Security for the Flow of Financial Data", at: http://www.iss.net/support/documentation/whitepapers/iss.php was used as reference.

---

78. For further information see Kellermann and Nishiyama 2003a.

79. http://www.iss.net/support/documentation/whitepapers/iss.php

80. Brian Krebs, "Internet Worm Hits Airlines, Banks," Washingtonpost.com; 1/26/2003; accessed at: http://www.washingtonpost.com/wp-dyn/articles/A46928-2003Jan26.html.

81. Kittipong Teeraruangchaisri, "Code Red and Code Red II: Double Dragons", SANS, 9/15/2001, accessed at: http://www.sans.org/rr/malicious/dragons.php.

82. Richard Stenger, "'Code Red' worm spreads, Pentagon reacts," CNN.com, 8/1/2001, accessed at: http://www.cnn.com/2001/TECH/internet/08/01/code.red/.

It is not easy for banks and financial institutions to safeguard their networks because new vulnerabilities are discovered daily, and their fixes/patches must be diligently applied to all systems. Vulnerability testing becomes essential in order to preserve the safety and soundness of the bank's networks. New connections to the Internet, modems, and virtual private networks (VPNs) create a multitude of new access points to a network whose risk is defined by its weakest link.

Penetration testing entails obtaining knowledge of existing vulnerabilities of a computer system or network and using that knowledge to attempt to gain access to resources on the computer or network while bypassing normal authentication barriers. It may also include exploiting vulnerabilities to gain increased authorization—for instance, to go from regular user to super-user. Penetration testing is good only on the day it was done (this is true for *all* security testing). Penetration testing is an excellent way of testing installed security measures, policies and procedures, and the effectiveness of a company's end-user security training programs. First, a company will be able to tell if security measures such as firewall and IDS systems are functioning properly and what skill level is required to circumvent them. Second, a company will gain insight into whether established policies and procedures allow its staff to detect and react to an intrusion properly. Third, a company can determine if additional training is required for its end-users.

Penetration testing should be performed at least annually, and more often if the system is subject to frequent application or operating system updates. Once a penetration test has been performed, ongoing vulnerability assessment should be performed to address newly discovered exploits. The frequency of the vulnerability assessment should be determined on the level of risk an organization is willing to accept. Given the speed at which new vulnerabilities and exploits are discovered, a vulnerability assessment should be performed semiannually and in many cases quarterly no matter what level of risk one is willing to accept.

Policy Management Software[83]

Security policies govern internal and external access to the network for each technology. These policies should address each aspect of the network and remain current. Is someone responsible for each security policy and procedure? How does each policy "owner" stay current? Do they attend security conferences? What are the qualifications for being in this position? What mechanisms are in place to keep policies up-to-date? Quality policy management is essential in preventing internal security gaps. Given that good e-security is a combination of people, processes and technology, banks should be implementing a policy approach that is governed by system wherein the policy and enforcement are dynamic. Bank policy vis-à-vis computer usage necessitates enforcement by a software program. The verbal policy dimension should be translated into machine code. This method of policy enforcement mitigates the insider threat dimension both premeditated and accidental. Once policy is built and subsequently amended, users must be educated and then regulated by a rule-set which is modular not static.[84] This security approach needs to take into account the privacy rights of the user on the system. Users should not only be identified once an alarm (policy violation) has occurred.

Business Continuity and Incident Response

The ability to react quickly to security incidents is an essential part of an overall security plan. An organization's ability to operate will depend on its ability to provide timely information to its clients in the form of electronic data. It is also essential to categorize information. Information from critical systems will surely receive a more direct and focused response than, for example, electronic information stored for office supplies. An organization needs the ability to react to and recover from security incidents as they arise with an effective and coordinated response, which in

---

83. The *Technology Risk Supervision Guidelines* to be released by the World Bank in September 2003 will define the correct policies necessary to retain safety and soundness in an open architecture environment.
84. Computer Associates, Tumbleweed and Policy vendor effective policy management software.

turn will minimize the cost and damage to the organization's infrastructure and to its image within the banking industry.

A security incident can be defined as an event that changes the security posture of an organization or circumvents security polices developed to prevent financial loss and the destruction, theft, or loss of proprietary information. It is characterized by unusual activity that causes the organization to investigate because the activity cannot be explained through normal operations. Some possible classifications for security incidents are these:

- Virus attacks (unable to clean, rename, or delete);
- Denial-of-service attacks;
- IDS alert notifications (false positives possible);
- Automated scanning tools.

Banking organizations must share in the responsibility of coordinating their response efforts with those of other financial institutions. Networking in a trusted environment and sharing incident information and detection/response techniques can be important to all of these organizations in identifying and correcting weaknesses. Gathering intelligence information from all sources is a critical part of information infrastructure protection. Having an information-sharing network in place can also help government agencies alert other agencies to potential and/or actual threats directed at the critical information infrastructure of nations.

Incident response within any organization must begin with management. Management is responsible for providing the support, tools, personnel, and financial backing needed to ensure the success of the incident response team. An incident response team must be perceived well by all concerned. Security awareness training and briefings for senior management are key components of a successful deployment of an incident response team.[85]

To maximize the full potential of the team, members must be available 24/7. Intrusion Detection Systems (IDS), network- and host-based, are playing a more critical role in identifying attacks and unusual activity. Alerts from such systems are generated at all hours of the day. An incident response team allows an organization to respond to alerts generated by automated systems 24/7. Monitoring systems and reviewing security alert information submitted by vendors is an important part of an incident response team's proactive duty. IDS systems, however, do not provide a complete solution to identifying and responding to incidents. An overall security plan is needed to ensure overall protection that would include an incident response mechanism.

An incident response team must also develop procedures. Clear definitions of each type of incident will enable members to react quickly and effectively. Procedures must detail the steps team members should take when alerted to an incident. Included within the procedures must be clearly defined investigative goals to be achieved before an incident can be closed. The team should also list and post contact information of key personnel and management to notify.

The team may need to contact other organizations to assist in the investigation. The bank must develop a policy that clearly describes the bank's position on the disclosure of incident information to the banking community as well as outside organizations such as the National Infrastructure Protection Center (NIPC), the Computer Emergency Response Team (CERT), FedCIRC, and commercial incident response teams. Bank organizations may designate an individual (job function) to coordinate the exchange of information. All team members must sign a nondisclosure form.

Tracking of security incidents can become a full-time job, because all incidents must be tracked. Incidents may remain open from a few hours to a few months, or even longer in some

---

85. Three good sources of information for building a Computer Security Incident Response Team: http://www.securityunit.com/pubs/index.htm SecurityUnit, Inc; http://www.cert.org/csirts/ CERT Coordination Center; http://www.cert.org/training/2002/creating_csirt.html Creating a Computer Security Incident Response Team

cases. The incident (case) record must contain all communications relating to the incident from the time it is opened to the time of closure. Depending on the type of incident, careful consideration should be given to collecting any data that may be relevant to the incident. Response team members should receive professional training in handling and collecting evidence (system logs and backup tapes) in case such evidence needs to be used in a court of law.

All system and user files should be backed up on a regular basis. Develop a plan that is broad enough to cover all the workstations and servers you have deployed. If you have regularly created checksums for all fields and have securely stored these checksums, you can plan to restore files from trusted backups against which the checksums are calculated. Backups should be centrally administered, with data copied from workstations via networks. Encryption tools can be used to protect data passing from a user's workstation to the central backup host. Backups must be made at least daily. The minimum requirements for most organizations are a full backup conducted on a weekly basis, and an incremental backup conducted every day. At least once a month, the backup media should be verified by doing a restore to a test server to see that the data is actually being backed up accurately.

The Ghost Site

As part of their business continuity process, financial institutions should develop an offline site as a preemptive measure to an interruption. This site should be fully functional and have the ability to "go live within minutes. The robustness of the ghost site is directly related to the business needs of the organization. At a minimum, the ghost site should provide appropriate communications to customers and be supported by a call center. This ghost site should consider all aspects of the business: Customers vendors, public relations, legal, marketing, investor relations, for example. It is imperative that its development team is designed from a cross-section of the organization. Discontinuity of operation is a threat to any organization and this exercise ensures management that they have a measured response for mitigating risk.

The Incident Response Plan

An incident response plan (IRP) is the primary document an organization uses to establish how it will identify, respond to, correct, and recover from a computer security incident. Every organization should have an IRP and should test it periodically.

All employees should be trained in the correct procedures to undertake in the event of a computer incident. An incident response plan might make the following points:[86]

1. The institution's security department, legal department, and public relations department should jointly develop and implement an incident response policy.
2. Incident response agencies responsible for an organization's site should be contacted. Some examples include:
   http://www.nipc.gov (National Infrastructure Protection Center)
   http://www.cert.org (Computer Emergency Response Team)
   http://www.cert.dfn.de/eng/csir/europe/certs.html (European Computer Emergency Response Teams)
   http://www.ectaskforce.org/Regional_Locations.htm (Electronic Crimes Taskforce)
   http://www.first.org/team-info/ FIRST (Forum of Incident Response and Security Teams)
3. Use out-of-band methods for communications (for example, through a phone call) to ensure that intruders do not intercept information.[87]

---

86. Provided by Bob Weaver of the New York Electronic Crimes Taskforce.
87. National Infrastructure Protection Center's advice.

4. Document your actions (for example, phone calls made, files modified, systems jobs that were stopped).[88]
5. Make copies of files the intruders may have left untouched (for example, malicious code, log files) and store them offline.[89]
6. Contact law enforcement officials. To ensure proper reporting during an e-security incident, please refer to the following URL: http://www.nipc.gov/incident/cirr.htm.

The term *incident determination*[90] describes the process used to define events as an "incident" and explains how each type of incident should be handled. Indicators that signal an incident may be categorized as Possible, Probable, and Definite. In addition, if there is a predefined set of conditions that constitute an incident, the incident will be handled in accordance with the plan once those conditions are determined to exist. Arguably, this is the most important section of the plan because it identifies certain situations or conditions and sets out in detail how to respond.

The term *incident notification* describes the procedures to be used in notifying the computer user population once an incident has been confirmed. This section of the plan identifies those who must be notified in the event of an incident and provides critical contact information and contact procedures. These are some elements that may be included in this portion of the plan:

- Internal components of the organization, including management, operations, security, public relations, and the general employee/user population.
- Computer security incident response organizations.
- Affected partners or other integrated entities.
- The organization's insurer, if the organization is insured through an e-risk policy
- Law enforcement at the local, state, and federal levels.
- News media and other public relations components.

Incident containment is the third area of the plan. It addresses the measures that must be taken to halt/mitigate the effects of the incident and to regain control of the affected networks, systems, and related components.

Damage assessment is a critical step once containment has been achieved. This phase assesses the damage that has been inflicted on the institution's assets. It should determine the scope of damage, the duration of the incident, the cause of the incident, and the identification of the responsible party.

Incident recovery is the next key element of the plan. It requires a comprehensive approach to returning networks and systems to normal operations. The following are vital activities that must be addressed during the recovery phase of incident response. First, the vulnerability that allowed the incident to occur should be mitigated. If removal of the vulnerability is not possible, then safeguards should be improved to mitigate additional damage. Second, all out-of-date detection mechanisms should be updated. Software, data, and services should be restored in accordance with approved procedures. System and network activity should be followed closely after restoration for any signs of a follow-up attack. Finally, during recovery, efforts must be made to restore confidence in the organization by its users, partners, and clients.

Reflection, or lessons learned, is the final section of the plan. This requires the institution to conduct a postmortem of the incident. The institution reviews what occurred, how it occurred,

---

88. Ibid.
89. Ibid.
90. In the next paragraphs, both the terms used for the plan and the descriptions of the terms, were contributed by Galaxy Computer Services Inc.

Box 6.3: SURVIVABLE SYSTEM DEVELOPMENT

Survivability analysis or business continuity helps to identify the essential functions or assets in the institution that must survive in the event of an attack or system failure. The delivery of essential services and the preservation of essential assets during a compromise, and the timely recovery of full services and assets following attack are among these functions. The organizational integration phenomenon that typifies the modern banking community is accompanied by elevated risks of intrusion and compromise.

It is essential to determine what elements in the institution's IT infrastructure are absolutely mission-critical—that is, what elements must be up and running within a certain time in order for business to continue. From this point forward one must envisage various compromises to the system so that contingency plans are in effect to cover all potential threats. The following sources on survivability will assist network architects in determining the impact of certain accepted risks.

The Carnegie Mellon Software Engineering Institute Network Systems Survivability Program uses incident data collected by the CERT as a basis for the institute's survivability research and for trend identification and the prediction of future problems. http://www.cert.org/nav/index_purple.html

The European Dependability Initiative (http://www.cordis.lu/esprit/src/stdepnd.htm) represents a major research effort within the European Union to address the critical infrastructure protection and survivability efforts of the member nations. There are plans for joint U.S./EU cooperation.

The National Infrastructure Protection Center (NIPC) is the U.S. government's focal point for threat assessment, warning, investigations, and response to attacks (http://www.nipc.gov).

Source: Joe McCleod of CERT.

how it could have been prevented, and what changes need to be made to ensure that such an event does not occur again. In addition, any related plans should be reviewed to determine whether any changes or lessons learned are applicable.

SELECTED PUBLIC E-SECURITY INCIDENTS

Date of Attack	Compromised financial and e-commerce entities	Name of hacker, group, or malicious tool	Various losses sustained because of the intrusion into the financial entity's networks
Sep. 18, 1995	Citibank[91]	Vladimir Levin	$ 10,000,000[92]
1999	Citigroup	Crime ring	Two funds transfers totaling approximately $37 million.[93]
Mar. 1, 2000	U.K., U.S., Thailand, and Canada's e-finance and e-commerce sites	Alias "CURADOR"	28,000 accounts compromised, with total losses exceeding $3.5 million.[94]
Mar. 15, 2000	Internet Trading Technologies[95]	Abelkader Smires	Denial-of-service attacks that caused major disruption of trading on the NASDAQ.

(*Continued*)

---

91. "Bank's Security Chains Rattled." Financial Times. Sept. 20, 1995. www.ft.com.
92. Of the $10 million lost, all but $400,000 was recovered.
93. From "Bank security falls victim to moles," Financial Times, http://news.ft.com/servlet/ContentServer?pagename=FT.com/StoryFT/FullStory&c=StoryFT&cid=1045511507743
94. National Infrastructure Protection Center Major Investigations Web site: www.nipc.gov/investigations/curador.htm.
95. National Infrastructure Protection Center Major Investigations Web site: www.nipc.gov.

(*Continued*)

Date of Attack	Compromised financial and e-commerce entities	Name of hacker, group, or malicious tool	Various losses sustained because of the intrusion into the financial entity's networks
Aug. 10, 2000	Bloomberg[96]	Oleg Zesev and Igor Yarimaka	Broke into the Bloomberg computer system in Manhattan in an attempt to extort $200,000.
Dec. 22, 2000	EggHead[97]	Eastern European groups	Hackers compromise database of thousands of credit cards; on Christmas Eve, many of the cards were then "salami sliced."[98]
2001	Hong Kong	Various Hackers	Eight cases of e-banking theft were recorded in the year involving the loss of over $4.4 mil.[99]
Mar. 8, 2001	40 domestic e-banking and e-commerce sites	Eastern European criminal syndicate	Intruders stole credit card account information and other data by exploiting a Windows NT security flaw; the National Infrastructure Protection Center labeled this attack the "largest Internet attack to date."[100]
Apr. 12, 2001	VISA	Eastern European groups	Intruders gained access to its computer network in the U.K. and later demanded ransom for data obtained in the virtual break-in; company received a ransom demand of £10 million.
Jun. 5, 2001	Central Texas Bank[101]	Vasilly Gorshov and Alexey Ivanov	They had access to the bank's system for six months before they were detected.
Jul. 6, 2001	S1 (a host company)[102]	Investigation ongoing	The compromise of more than 300 banks and credit unions whose systems were hosted by S1.[103]

96. National Infrastructure Protection Center Major Investigations Web site: www.nipc.gov/investigations/bloomberg.htm.

97. Sullivan, 2001.

98. National Infrastructure Protection Center briefing, August 2001.

99. http://www.info.gov.hk/police/aahome/english/statistics/download/200201/crimebrief_eng.doc.

100. SANS Institute Alert, March 8, 2001.

101. Predictive Systems "Global E-review," August 2001. www.chron.com/cs/cda/story.hts/metropolitan/929311.

102. First reported by www.securityfocus.com.

103. A compromise is defined as access to a person's computer systems and databases without his or her explicit knowledge and consent. S1 had an impressive client list, from E*Trade to FleetBoston Financial Corp.

Date of Attack	Compromised financial and e-commerce entities	Name of hacker, group, or malicious tool	Various losses sustained because of the intrusion into the financial entity's networks
Jul. 14, 2001	Australia's Online Trading Systems	Black Orifice—Trojan Horse	Account data of more than 40,000 of their clients was compromised.
Aug. 21, 2001	Riggs Bank, First Virginia Banks, SunTrust, and Visa	Investigation ongoing	The account information of more than 4,000 account holders from these banks who used Visa debit cards was compromised; banks were forced to cancel all debit cards.[104]
Sep. 20, 2001	Deutsche Bank[105]	Nimda worm	Unknown—costs of breaches indeterminable.
Feb. 7, 2002	U.S. Treasury Direct[106]	Louis Lebaga	$158 million—Lebaga was apprehended only after attempting to steal $1.3 billion more five days later.
Mar. 1, 2002	Prudential Insurance Company	Donald McNeese	McNeese was arrested for the theft and credit card scam stemming from the hack of Prudential's database, compromising 60,000 personal records of employees there.[107]
Apr. 5, 2002	State of California, Payroll database	Investigation Ongoing	The hacker copied 265,000 state employee account names and social security numbers, thus making them vulnerable to ID theft.[108]
Apr. 12, 2002	Republic Bank	Investigation Ongoing	The hacker copied 3,600 bank customer account names and files, thus making them vulnerableto ID theft; by exploiting SI's (the hosting company's) servers, he was able to compromise the accounts of these customers.[109]

(*Continued*)

104. Sara Goo of the *Washington Post* first broke this story. www.idg.net.
105. National Infrastructure Protection Center. www.nipc.gov. These intrusions were perpetrated to steal proprietary databases, which were then sent to the heads of these banks with extortion demands.
106. The National Infrastructure Protection Center reported that the worm was distributed from unknown sources and is said to have disrupted and infiltrated networks worldwide. www.zdnet.com.
107. U.S. District Court Arrest Warrant Case # 02-841.
108. U.S. Department of Justice, 2002.
109. www.newsbytes.com/news/02/175977.html.

(*Continued*)

Date of Attack	Compromised financial and e-commerce entities	Name of hacker, group, or malicious tool	Various losses sustained because of the intrusion into the financial entity's networks
Jun. 19, 2002	Singaporean Bank DBS	A Chinese National[110]	The hacker siphoned over $31,000 from 21 various accounts, transferred $35,000 into his own account, withdrew the money at a bank branch and then fled the country. The whole operation took less than two hours.
Jul. 2002	Australian BPay Electronic Funds Transfer	Investigation Ongoing	Over 100 customers lost approximately A$150,000 (US$85,000) each.[111]
Aug. 2002	Daewoo Securities	Investigation Ongoing	Hackers penetrated a bank's security system and illegally sold 5 million shares of Delta Information and Communications stock worth approximately $21.7 million. [112]
Sep. 18, 2002	Unidentified bank, possibly Citibank	Ko Hakata and Goro Nakahashi	Hakata and Nakahashi used computers from a Tokyo cybercafe to steal $141,000 from online accounts.[113]
Oct. 21, 2002	Internet Root Servers	Investigation Ongoing	Largest ever Distributed Denial-of-Service (DDOS) attack, conducted on 13 root servers.[114]
Dec. 14, 2002	TriWest Healthcare Alliance, a Pentagon contractor	Gary McKinnon	Accused of stealing a database containing 500,000 medical records from a Defense Department contractor. Stolen data included social security numbers and personal medical records for military personnel.[115]

---

110. The Economic Times http://economictimes.indiatimes.com/articleshow.asp?artid+14588
111. Borneo Post http://www.saga.net.my/headlines/2002/july/024.htm
112. BBC News, "South Korea probes online dealing fraud," 8/26/2002, accessed at: <http://news.bbc.co.uk/2/hi/business/2217584.stm>.
113. The Mercury News, http://www.siliconvalley.coms/mld/siliconvalley/business/special_packages/security/5331143.htm
114. Washington Post http://www.washingtonpost.com/wp-dyn/articles/A828-2002Oct22.html
115. MSNBC http://www.msnbc.com/news/853426.asp.

Date of Attack	Compromised financial and e-commerce entities	Name of hacker, group, or malicious tool	Various losses sustained because of the intrusion into the financial entity's networks
2002	Equifax Inc., Experian Information Solutions Inc., and Trans Union LLC	Philip Cummings	Accused of massive identity theft of over 30,000 victims from help desk of Teledata Communications Inc. Stolen information included customer password and codes, which were used to obtain creditreports. Credit reports were then sold to third parties for $30 each.[116]
2002	H&R Block	Ivy Johnson, former H&R Block manager	The former H&R Block manager has been charged with mail and credit card fraud, for the identity theft of at least 27 customers.[117]
Jan. 25, 2003	Bank of America, American Express, Countrywide Financial Corp., airlines, and other databases	Sapphire worm (aka Slammer)	By attacking a Microsoft SQL Server 2000 vulnerability, 13,000 of Bank of America's ATMs were affected. Estimates are that at least 160,000 total databases were infected with the worm.[118] Countrywide Financial Corp. was forced to shut down their Web site for a day.[119] The Australian Amex site also had to be taken down for a period during the attack.[120]
Jan. 29, 2003 (reported)	Italian banking system	Italian hackers	Hackers stole the credit card information of an estimated 5,000 customers, and used these cards for purchases.[121]

(*Continued*)

---

116. ComputerWorld http://www.computerworld.com/securitytopics/security/cybercrime/story/0,10801,76252.00.html

117. The New York Times http://nytimes.com/2003/01/03/nyregion/03THEF.html

118. Brian Krebs, "Internet Worm Hits Airlines, Banks," Washingtonpost.com, 1/26/2003; accessed at: "http://www.washingtonpost.com/wp-dyn/articles/A46928-2003Jan26.html".

119. MSNBC, "Virus-like attack slows Web traffic;" 1/27/2003; accessed at: http://www.msnbc.com/news/864184.asp.

120. Julian Bajkowski, "Australian Amex site made 'unusable' by Slammer worm," Computerworld, 2/3/2003; accessed at: http://www.computerworld.com/developmenttopics/websitemgmt/story/0,10801,78140,00.html.

121. Security News Portal (from the www.repubblica.it), "Major Italian Banking and Credit Card Hacking Organization Smashed by Police," 1/29/2003, accessed at: http://www.securitynewsportal.com/cgi-bin/cgi-script/csNews/csNews.cgi?database=JanV%2edb&command=viewone&id=82&op=t.

(*Continued*)

Date of Attack	Compromised financial and e-commerce entities	Name of hacker, group, or malicious tool	Various losses sustained because of the intrusion into the financial entity's networks
Feb. 2003	EBay	Investigation Ongoing	A hacker stole eBay users' personal financial information using a university computer system to which he had no affiliation.[122]
Feb. 2003	Visa, Mastercard, American Express	Investigation Ongoing	Hackers stole approximately 8 million credit card numbers from a database.[123]
Mar. 2003	Commonwealth NetBank (Australia)	Investigation Ongoing	Alternative website was created, when information was input it was sent to a third party rather than the bank.[124]
Mar. 14, 2003	Discover Card	Investigation Ongoing	Emails were disseminated to Discover customers containing a links to a spoofed website; when customers submitted their bank account information, it would be sent to the criminal's email address.[125]
Apr. 2003	Australia/New Zealand Banking Group (ANZ Bank)	Investigation Ongoing	Combination of methods, including spoofed email and spoofed website with "tweaked log-in scripts."[126]
May 2003	Bank of America	Investigation Ongoing	Combination of spoofed email andspoofed website. Approximately 75 customers rendered their information.[127]
Jun. 2003	Banking customers in China, Hong Kong	Investigation Ongoing	A website belonging to a fake bank, www.banquedenationale.com, attempt to lure sensitive account information.[128]

122. Associated Press, "FBI Seeks Hacker Who Stole Credit Card Numbers From eBay Users," Washingtonpost.com, 2/7/2003; accessed at: http://www.washingtonpost.com/wp-dyn/articles/A39049-2003Feb7.html.

123. Jonathan Krim, "8 Million Credit Card Accounts Exposed," Washingtonpost.com, 2/19/2003; accessed at: http://www.washingtonpost.com/wp-dyn/articles/A27334-2003Feb18.html.

124. Commonwealth NetBank Incident: http://www.smh.com.au/articles/2003/03/29/1048653901522.html

125. Discover Incident: http://www.pcworld.com/news/article/0,aid,109829,00.asp

126. Australia Incident: http://www.computerweekly.com/Article120875.htm

127. Bank of America http://www.pcworld.com/news/article/0,aid,110725,00.asp

128. Hong Kong Bank http://www.info.gov.hk/hkma/eng/press/2003/20030619e3.htm

Date of Attack	Compromised financial and e-commerce entities	Name of hacker, group, or malicious tool	Various losses sustained because of the intrusion into the financial entity's networks
Jul. 2003	Absa Bank, South Africa	Johannes Jacobus Fourie	With the help of computer spyware, Fourie stole approximately R500,000 from customer accounts in South Africa's largest bank.[129]
Jul. 2003	Wells Fargo	Investigation Ongoing	Contained a spoofed email with an attachment carrying the Trojan horse virus. The virus collected passwords and sent them to a third party. [130]
Jul. 26-27, 2003	Kearney Bank	Malaysian crime ring	A Malaysian crime ring hacked into the Nebraska bank's computer system, and made illegal charges on customer accounts by attacking the Visa Check Card program. [131]
Aug. 2003	Bank of Montreal	Investigation Ongoing	Hackers sent spam stating they were bank representatives informing customers of a chance to win $500. A link was placed within the email to take customers to a false BMO bank site in which customers had to enter bank information and PIN numbers. The link also contained the Trojan horse virus. [132]
Sep. 2003	Paypal/Ebay	Investigation Ongoing	Utilized a spoofed paypal email address linking to www. paypalwarning.org, a site unrelated to the official paypal website. [133]

(Continued)

---

129. John Leyden, "Trojan infection linked to SA Net bank thefts," The Register, 7/21/2003; accessed at: http://www.theregister.co.uk/content/6/31848.html.

130. Wells Fargo Response http://www.wellsfargo.com/jump/fraud_prevention.jhtml http://www.nwfusion.com/newsletters/ecomm/2003/0728ecom2.html

131. USA Today, "Counterfeit Ring Hacks Nebraska Bank's Computer," USA Today, 7/23/2003; accessed at: <http://www.usatoday.com/tech/news/computersecurity/2003-07-23-ne-hack_x.htm>

132. Ebay/ Paypal hit again http://www.internetnews.com/IAR/article.php/3075041

133. Bank of Montreal http://www.workopolis.com/servlet/Content/fasttrack/20030912/RBMOO12?section=Dot-com

(*Continued*)

Date of Attack	Compromised financial and e-commerce entities	Name of hacker, group, or malicious tool	Various losses sustained because of the intrusion into the financial entity's networks
Sep. 2003	Barclays	Investigation Ongoing	False emails concerning Barclays new security policy were sent to random customers directing them to a Barclays link which would then take them to one of eight spoofed Barclays websites where customers were prompted to input bank and credit information. [134]
Oct. 2003	Stock market	Van Dinh	Dinh used keystroke loggers to steal U.S. brokerage firm customer accounts, and then used a victim's account identity as a means to unload Dinh's falling stocks. [135]

134. Barclays http://www.guardian.co.uk/business/story/0,3604,1042006,00.html http://www. theregister.co.uk/content/55/32796.html

135. BBC News, "US Hacker Accused of Massive Fraud", accessed on 10 Oct 2003 at http://news.bbc. co.uk/1/hi/business/3180358.stm.

TYPES OF E-FRAUD

The problem of fraud is not new, however, digital capabilities enhance the speed, reach, and magnitude with which crimes are executed. Through the Internet, a criminal can launch a single attack from a computer located in one part of the world and, within seconds, victimize countless computer users worldwide. Most often, these acts of cyber fraud are conducted for the purpose of yielding a financial gain for the criminal. Financial institutions are thus vulnerable to often-undetectable, global, and virtually instantaneous attacks on internal systems and proprietary information. Banks and vendors with weak security controls are susceptible to business disruptions, theft of data, sabotage, corruption of key records, and fraud (see Annex A for a detailed listing of major e-security incidents made public). Additionally, the development of wireless technologies to access the Internet further compound the problem by enabling foreign governments, terrorists, criminals, and hackers, singly or in concert, to operate in countries that primarily use advanced open network infrastructures without adequate security protocols in place (please see Annex F for wireless vulnerabilities).

What follows is an explanation of how traditional fraud has evolved due to the Internet, and how these incidents of e-fraud impact financial service providers.

Unauthorized System Access

The open network architecture of the Internet enables millions of users to be interconnected on a single digital network. As a result, the number of doorways through which malicious users can obtain unlawful access to remote computer systems also increases. Most instances of e-fraud begin with an unauthorized system access. In 2003, suspected activity reports (SAR) statistics for computer intrusions show 3,229 incidents, with losses totaling over US$2.2 billion.[136]

---

136. This data was taken from the United States Federal Bureau of Investigations (FBI), Suspicious Activity Report (SARS) Statistics, 2003.

Obtaining Unauthorized System Access: The Targets

The key ways with which criminals or illegitimate Internet users can obtain unauthorized system access is through vulnerabilities in: a system's network infrastructure, digital end-user devices, software applications, or human error.

First, vulnerabilities in the network system infrastructure can provide criminals with unauthorized system access. In making the shift from legacy mainframe computer systems to digital networked systems, organizations lose the security layer provided by closed, analog transmission systems. Particularly relevant to the banking community, many key payment systems are making this converting from legacy to open network architecture without realizing that they are exposing themselves to significant vulnerability of theft, corruption, or unauthorized access. In a specific example, SWIFT, the global bank wire transfer system, made the switch from legacy mainframe computers to networked computers. In doing so, SWIFT's money transfers take place via the transmission conduit of the Internet, open and potentially vulnerable to exploits by hackers in cyberspace, especially in the absence of a layered security system.[137]

Next, the transmission of information in digital form creates new vulnerabilities, and digital devices can be manipulated to profit from these weaknesses. For example, while wireless infrastructures offer a fast and relatively inexpensive way to bring financial services to remote regions, this increased provisioning of financial services through the open airwaves of the wireless networks creates new threats to sensitive financial information. The ubiquity of transmissions over wireless devices increases the threat of message interception and alteration attributable to vulnerabilities inherent in this type of technology (see Annex F on wireless vulnerabilities). Hackers can initiate man-in-the-middle attacks whereby a rogue computer intercepts and alters messages—such as sensitive financial data—as they transmit between cellular towers and devices.

Third, software applications create doorways where illegitimate users can obtain unauthorized system access. Software applications are attractive because new technologies give organizations the ability for more efficient ways of conducting business. File sharing applications, voice over Internet protocol (VOIP), Instant Messaging,[138] Microsoft Office software, even Internet browsers are ways in which the digital transformation alters business functions. Each of these technologies, however, are inherently vulnerable because their interoperability with the Internet creates an open network environment, and thus entry ways through which hackers can pilfer sensitive information or otherwise enter a user's computer system.

Finally, there are many instances where social engineering or human error creates openings for those with malicious intent to gain access to a system. Through even a single phone call, where a criminal pretends to be a company's systems administrator, he or she can often obtain the information necessary to obtain access to the company's computer systems. On the other hand, the human threat increases with the risk of insider threats to an organization, particularly since digital capabilities facilitate the transportation of large amounts of sensitive data in and out of an organization's physical walls.

Obtaining Unauthorized System Access: The Tools

Hacking is an endemic method of committing cyber crime, and a common way in which financial customers accounts are illegitimately accessed. The United States Financial Intelligence Unit's (FINCEN) most recent report depicts a 300 percent surge in hacking upon US banks over the past 8 months; 3,229 Suspicious Activity Reports (SARs) for computer intrusions were reported between September 15, 2002 to September 15, 2003.

Hacking is conducted through an unauthorized access of computer systems, generally when vulnerabilities in systems, applications, and devices are exploited through various forms

---

137. For further information see iDefense Inc. "A Security Overview of the SWIFT Financial Services Network," June 2003, Reston, VA.

138. For further information on the vulnerabilities of IM, please see Nishiyama 2003.

Box B.1: VOICE-OVER-IP (VOIP)

VOIP enables real-time voice communication over IP networks rather than the Public Switched Telephone Network (PSTN). Strong evidence exists that this technology is proliferating on a grand scale. The International Telecommunications Union (ITU) predicts: "By 2004, it could account for up to 40 per cent of all international traffic" (ITU 2002)

VOIP is vulnerable not only because of risks inherent within the technology itself, but also because convergent technologies amass weaknesses from multiple technologies. For example, VOIP carries risks that exist in traditional telephone networks, or "plain old telephone service" (POTS), such as the threat of wiretapping, people hijacking the phone network to get free calls, or network failure. Furthermore, VOIP is susceptible to dangers that exist in mobile phones; the nature of bits traveling through open air make mobile phones especially prone to hacks. To make matters worse, criminals and hackers have a good chance of remaining anonymous on a wireless network due to the transient nature of airwaves. Celltracker tools facilitate eavesdropping on cellular transmissions, and hackers and criminals can intercept data as they travel in that vulnerable zone between legitimate users and a cell tower. Though eavesdropping on phone calls might not pose a terribly great risk, the risk is exponentially greater when sensitive data, such as credit card and user identity information, travels through the airwaves while engaging in e-commerce activities.

When Internet and telephone technology are combined to make IP telephony possible, the risks and vulnerabilities are exponentially greater. Malicious viruses, hackers, identity theft, data interceptions, are all dangers to Internet communications. Additionally, convergence facilitates the return of old threats such as war dialing, where hackers would locate and penetrate open modems on the network. However, when applied to VOIP, the hacker will get more information than just voice. The phones over the IP networks can carry sensitive data such as identity and financial information.

Other points of vulnerability in the VOIP system include the operating system (OS), because VOIP systems run atop inherently vulnerable software such as Microsoft NT (Lemon 2001). The danger of exposing VOIP to these network holes is that transmissions are not simply limited to voice. New e-finance and e-commerce applications increasingly encourage the transmission of sensitive data using VOIP as a vehicle.

Additional risks within the VOIP network structure include the gateways and signaling. Gateways are particularly risky because they can expose data during the conversion between digital packets on the IP network to voice on the PSTN (Vijayan 2002). Meanwhile, the risk in signaling is that the actual signaling data, such as address and session information, is sent together with the digitized voice itself. This means it is much easier for a hacker to break into a VOIP transmission and retrieve the information necessary to modify a communication session for malicious purposes. Traditionally, on the PSTN, signaling information and the actual communications data are carried separately, acting to some extent as a safeguard against network intruders who want to conduct malicious network manipulations (Arkin 2002). Convergent communications devices can effectively combine the vulnerabilities found across numerous systems, thereby resulting in multiple points of vulnerabilities that compromise the security of sensitive information.

Source: Authored by Yumi Nishiyama, World Bank Integrator Group. The data was compiled from a variety of sources. Sources include the International Telecommunications Union (ITU) website. Additional research material includes: Lemon 2001, Vijayan 2002, and Arkin, 2002.

of malicious code. Viruses, worms, and denial-of-service attacks are several common tools that allow hackers to remotely enter a computer system and obtain access to system processes.[139]

Viruses are computer-transmitted malicious code that can swiftly compromise a system's integrity. They spread by attaching themselves to such things as e-mails and shared computer disks. Once they set up residence in a system, it is virtually impossible to kill it without replacing

---

139. For further information, see Kellermann and Nishiyama 2003a.

the infected parts of the system. Viruses did not exist before the early 1980s, and only recently have countries implemented legislation making the infection of a system with a virus a crime.[140]

Worms, an acronym for Write Once Read Many, are another form of malicious code that, unlike viruses that attach themselves to transport vehicles, self-replicate once written to a computer

---

Box B.2: CASE STUDY—BUGBEAR.B

In September 2002 a worm called Bugbear was unleashed, giving hackers access to computers to execute code and erase files. Several months later, in June 2003, security experts identified a more malicious variation of the original worm called Bugbear.B. Bugbear.B is programmed to target the Financial Sector. In particular, it is programmed to steal credit card and authentication information from networks.

Bugbear.B proliferates in two ways. First, it acts as a parasite. It disguises itself as a seemingly innocuous email attachment or it can attach itself to software so that the Bugbear.B code launches when a software program is executed. Certain vulnerabilities in Microsoft Outlook code permits the worm to automatically execute the email program, so that users may not even know an attack is being launched from their machine.

Second, Bugbear.B spreads through computer networks. Characteristic of any worm, it creates back doors through which hackers can enter and re-enter a system for future attacks. Bugbear.B then enters through the back door and listens on port 1080/tcp for sensitive information as an insider. This particular port, also known as the SOCKS port, enables networked Internet connections, but also acts as a tunnel through firewalls. In other words, data packets have a protected path into a networked system, untouchable by such things as an IDS. Legitimate programs use this port, including Internet Relay Chat (IRC); it has also been used to facilitate the dissemination of spam. Bugbear.B takes advantage of this system configuration to propagate itself through the network on its own device, without the help of email transmissions.

Negative manifestations of Bugbear's code include something as seemingly innocuous as sending data to printers so that it prints pages of illegible code, to more threatening actions such as pilfering sensitive user information for monetary gain. Bugbear.B shuts down or bypasses both anti-virus software and firewalls. Once inside a system, Bugbear.B will listen for such information as user names, passwords, and credit card numbers. It can also gather this data by installing a key-logging program onto the machine, a technology that stores a user's keystrokes.

Specific to the financial industry, Bugbear.B apparently contains the names of approximately 1300 financial institutions. When username or password data from emails match the name of any financial institution, Bugbear opens a backdoor and activates key logging for the purpose of obtaining sensitive user information. Once this data is acquired, Bugbear sends the data to one of several email addresses written into its source code.[141] Protection against this code entails downloading and running an anti-virus specially formulated against the Bugbear worm.

The Bugbear example illustrates the potentially catastrophic consequences of malicious code. It also demonstrates the dire need for multiple layers of security, as well as policies that support diligent oversight of security systems.

Source: Authored by Tom Kellermann and Yumi Nishiyama, World Bank Integrator Group. For further information see Kellermann and Nishiyama 2003a. Ted Bridis describes the Bugbear problem in an article titled, "Government Warns Banks About Virus-Like Infection," June 9, 2003, Association Press (http://www.securityfocus. com/news/5610). Additional information was gathered from the Computer Emergency Response Team Coordination Center (CERT/CC) website at http://www.cert.org.

---

140. Robert J. Morris wrote a computer program known as a worm that brought 10-20 percent of U.S. computers to an abrupt halt in 1988. "Hackers break into California state computers." May 27, 2002, Associated Press.

141. Bridis, Ted, "Government Warns Banks About Virus-Like Infection," June 9, 2003, Association Press, http://www.securityfocus.com/news/5610.

TABLE B.1: POTENTIAL LOSSES FROM A DENIAL-OF-SERVICE ATTACK

Business type	Brokerage firm	Credit card authorization company	Automated teller machines	Major online auction site
Exposure/Hour	$6.5 million/hr	$2.6 million/hr	$14,500/hr in fees	$70,000/hr

Source: Red Herring, December 2000.

system. Box B.2 illustrates the recent example of the Bugbear worm, and its consequent effects on the financial industry.

A denial-of-service attack (DOS) occurs when hackers send malicious code through emails, vulnerable software, etc. in order to overwhelm and shut down system processes. Table 3 suggests that denial of service can cost an average-size brokerage firm $6.5 million an hour or a credit card authorization company $2.6 million an hour. Moreover, these estimates do not include the costs of damage to reputation.

Whether worm, virus, or other means, there is an increased threat to online services on account that many of today's attacks tools are automated. Criminals can use pre-made tools found publicly on the Internet. Many of these tools contain advanced scanning patterns to quickly locate system vulnerabilities, and can even generate new attack cycles by exploiting vulnerabilities while the tools scan. Moreover, the Internet has provided criminals with a new way in which to coordinate a large number of attacks tools, and share information on the most efficient means of executing crimes online. Figure B.1 illustrates the dramatic rise in computer incidents over the past twelve years.

Conducting E-Fraud

There are numerous ways in which criminals have exploited computer users once gaining unauthorized access to their computer systems. Types of fraud that directly impact financial services

FIGURE B.1: COMPUTER INCIDENTS 1990-2002

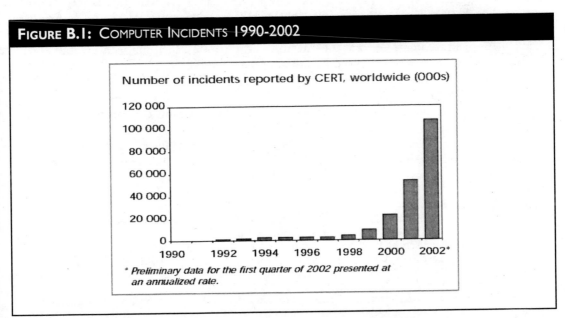

Number of incidents reported by CERT, worldwide (000s)

* Preliminary data for the first quarter of 2002 presented at an annualized rate.

Source: Computer Emergency Response Teams Co-ordination Centre (CERT/CC).

Box B.3: IDENTITY THIEF: ABRAHAM ABDALLAH

The most infamous of all identity thieves was Abraham Abdallah, a Brooklyn busboy. When police arrested him in March 2001, he had *Forbes* magazine's issue on the 400 richest people in America, as well as Social Security numbers, credit card numbers, bank account information, and mothers' maiden names of an A list of intended victims drawn from the issue, including Steven Spielberg, Oprah Winfrey, and Martha Stewart. Abdallah is accused of using Web sites, e-mail, and offline methods to try to steal the celebrities' identities as well as millions in assets. In May 2001, the Justice Department said in a statement to a congressional panel on Internet fraud, "Identity theft is the nation's fastest-growing white-collar crime." John Huse Jr., the Social Security Administration's inspector general, testified that the misuse of Social Security numbers in fraudulent activity is a "national crisis."

Source: New York Electronic Crimes Taskforce 2001.

---

institutions include, but are not limited to: identity theft, credit card theft, customer financial account access, and extortion. Almost always, financial gain is the primary incentive for criminals to commit these types of fraud.

Identity theft can be understood to be a general umbrella term to describe situations in which criminals pose as their victim in order to conduct malicious acts. Identity theft is the number one crime in the United States. The Federal Trade Commission reports that this type of crime affected 27 million people between 1998-2003, at a clean-up cost of 30-60 hours per incident.[142] Furthermore, reported incidents are projected to more than double, from 700,000[143] in 2001 to 1.7 million in 2005, and the costs to financial institutions globally will increase 300 percent each year, to more than $221 billion in 2005.[144] Disturbingly, these numbers do not take into account the wide range of social costs associated with this crime, such as litigation expenses, or the lost hours to redeem one's name or credit information. Box B.3 provides a graphic example of how pervasive a problem identity theft has become.

The pervasive diffusion of online credit card payment systems creates a prime target for cyber criminals. Illicit Internet users lure victims to give their credit card information in illegitimate emails, or by hacking into various organizations' databases or computer systems.[145] In February 2003, a hacker stole approximately 8 million Visa, Mastercard, and American Express credit card numbers from an e-commerce company's database (Krim 2003). In a similar incident in 2001, a compromised database resulted in the data theft of over 4,000 debit card accounts for several large financial organizations, including Riggs Bank and Visa.[146]

In addition to stealing identity or account information in order to commit financial crimes, illicit Internet users have directly accessed financial customer accounts to pilfer money. A fraud scheme that Australian police say may have netted millions of dollars, has shaken faith in one of the country's largest electronic banking systems. Almost 3 million Australians registered for Internet and telephone banking are being asked to check their accounts for irregularities following

---

142. Sullivan, Bob, "FTC: Millions hit by ID theft," MSNBC.com Mobile, accessed on Sep. 4, 2003 at http://www.msnbc.com/news/MobileChannel/960638.asp?s=TECH.

143. This figure represents a yearly trend within the United States only.

144. Published in a 2003 report by the Aberdeen Group www.csoonline.com

145. For additional information on a fraud trend called "phishing," please see Kellermann and Nishiyama 2003b.

146. SWD Staff, "Cracker Intercepts Visa Credit Card Data", Information Security Magazine, 9/10/2001, vol. 3, no. 69; accessed at: <http://infosecuritymag.techtarget.com/2001/sep/digest10.shtml#news4>.

security breaches involving the BPay electronic funds transfer system. To date, over 100 customers have lost upwards of $150,000 each.[147]

The shift of financial services to the Internet can, itself, be manipulated to commit crimes. The digital infrastructure is not only a transmission tool, but more importantly, serves as the critical foundation on top of which many of the world's industries operate. In other words, while digital trading of stocks and bonds can potentially reap innumerable benefits, it has also creates new risks. In March 2000, a hacker by the name of Abdelkader Smires launched a denial-of-service attack from his computer to a trading company where he worked.[148] Smires proceeded to crash the company's computer servers for three days, and, because of the massive quantity of NASDAQ trades the company handled, the ripple effect was that Smires' action caused major disruptions to trading on NASDAQ. Additional vulnerabilities exist in the shift to stocks and bonds trading online. In a recent example, a 19-year old hacker by the name of Van Dinh, used keystroke loggers to obtain a trading company customer's account information.[149] Dinh was then able to use the victim's online account to manipulate stock sales.[150]

Finally, all of the digital methods of fraud described above can be used to enhance traditional forms of fraud. Extortion is a key example of this. Law enforcement agencies have documented that Eastern European organized hacker groups have penetrated hundreds of banks worldwide over time. Several Kazakhstan nationals were caught for attempting to use alleged vulnerabilities in the Bloomberg website in exchange for $200,000 from Michael Bloomberg.[151] The FBI's computer crimes division, the National Infrastructure Protection Center (NIPC), notes that many financial service providers pay off extortion demands for fear of risking their reputations and losing their customer bases to competitors. The Creditcards.com hacking incident of 2000 is just one such example of extortion.[152] In this case, hackers penetrated a database containing 55,000 credit card numbers and then demanded that the company pay them a large sum of cash to protect against the posting of those numbers. Customer numbers were posted online for at least 2 days, costing the company up to $20 per customer to issue new cards.

In sum, these select incidents illustrate the dire need to parallel the rising e-commerce capabilities with heightened security measures. While the financial institutions rapidly shift to digital capabilities, it is evident that the Internet is vulnerable. Illicit users will continue to target these vulnerabilities for their own financial gain. Digital capabilities in fact, facilitate fraud through its globally networked structure, and through the reach, speed, and magnitude of crimes committed online. Moreover, the Internet allows criminals to remain relatively anonymous; there are countless e-fraud incidents that have never been solved, and many more that have yet to be detected. To take e-fraud capabilities a step further, even when criminals succeed in reaping a financial gain, the Internet can then be used to the launder money.

---

147. First reported in an article entitled "Australian bank scam may have siphoned millions," accessed at: http://business-times.asia1.com.sg/news/story/0,2276,51947,00.html

148. National Infrastructure Protection Center Major Investigations Website: www.nipc.gov; see also, Ann Harrison, "Database programmer arrested for attack on Wall Street employer's systems," *Computerworld*, Mar. 17, 2000.

149. BBC News, "US Hacker Accused of Massive Fraud", accessed on Oct. 10, 2003 at http://news.bbc.co.uk/1/hi/business/3180358.stm.

150. Dinh used the victim's trading account to offload Dinh's own falling Cisco stocks at a higher value.

151. Disabatino, Jennifer, "Suspects Nabbed in Bloomberg Extortion Case," *Computerworld*, Aug. 21, 2000, accessed on Oct. 10, 2003 at <http://www.computerworld.com/industrytopics/financial/story/0,10801,48794,00.html>.

152. Sandoval, Greg and Stephen Shankland, "Company says extortion try exposes thousands of card numbers," CNet News.com, Dec. 12, 2000, accessed on Oct. 10, 2003 at <http://news.com.com./2100-1017_3-249772.html?tag=prntfr>.

Electronic Money Laundering

Many governments acknowledge the large inherent difficulty in estimating the full magnitude of the global money-laundering (ML) problem. For example former IMF Director Michel Camdessus estimated the global volume of ML at between two to five percent of global GDP, a range encompassing $600 billion to $1.8 trillion. One example of how this phenomenon is growing via the Internet is the operation of E-gold.[153] This site provides users with an electronic currency, issued by E-gold Ltd., a Nevis corporation, 100 percent backed at all times by gold bullion in allocated storage. E-gold was created in response to a need for a global currency on the World Wide Web. E-gold operates in units of account by weight of metal, not US dolloars or any other national currency unit. Weight units have a precise, invariable, internationally recognized definition. Additionally, precious metals, gold in particular, enjoy a long history of monetary use around the world. Thus, E-gold is being used for international transactions. Here a non-financial institution is becoming a de facto money remitter or intermediary. No real records are stored, few diligence standards are followed, no specific reports on suspicious activity are filed, etc. E-gold sells the ability for people to exchange money, thus circumventing the financial institutions and their corresponding oversight/regulatory mechanisms. Intangible services like consulting are common facades for the disbursement of funds between organized criminal syndicates. These entities usually establish themselves in jurisdictions where secrecy laws prevent adequate disclosure. For example, e-gold utilizes the Internet and nations like Luxemburg and other neutral regimes to base their servers. Sources in the United States Financial Intelligence Unit, FINCEN, indicate that these types of online entities are becoming the preferred method of money laundering.[154]

In sum, several pervasive venues for electronic attacks in the area of e-financial services have been publicly documented, but continue to be problematic. The most frequent problems in this arena are: (i) insider abuse, (ii) identity theft, (iii) fraud, and (iv) breaking and entering, often conducted by hackers. Though these areas must be addressed and risks mitigated, there continues to be a relative lack of accurate information about intrusions and associated losses. This deficiency in reporting intrusion to regulators and law enforcement is the fundamental reason why issues related to e-security are not recognized as an immediate priority. In the United States, a 2001 CSI/FBI Computer Crime Survey identified the following five major reasons organizations did not report electronic intrusions to law enforcement:

- Negative publicity;
- Negative information competitors would use to their advantage—for example, to steal customers;
- Lack of awareness that they could report events;
- Decision that a civil remedy seemed best;
- Fear among IT personnel of reporting incident because of job security.

Public awareness is the critical first step. However, e-security must be addressed and prioritized so that positive externalities from the diffusion of new technologies can be embraced, rather than wreaking further havoc from new methods of cyber crime.

---

153. For additional information, please see e-gold website at: http://www.e-gold.com/.
154. Information taken from authors interview with anonymous FINCEN agent.

WORLDWIDE E-SECURITY INDUSTRY

Today's e-security industry boasts an ever-growing array of companies. The types and numbers of choices can be confusing for the expert and overwhelming to the novice. These companies are involved in every facet of securing the networks used by financial services providers. They range from those that provide active content filtering and monitoring services (even virus detection companies are an example) to those that undertake intrusion detection tests, create firewalls, undertake penetration testing, develop encryption software and services, and offer authentication services.

In scope, the e-security industry increasingly is becoming a worldwide presence as it grows parallel with the expanding connectivity to the Internet. The growing integration of technologies among the Internet, wireless, Internet provider (IP), telephone, and satellite will also present new challenges for e-security and the structure of the financial services industry and e-finance.

From the vantage point of financial services providers, the earlier that security is built into a system's design process, the greater will be their return on investment in security-related services. For example, studies show that spending $1 to fix a vulnerability during the system design process saves $99 of the $100 that must be spent later when the system is implemented (See Berinato 2002; Soo Hoo 2001). This cost avoidance or cost savings makes or breaks many IT projects. The increasing extent to which technology platforms drive financial services and the increasing rates at which computer e-security incidents are occurring emphasize the importance of using risk management in making business decisions to avoid greater future losses.

Electronic Security Vendors

A rich variety of vendors operate in what is becoming a global industry for e-security. Many types of companies operate in this industry. In the United States alone, $5.1 billion in security software

FIGURE C.1: E-SECURITY INDUSTRY AND E-FINANCE

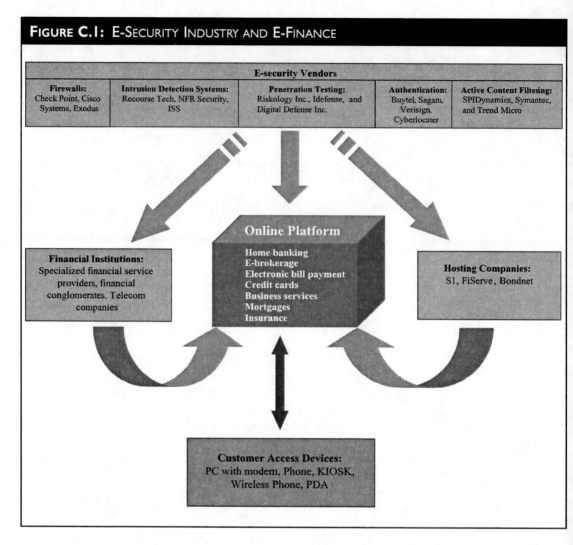

was sold in the year 2000—a 33 percent increase over the prior year.[155] These companies are involved in every facet of securing the wide area networks over which financial services are provided. The following is a brief description of the major categories of vendors (see also Figure C.1).

Active Content Monitoring and Filtering. These companies produce tools that examine a system for potentially destructive content material entering a network. The tools monitor all content trying to enter a network for malicious codes, or other harmful attributes. Trojans, worms, and viruses are methods used to deploy an attack once the perpetrator enters the system. Viruses are programs that infect other programs on the same system by replicating themselves. Virus scanners are critical in mitigating these attacks. Vendors of virus scanners provide software that scans and cleans networks and is periodically updated.

Intrusion Detection Systems Vendors. These companies provide products to monitor network traffic and alert the systems administrator with an alarm when someone or something is attempting to gain unauthorized access to a system.

Firewall Vendors. These companies provide a virtual "security guard" that sits at the gate of the customer's facilities. A firewall is a system that enforces the access-control policy between two networks. Vendors create these virtual guards to protect a network's integrity.

---

155. See Cunningham, "Digital Security: Heightened Risks Demand Innovation," *Red Herring*, July 2001.

Penetration Testing Companies. These entities provide "teams" to simulate attacks on a network to test for the system's inherent weaknesses. They then patch the holes found during the simulated attacks. Typically, vulnerability-based scanning tools provide a current snapshot of a system's vulnerabilities.

Cryptographic Communications Vendors. This form of security enables the client to protect its communications by inserting the data into an encryption envelope. Encryption uses complex algorithms known as a "key" to shield messages transmitted over public channels. It provides safe passage from point A to point B. When the message reaches its destination, the recipient uses another algorithmic key to open it. It is highly recommended for use by mobile workforces and/or large non-centralized corporations or institutions.

Authentication Vendors. These vendors provide tools that ask users such questions as "Who are you?" and "Are you allowed to do that?" A user is permitted access the system only if it answers these questions correctly. This type of service can be broken into four general categories: passwords, tokens or smart cards, biometrics, and encryption.

Links to E-Finance

In October 2002, a yet unknown source launched a Distributed Denial-of-Service (DDOS) attack on the Internet's thirteen root servers. While the Internet is essentially perceived to be a decentralized network of networks, the root servers act as the sole circulatory mechanism for the infrastructure, making the critical translation between domain names and IP addresses so that Internet addresses can be understood by computers from points of origin to destination. The thirteen root servers are then connected to key Network Access Points (NAPs), or Internet Exchange Routes, which route traffic at critical junctures. The Internet backbone is comprised of these parts. ISPs around the world are connected together via the NAPs, thereby creating an interconnected network of computers. It is at this level that individual users, organizations, and application service providers (ASPs) connect the Internet.

The above example bears particular relevance to the financial sector, for had the root servers completely crashed during the 2002 attack the entire Internet backbone would have disabled the infrastructure, shutting down all processes replying on it—including financial, transportation, communication, and other critical infrastructure uses. This scenario clearly demonstrates the interconnected, interdependent, and complex nature of today's critical infrastructures and the vital role of e-security, and the companies that provide these services in protecting us from major disruptions.

Because e-security companies are becoming increasingly global in nature, it is important, when designing public policy, to understand the links between such companies and the finance industry. Figure C.1 provides a stylistic example of some of the links among the many types of vendors of e-security services and financial services providers.

Figure C.1 also shows a potentially disturbing reality about the e-security industry. One vendor may provide multiple services to several interlinked customers. For instance, a vendor may provide security to the financial services provider's online platform. This same vendor also may provide security services directly to the bank for its offline computer systems. In addition, it may supply security services to the hosting company. Telecommunication companies in many emerging markets provide hosting—or what many refer to as "e-enabling services"—to the banking community. By establishing a convenient online platform that customers can access through a variety of electronic devices, these hosting companies (e.g., ISPs) have become targets for organized crime.

In many emerging markets, the telecommunications company may have an interest in or own outright the ISP provider and the hosting company. Disturbingly, it may provide various forms of financial services as well. Moreover, many telecommunications companies also have multiple interests in many different forms of technology providers, from fixed-line telephony to wireless to satellites. This monopolistic industry structure should raise concerns—it signifies the need to discuss and debate difficult public policy issues now, such as competition policy, and how these issues might be addressed in designing new legal and regulatory elements of the present frameworks (see Claessens, Glaessner, and Klingebiel 2002).

Along with a complex, concentrated, cross-linked telecommunications organizational structure, convergence in technologies will present special challenges in the design of public policies relating to e-security. Specifically, increasing points of vulnerability will emerge, and any well-designed e-security system must address them. These new points of vulnerability might include the potential interfaces between customer access devices, such as a PC with modems, land-line phones that can be linked with any Internet platform through voice recognition, wireless phones, or personal digital assistants (PDAs) with an online platform. The point at which the message leaps from one channel to another is the point at which it is most vulnerable. Hence, financial services providers will need to address a much wider array of risks and expend effort to define liability; public policymakers will need to examine the impacts of potential weaknesses, given what is already a complex e-finance industrial structure.

The need to secure systems against physical risks that involve the use of multiple technologies in different locations runs up against the fact that the more distributed and decentralized a network is, the more vulnerable to interception and unauthorized access at the point of interface. As technologies converge, developing effective standards to secure such points of interface will become increasingly more important.

One example of how convergence of technologies creates vulnerability occurs when a wireless Groupe Spécial Mobile (GSM) phone is used to initiate a transaction through an interface with the Internet (e.g., via indicating transactions on the online platform of the financial services provider). Specifically, a secure way of integrating between the two technologies—GSM and the Internet—is needed. This typically requires seamless connectivity and an integration of standards, including those for worldwide security, that are not in place today. Wireless messages have to travel through a gateway,[156] which channels them to a wired network (e.g., the Internet) for retransmission to their ultimate destination. At the gateway, the message sent and encrypted in GSM using what is called Wireless Application Protocol (WAP) and the associated use of Wireless Transport Layer Security (WTLS) must be converted into the industry standard for secure messaging over a wired network—secure socket layer (SSL). At this point (in the gateway), the message will be unencrypted before being re-encrypted, and there is vulnerability.

---

156. For more detailed analysis of this problem, see Annex F

Box C.1: EVOLUTION OF TECHNOLOGY AND INTERNATIONAL STANDARDS

A fundamental security dilemma is embedded in global information networks. The global IT network infrastructure (i.e., the physical machinery that allows electronic linkages on a global scale) is on the one hand most secure and immune to destruction by natural disasters or terrorist and cyber-criminal attacks when it is most distributed and decentralized. After the great Kobe earthquake and the destruction of all fiber optic connections in the city during that natural disaster, the Japanese government proceeded to install satellite VSAT[157] terminals at post offices throughout the country to ensure the basic integrity of national communications.

On the other hand, the most distributed networks are most vulnerable to interception and unauthorized access. Often maximum vulnerability to interception exists at the point where fiber, coax, satellite, and terrestrial wireless systems interconnect. Air interface standards are but one example of modern telecommunications and IT systems open to interception.

A few years ago, telecommunications were projected to follow the model known as the "Negroponte Flip," whereby all narrowband traffic would go onto wireless (and largely mobile) systems, but all broadband service (in order to conserve frequency) would go onto fiber networks. This model was focused on the United States rather than the rest of the world, and it was technology-driven. In fact, the popularity of wireless systems (both satellite and terrestrial wireless) has continued to increase, and the market has demanded more and more Direct Broadcast Satellite (DBS) satellite entertainment service and broader band wireless now in the form of third generation systems and soon fourth generation systems. The market has thus actually followed the trend of the so-called Pelton Merge, which calls for continued improvement of "seamless interface standards" that allow the smooth interconnection of fiber, coax, terrestrial wireless, satellites, and other new and evolving technologies such as high altitude platforms. The challenge is thus to develop standards that allow easy and reliable interconnection and yet also protect security.

One example of a standard is the ISO seven-layer model of telecommunications. The current standard, however, does not really treat the security issues in the seamless interface between these technologies. Hence, it is necessary to consider the creation of a new layer that is truly secure, based on a 256- or even 1024-bit code that is constantly updated. Further study would be needed to determine whether the ultimate solution is a separate layer or the reengineering of part of an existing layer that could be devoted to this task. The extension of security identification module (SIM) smart cards that could be used throughout the world would also be a major step forward.

Source: Dr. Joseph Pelton, Executive Director of the Clarke Institute.

---

157. Very Small Aperture Terminal (VSAT), but more simply put it describes a small satellite terminal that can be used for one-way and/or interactive communications via satellite.

RISK MANAGEMENT: A BLUEPRINT FOR LAYERED SECURITY[158]

This Annex provides technical information to complement the material in Chapter 6. We identified 12 core layers of proper security which we believe are essential for maintaining the integrity of data and mitigating the risks associated with open architecture environments, and in many instances, actual implementation of a specific layer need not entail large capital investments or outlays. The Chief Information Security Officer (CISO) has the critical role of overseeing that the 12 layers are carried out and implemented in accordance with the best practices

1. **Risk Management**—A broad-based framework based upon CERT's OCTAVE paradigm for managing assets and relevant risks to those assets.
2. **Cybernetic Intelligence**—Experienced threat and technical intelligence analysis regarding threats, vulnerabilities, incidents, and countermeasure should provide timely and customized reporting to prevent a security incident before it occurs.

---

158. The annexes to this paper were created to be a comprehensive blueprint for adequate, layered, electronic security. The contributors and reviewers came from the e-security industry, the law enforcement community, and academic institutions. The reviewers of these annexes believe that the procedural guidelines for e-security outlined in the annexes are state-of-the-art as of June 2003. These reviewers were Dave Thomas, Chief Investigator for the FBI Computer Crimes Division; Keith Schwalm, Director of Infrastructure Protection, President's Critical Infrastructure Protection Board; Jim Nelms, Chief Security Officer, World Bank Treasury; Rick Fleming, Vice President of Security Operations for Digital Defense Inc.; Linda McCarthy, Executive Security Advisor to Symantec Inc.; Simon Martinez, Director of the Federal Deposit Insurance Corporation's Computer Security Incident Response Team; Gary Sullivan, President of Galaxy Computer Services Inc.; Chris Bateman, Technical Analyst for the Computer Emergency Response Team; Dorothy Denning, Professor of Computer Engineering at Georgetown University; Joseph Pelton, Executive Director of the Clarke Institute; Stephanie Lanz, Visiting Research Scholar at the Center for Emerging Threats and Opportunities at Quantico VA.; John Frazzini, Special Agent for the Secret Service Financial Crimes Division; Tracey Vispoli, Vice President of CHUBB, and Bill Worley, HP fellow, Chief Scientist for Hewlett Packard, Inc.

3. **Access Controls/Authentication**—Establish the legitimacy of a node or user before allowing access to requested information. The first line of defense is access controls; these can be divided into passwords, tokens, biometrics, and public key infrastructure (PKI).
4. **Firewalls**—Create a system or combination of systems that enforces a boundary between two or more networks.
5. **Active Content Filtering**—At the browser level, it is prudent to filter all material that is not appropriate for the workplace or that is contrary to established workplace policies.
6. **Intrusion Detection System (IDS)**—This is a system dedicated to the detection of break-ins or break-in attempts, either manually or via software expert systems that operate on logs or other information available on the network. Approaches to monitoring vary widely, depending on the types of attacks that the system is expected to defend against, the origins of the attacks, the types of assets, and the level of concern for various types of threats.
7. **Virus Scanners**—Worms, Trojans, and viruses are methods for deploying an attack. Virus scanners hunt malicious codes, but require frequent updating and monitoring.
8. **Encryption**—Encryption algorithms are used to protect information while it is in transit or whenever it is exposed to theft of the storage device (e.g. removable backup media or notebook computer).
9. **Proper Systems Administration**—This should be complete with a list of administrative failures that typically exist within financial institutions and corporations and a list of best practices.
10. **Vulnerability Testing**—Vulnerability testing entails obtaining knowledge of vulnerabilities that exist on a computer system or network and using that knowledge to gain access to resources on the computer or network while bypassing normal authentication barriers.
11. **Policy Management Software**—A software program should control Bank policy and procedural guidelines vis-à-vis employee computer usage.
12. **Business Continuity/Incident Response Plan (IRP)**—This is the primary document used by a corporation to define how it will identify, respond to, correct, and recover from a computer security incident. The main necessity is to have an IRP and to test it periodically.

Risk Management

The BITS Financial Services Security Laboratory is a testing facility. It was launched in July 1999 to test products and services that strengthen the security of electronic payment systems and related e-commerce technologies. The criteria established by BITS needs to be strengthened. The annexes to this monograph serve to depict the minimum technological baseline that banks should incorporate into their information technology (IT) security. Based on both the BITS recommendations (see box 1 in this annex) and the 14 recommendations from the Electronic Banking Group (see box 4.1), these annexes provide a blueprint for "true" layered security.

Access Controls/Authentication

1. Users should be required to issue both a user ID and a password at the time of logon.
2. File and directory access control should be set according to the sensitivity and use of the files and directories.
3. Users should be granted rights and privileges to available system resources only on a need-to-know, need-to-use basis.
4. The host system should be able to identify both the workstation and the workstation connection point (i.e., location) at logon.
5. Data access control should be determined at the appropriate level in each division.
6. File access privileges should be identified as read, read-only, write (with separate add and update levels), execute, execute-only, create, rename, delete, change access, and none.

Box D.1: BITS MASTER SECURITY CRITERIA

- **Identification:** The system shall have the capability of associating a user with an unambiguous identifier by which the said user shall be held accountable for the actions and events initiated by that user.
- **Nonrepudiation:** The system shall have the capability of preventing users from successfully denying actions and events of users acting in the role of a sender or receiver.
- **Authentication:** The system shall offer features to verify the claimed identity of a user before allowing system access to the said user.
- **Authorization:** The system shall offer features to support the following restrictions:

  - No user shall be allowed access to the system without identification and authentication;
  - No user shall be allowed access to a resource of the system unless specifically authorized.

- **Confidentiality:** The system shall offer features to ensure that sensitive information shall be communicated and stored in a way such that only authorized users are allowed access.
- **Data Integrity:** The system shall offer features to ensure that either:

  - The data shall not be modified or altered without authorization in either storage or in transit; or
  - Any unauthorized modification of data shall yield an auditable security-related event.

- **Audit:** The system shall offer features to support the following functions:

  - Maintain a history file (e.g., audit log) that records all security-related events pertinent to establishing an audit trail for a "post-mortem" analysis of a suspected security breach;
  - Ensure integrity of the audit log;
  - Generate customized audit reports;
  - Protect audit log from unauthorized[un okay?] access;
  - Support administrator-selectable alerts for specified security related events;
  - Support audit records of administrative events.

- **Data Disposal:** The system shall ensure that there is no residual data exposed to unauthorized users as resources are allocated to those data objects or released from those data objects.
- **System Integrity:** The system shall offer features to support the following functions:

  - Perform integrity checks for system function;
  - Retain the security parameters after the occurrence of events such as system restart, disaster recovery, arrival of sensitive dates, et cetera;
  - Provide the backup capability to restore the system, when necessary, to a well-defined state;
  - Ensure the security features are always invoked and may not be bypassed unless authorized and configured to do so.

- **Security Administration:** The system shall offer features to selectively authorize a highly privileged user (as security administrator) to perform day-to-day activities.
- **Guidance:** The vendor shall supply the following product support capabilities: a cogent security-related document for administration that would be made available as a hard copy or an electronic file, as an entity unto itself, and not fragmented throughout the manuals.

7. System resource access should be assignable on an individual, group, or public basis.
8. The user ID format should be seven (7) characters. The remaining characters should be alphanumeric special characters (e.g., *, %, @), which are even more secure than numeric. This format should be applied to all platforms the user is authorized to access.
9. System passwords should be a minimum of 6 up to a maximum of 16 characters long.
10. System passwords should be changed at least every 90 calendar days.
11. System passwords should not be reused within the last 10 passwords.

Box D.2: THE FUTURE OF ACCESS CONTROLS

Advanced biometric technologies are currently operational in a number of retail locations, providing an instant and secure biometric authentication mechanism that can be implemented in any banking, government, retail, or corporate environment. Pay By Touch^{SM} is one such system that provides authentication by means of scanning the fingerprint of a user and comparing the scanned image to previously stored fingerprint templates. An employee of the organization using this system initially authenticates the individual's identity using standard methodologies, a procedure required in order to maintain data integrity. The individual chooses a PIN number which acts as both a secondary authentication check and a "search code." The combination of the biometric and the search code enhances non-repudiation, virtually eliminating any authentication error.

Once the individual has been enrolled, he/ she will be recognized anywhere Pay By Touch^{SM} is in use. Subsequent transactions require only placement of the enrolled finger and entry of the PIN number in order to automatically access the individual's payment, loyalty, identification cards, or anything else the individual chooses to enroll. A combination of DUKPT and 3DES encryption is used to create an extremely secure environment. Advanced applications of biometric technologies have the potential to improve not only authentication and non-repudiation, but also, to improve throughput and revenue at the point of sale.

Source: Eric Bachman, COO, Pay By Touch (formerly Solidus Networks).

---

12. There should be no echoing of password positions, actual characters used, or dummy characters (e.g., display of asterisk for each password character position).
13. New system passwords should always be entered twice for verification.
14. Attempts by general users to enter a correct password should be limited to five (5) attempts, after which the system will disable the account.

Firewalls: Recommendations for Proper Firewall Configuration

1. The firewall should be placed in between your network router and your network or given application.
2. It is important to minimize and limit any network protocol that is not required by your organization. As an example, if you are not using Novell, then IPX should not be allowed to traverse your network.
3. Routers need proper configuration. The most common mistake in configuring firewalls is to allow servers that should accept only inbound connections—for example, Web servers—to make outbound connections. This is important because if your Web server is compromised as a result of a security breach and the firewall is configured to not allow that server to initiate a connection to another system, then the hacker has found a dead-end connection. Effectively, the hacker cannot further compromise your systems using that Web server.[159] Routers are capable of filtering packets as well. According to Peter Tippett, Chief Technical Officer of Trusecure Inc.: "Over 92 percent of routers have turned their default feature off. This feature, which exists in all Cisco routers, is typically disallowed due to the existence of an Any/Any rule that turns this safety feature off. If the rule for the router is changed to Default/Deny, your router becomes, in essence, an extra packet firewall, thus reducing risk to your business by 2,000 percent."
4. Firewalls need to remain current. They should be updated like virus scanners and patches at regular intervals, when a serious vulnerability has been discovered, and when a patch is available.

---

159. Contributed by Rick Fleming, Vice President of Security Operations for Digital Defense Inc.

5. Ingress and egress filtering should be used. Spoofing Internet protocol (IP) addresses is a common method used by attackers to hide their tracks when they attack a victim. For example, the very popular smurf attack uses a feature of routers to send a stream of packets to thousands of machines. Each packet contains a spoofed source address of a victim. The computers to which the spoofed packets are sent flood the victim's computer, often shutting down the computer or the network. Performing filtering on traffic coming into your network (ingress filtering) and going out (egress filtering) can help provide a high level of protection. The filtering rules[160] are as follows:

- Any packet coming into your network must not have a source address of your internal network.
- Any packet coming into your network must have a destination address of your internal network.
- Any packet leaving your network must have a source address of your internal network.
- Any packet leaving your network must not have a destination address of your internal network.
- Any packet coming into your network or leaving your network must not have a source or destination address of a private address or an address listed in RFC1918 reserved space. These include 10.x.x.x/8, 172.16.x.x/12, or 192.168.x.x/16, and the loopback network 127.0.0.0/8.
- Block any source-routed packets or any packets with the IP options field set.
- Reserved, DHCP auto-configuration, and Multicast addresses should also be blocked:

  - 0.0.0.0/8
  - 169.254.0.0/16
  - 192.0.2.0/24
  - 224.0.0.0/4
  - 240.0.0.0/4

6. Rate-limiting filters should be employed.
7. If users are allowed to connect from the Internet to the internal network, the access should be restricted to either a virtual private network (VPN) or an encrypted software session.[161]
8. Security policies should be put in place that control both internal and external access to the network. Security policies should not allow the needs of IT and specific applications to dictate—for example, if one needs to access a system internally using a wireless laptop and the systems administrator places the access point outside of the firewall. This is a configuration error. As recent Nimda and Code Red worms taught us, a firewall reduces the number of hack attempts, but it does not eliminate them.
9. The list of what a systems administrator should allow/disallow through the firewall depends on many factors. The critical factor is where on the network the firewall sits. For example, a firewall positioned between a Web server and an application layer will pass one set of protocols, and a DMZ firewall that sits in front of the mail server will pass a completely different set. In either case, the system should be designed to allow through a limited set of well-behaved telecommunications protocol (TCP) ports.[162] However, if the firewall is guarding the corporate network, only authenticated protocols should be given access to bolster security. And, when configuring a firewall, any protocol that is not

---

160. Input provided by the SANS Institute.
161. Ibid.
162. Contributed by Peter Penfield of Cisco Systems.

required for the organization to function properly should be disallowed. Moreover, proper configuration dictates that only the minimum set of protocols be allowed access to the minimum set of specific hosts that are needed to run the network. The system denies all and logs those packets that are dropped. By blocking traffic to these ports at the firewall or other network perimeter protection device, you add an extra layer of defense that helps protect you from configuration mistakes. Note, however, that using a firewall to block network traffic directed to a port does not protect the port from disgruntled coworkers who are already inside your perimeter or from hackers who may have penetrated your perimeter using other means. According to the SANS Institute, the following ports should be blocked:[163]

- Login services—telnet (23/tcp), SSH (22/tcp), FTP (21/tcp), NetBIOS (139/tcp), rlogin et al. (512/tcp through 514/tcp)
- RPC and NFS—Portmap/rpcbind (111/tcp and 111/udp), NFS (2049/tcp and 2049/udp), lockd (4045/tcp and 4045/udp)
- NetBIOS in Windows NT—135 (tcp and udp), 137 (udp), 138 (udp), 139 (tcp). Windows 2000—earlier ports plus 445(tcp and udp)
- X Windows—6000/tcp through 6255/tcp
- Naming services—DNS (53/udp) to all machines that are not DNS servers, DNS zone transfers (53/tcp) except from external secondaries, LDAP (389/tcp and 389/udp)
- Mail—SMTP (25/tcp) to all machines that are not external mail relays, POP (109/tcp and 110/tcp), IMAP (143/tcp)
- Web—HTTP (80/tcp) and SSL (443/tcp) except to external Web servers; may also want to block common high-order HTTP port choices (8000/tcp, 8080/tcp, 8888/tcp, etc.)
- "Small Services"—ports below 20/tcp and 20/udp, time (37/tcp and 37/udp)
- Miscellaneous—TFTP (69/udp), finger (79/tcp), NNTP (119/tcp), NTP (123/udp), LPD (515/tcp), syslog (514/udp), SNMP (161/tcp and 161/udp, 162/tcp and 162/udp), BGP (179/tcp), SOCKS (1080/tcp)
- ICMP—block incoming echo request (ping and Windows traceroute); block outgoing echo replies.

Active Content Filtering

A list of the greatest content- and protocol-related threats to network systems follows.

1. Hostile Active X
2. Javascript
3. Remote Procedure Calls (RPCs)
4. Perimeter-based security (PBS)
5. Berkeley Internet Name Domain (BIND): The following steps should be taken to defend against the BIND vulnerabilities:[164]

- Disable the BIND name daemon (called "named") on all systems that are not authorized to be DNS servers. Some experts recommend you also remove the DNS software.
- On machines that are authorized DNS servers, update to the latest version and patch level. Use the guidance contained in the following advisories:

---

163. Refer to www.sans.org/top20.htm.
164. The SANS Institute, www.sans.org/top20.htm.

> For the NXT vulnerability: http://www.cert.org/advisories/CA-99-14-bind.html. For the QINV (Inverse Query) and NAMED vulnerabilities: http://www.cert.org/advisories/CA-98.05.bind_problems.html http://www.cert.org/summaries/CS-98.04.html.

- Run BIND as a nonprivileged user for protection in the event of future remote-compromise attacks. (However, only processes running as root can be configured to use ports below 1024—a requirement for DNS. Therefore you must configure BIND to change the user ID after binding to the port.)
- Run BIND in a root directory structure for protection in the event of future remote-compromise attacks.
- Disable zone transfers except from authorized hosts.
- Disable recursion and glue fetching to defend against DNS cache poisoning.
- Hide your version string.

6. Simple Network Management Protocol (SNMP) default community strings[165]:

- If you do not absolutely require SNMP, disable it.
- If you must use SNMP, use the same policy for community names as used for passwords. Make sure that they are difficult to guess or crack, and that they are changed periodically.
- Validate and check community names using snmpwalk. Additional information can be found at http://www.zend.com/manual/function.snmpwalk.php.
- Filter SNMP (Port 161/UDP) at the border-router or firewall unless it is absolutely necessary to poll or manage devices from outside of the local network.
- Where possible, make MIBs read-only.

7. JVM vulnerability[166]
8. Sendmail[167]—The following steps should be taken to protect Sendmail: Upgrade to the latest version of Sendmail and/or implement patches for Sendmail; http://www.cert.org/advisories/CA-97.05.sendmail.html. Do not run Sendmail in daemon mode (turn off the -bd switch) on machines that are neither mail servers nor mail relays.
9. Internet Message Access Protocol (IMAP) and Post Office Protocol (POP)
10. Sadmind and mountd: Sadmind allows remote administration access to Solaris systems, providing a graphical user interface for system administration functions. Mountd controls and arbitrates access to NFS mounts on UNIX hosts. The following actions[168] will protect against NFS vulnerabilities, including sadmind and mountd:

- Wherever possible, turn off and/or remove sadmind and mountd on machines directly accessible from the Internet.
- Install the latest patches:
  For Solaris Software, http://sunsolve.sun.com;
  For IBM AIX Software, http://techsupport.services.ibm.com/support/rs6000.support/downloads, http://techsupport.services.ibm.com/rs6k/fixes.html;
  For SGI Software, http://support.sgi.com/;
  For Compaq (Digital UNIX), http://www.compaq.com/support.

---

165. For more comprehensive information regarding this vulnerability refer to: http://www.cert.org/advisories/CA-2002-03.html

166. There is a JVM patch that will prevent the copying of Web sites visited as well as the copying of passwords typed.

167. Sendmail is the program that sends, receives, and forwards most electronic mail processed on UNIX and Linux computers.

168. The SANS Institute, www.sans.org/top20.htm.

- Use host/IP-based export lists.
- Set up export file systems for read-only or no suid where possible.
- Use nfsbug to scan for vulnerabilities.

11. E-mail

- Filter all .exe attachments.
- Filter all .doc attachments.
- Consider filtering all arriving and departing e-mail by a spam threshold (greater than 40 identical messages blocked and source traced, if inside the network).

Intrusion Detection Systems

Box D.3: Next Generation Intrusion Detection Systems

Advanced intrusion protection systems (IPS) go beyond the static monitoring of packets for system breaches, as inherent in traditional intrusion detection systems. One company has developed a patent pending IPS that is an adjunct to existing intrusion-based methodologies. The technology does not rely on either signatures or anomaly detection, but instead, identifies basic building blocks of activities that may be differentiated with pattern classification techniques on the fly. When the application determines non-legitimate intent, it is capable of automatically tracking the user or blocking continued access.

All users in a network are assessed multiple times per second for entire sessions by user-assigned neural network assessment engines. A single assessment consists of collecting user activities as a whole, submitting activities to the assessment engine, automatically rating overall activity on the two behavioral dimensions of expertise and deception, and providing an assessment result that falls within a two dimensional grid. If a user' activities result in a behavioral rating in the tracking region, the user's behavior and associated activities will be tracked for the duration of the session. If a user's activities result in behavior falling within the blocking region, the IPS directs the firewall to block continued access for that user. Associated with the tracking and blocking functions is a very low false positive rate. Because the IPS converts activities that are associated with both legitimate and non-legitimate use into classes of behaviors that can be differentiated with the assessment engine, the IPS can properly classify misuse intent from legitimate use.

There are several advantages of this new technology. First, although specific building block activities are monitored, the assessment engine can assess any possible combination of the detectable activities. This means that any new form of attack that is comprised of elements of the building block activities may be assessed for malicious intent. Unlike anomaly detection, these assessments are not norm based which may lead to false positives, but are based on actual expertise and deception dimensions. Second, the IPS does not require tuning. One places the IPS in the rack, configures it, and can walk away. Occasional monitoring may result in altering critical regions, only if desired. There are significant savings in staff resources. Third, and in development, the behavioral "prints" may be compared to determine if a user may be attacking from more than one IP or if there is a coordinated attack. Although a user may change actual activities, the expertise and deception associated with the activities may present very similar patterns. In short, the IPS is a behavior analysis technology that successfully characterizes network activity with behavioral meaning and intent.

Source: Gary M. Jackson, PhD, CEO and President, Psynapse Technologies Inc.

Virus Scanners
Best Practices to Prevent Outbreaks in Your System Due to Worms and Viruses[169]

1. Understand that mass mailing worms *will* come from someone you know.
2. Do not open unknown e-mail attachments.

---

169. This section was provided by Peter Tippet, Chief Technical Officer of Trusecure Inc.

Box D.4: SQL VULNERABILITY

Microsoft's SQL Server is a relational database system based upon the structured query language (SQL) standard. It holds the position as one of most widely used databases. On January 25, 2003, a buffer overload vulnerability in the MS SQL Server resulted in the widespread execution of a malicious code from a yet unknown source. Known by names such as Sapphire, Slammer, and SQLSlammer, this worm worked on a stack buffer overflow vulnerability. This type of vulnerability is common, and occurs when large quantities of data are sent to a system—so large that the sent code extends beyond its limited length, and overwrites disk data. With the Slammer worm, this allowed arbitrary code to be executed in order to shut down an entire server. Once a server was infected with the worm, the code self-propagated by sending 375 byte packets to randomly chosen IP addresses, targeting other port UDP port 1434 for infection.[170] To get a sense for the speed at which this transpired, it took 10 minutes for the worm to spread around the world.[171] Sapphire was responsible for numerous network outages, among which South Korea was the most egregious case with nearly all Internet service lost to the majority of users during the attack. Financial systems and transportation systems were among the numerous industries that experienced negative ramifications of the attack. Bank of America suffered a network outage of 13,000 of its ATMs.[172] The Australian AMEX site was taken down until the evening of the 26th on account of damages.[173] It is important to note that although perceived to be merely a denial of service attack. The Slammer worm installed a stealth program (backdoor) into every operating system it infected, thus allowing the perpetrators to reenter every machine they compromised at will.

Last year, another vulnerability in MS SQL Server threatened both Denial of Service attacks and the e-mail dissemination of an infected server's passwords and network configurations.[174] Called Spida or SQLSnake, this worm would attack a vulnerability found in servers containing MS SQL's default network settings. Once inside a machine, the worm would copy IP configurations and password files to a temporary location that it would later access through the creation of a guest account.[175] These two SQL vulnerabilities illustrate the dire need to mitigate system risks through proper configuration and maintenance of a network.

Source: Authored by Yumi Nishiyama, World Bank Integrator Group. The data was compiled from a variety of sources. These include: National Infrastructure Protection Center (NIPC) Advisory 03-001.1, "Worm Targets SQL Vulnerability," 27 Jan 2003 (http://www.nipc.gov/warnings/advisories/2003/03-001.1updates.htm). Reuters, "SQL Slammer Worm Spread Worldwide in 10 Minutes," *Forbes.com*, 4 Feb 2003 (http://www.forbes.com/technology/newswire/2003/02/04/rtr870187.html). Julian Bajkowski, "Australian Amex site made 'unusable' by Slammer worm," *Computerworld*, 3 Feb 2003 (http://www.computerworld.com/developmenttopics/websitemgmt/story/0,10801,78140,00.html).

3. Do not connect to Web-based e-mail from the country systems—Hotmail, AOL, or Yahoo, for example.
4. Check to see that your anti-virus product is updated at least monthly.
5. Use plain text format for e-mail (not HTML) to prevent embedded malicious code.
6. Use Rich Text Format (.rtf) or plain text (.txt) for your documents instead of document (.doc) format.

---

170. National Infrastructure Protection Center, "Worm Targets SQL Vulnerability," Advisory 03-001.1, 1/27/2003, accessed at: http://www.nipc.gov/warnings/advisories/2003/03-001.1updates.htm.

171. Reuters, "SQL Slammer Worm Spread Worldwide in 10 Minutes," Forbes.com, 2/4/03, accessed at: http://www.forbes.com/technology/newswire/2003/02/04/rtr870187.html.

172. Ibid.

173. Julian Bajkowski, "Australian Amex site made 'unusable' by Slammer worm," Computerworld, 2/3/2003, accessed at: http://www.computerworld.com/developmenttopics/websitemgmt/story/0,10801,78140,00.html.

174. National Infrastructure Protection Center, "Microsoft SQL Worm Spida," Advisory 02-003, 5/22/2002, accessed at: http://www.nipc.gov/warnings/advisories/2002/02-003.htm.

175. Ibid.

7. Save a document received as an attachment to disk and scan it before opening.
8. Consider putting an alias as the first entry in your e-mail address book that will send a message to your system administrator or trusted antivirus lab as an early warning mechanism for a mass mailer outbreak.
9. Set Internet Explorer security settings in the Internet Zone to *High*.
10. Set Internet Security settings to disable ActiveX and Active Scripting. Javascipt settings should be placed on disable or prompt.
11. Disable Open and/or Preview panes if implementing Outlook Express.

For System Administrators
1. Filter executable attachments at the e-mail.
2. Subscribe to one of the following mail lists to be proactive and to receive early warnings for newly discovered malicious code:
   http://www.cert.org
   LISTSERV@lehugh.edu
   http://www.ntbugtraq.com
   http://www.2600.com
   http://www.dhs.gov
   listserv@netspace.com
   linux-security-request@Redhat.com

Encryption[176]
Encryption/Decryption
Symmetric and asymmetric key encryption both are used to scramble data so completely that an attacker lacking the correct "key" is unable to determine the punctuation or control, or video and audio images.

The process of scrambling the data is called "encrypting," or "enciphering" the data. The reverse operation, to unscramble the data back to its original form, is called "decrypting," or "deciphering" the data. The original unscrambled data is called "clear" text, signifying that the meaning of the text is "clear." The scrambled data is called "cipher" text, signifying that the meaning of the data has been obscured.

There are many different algorithms[177] for encrypting and decrypting. All algorithms for encrypting and decrypting take two input arguments, and produce as output the encrypted or decrypted data, respectively. The first input argument is the data to be encrypted or decrypted. The second argument is called the "key." Best practice deems the secrecy of an encryption and decryption scheme to inhere solely in the key. To describe encryption or decryption, we shall write:

$$\text{Cipher-text} = \text{Encrypt(Clear-text, Encrypt-key)};$$

$$\text{Clear-text} = \text{Decrypt(Cipher-text, Decrypt-key)};$$

This denotes the content or meaning of the original unscrambled data. The data itself can be any form of digitized information — letters or numbers of any language, special symbols for words.

The principle that secrecy must inhere solely in the key was first articulated in January and February 1883, in a book entitled *La Cryptographie Militaire*, first published as two installments

---

176. Inputs for this section were contributed by Bill Worley, HP fellow, Chief Scientist for Hewlett Packard, Inc.
177. Also called "Ciphers."

in the *Journal des Sciences Militaries*. The author, born Jean-Guillaume-Hubert-Victor-François-Alexandre-Auguste Kerckhoffs[178] on 19 January 1835, and the same publisher later in 1883 reissued Kerkhoffs's book as a paperback.[179] Kerkhoffs's 64-page book, widely regarded as one of the most famous, concise, and important books on cryptology, remains a guiding influence to this day.

Symmetric Key Encryption

For symmetric key encryption, both the sender and receiver of encrypted messages employ the same secret key. That is, in the formulas: Encrypt-key = Decrypt-key. For example, if the secret key were the word "applesauce", the equations would be:

$$\text{Cipher-text} = \text{Encrypt(\ Clear-text, ``applesauce''\ )};$$

$$\text{Clear-text} = \text{Decrypt(\ Cipher-text, ``applesauce''\ )}.$$

Of course, the keys that actually would be used by systems would be nothing so simple as an English language word. Rather, they would be long, randomized bit strings. The actual lengths of keys are determined by the specific symmetric cipher. The actual binary values of keys are generated by processes that ensure that these values are sufficiently random and unpredictable. Symmetric ciphers are of two basic types: "block" and "stream." A block cipher encrypts or decrypts a single, fixed-size block at a time. The size of a block is defined by the specific block cipher. A streaming cipher generates a sequence of binary values that are XOR'ed[180] with the Clear-text or Cipher-text.[181] The size of each binary value generated by a stream cipher is defined by the specific stream cipher.

The names, key lengths, and block/stream-element lengths of some important symmetric ciphers are shown in the table below. The newest of the symmetric ciphers is the Advanced Encryption Standard (AES). On 6 December 2001 it was approved as FIPS 197, effective 26 May 2002. The cipher was selected on 2 October 2000 as the winner of an extensive cipher design and evaluation competition run by the National Institute of Standards and Technology (NIST).[182]

Cipher Name	Acronym	Key Length (bits)	Data Length (bits)	Type
Data Encryption Standard FIPS 46	DES	56	64	Block
Data Encryption Standard (export restricted)	DES 40	40	64	Block
Triple DES	3DES	$3 \times 56, \sim 112$ [183]	64	Block
Advanced Encryption Standard FIPS 197	AES	128, 192, 256	128	Block
Rivest Cipher 4	RC4	Variable	Byte Stream	Stream

---

178. He later shortened his name to simply: Auguste Kerkhoffs.

179. David Kahn, *The CODE-BREAKERS*, Scribner, 1967, 1996.

180. XOR is the exclusive OR logical operation: $(0 \text{ XOR } 1) = (1 \text{ XOR } 0) = 1; (0 \text{ XOR } 0) = (1 \text{ XOR } 1) = 0;$

181. The same stream value can be used both for encryption and decryption. This works because XOR operands can be ordered and grouped arbitrarily, the XOR of any value with itself is zero, and the XOR of zero with any value yields the value itself. In symbolic terms:
Cipher-text = Clear-text XOR str-val;
Clear-text = Cipher-text XOR str-val = (Clear-text XOR str-val) XOR str-val =
        Clear-text XOR (str-val XOR str-val) = Cleart-text XOR 'zero' = Clear-text.

182. The finalist ciphers were named MARS, RC-6, Rijndael, Serpent, and Twofish. The selected winner was Rijndael (pronounced: "Rain-doll"), named after portions of the names of the two inventors.

183. Three 56-bit keys are used, but a known attack reduces the effective key strength to 112 bits.

Symmetric key ciphers execute at high speed. On grounds of security and performance, symmetric ciphers rank very highly. For any confidential, high-volume data interchange, symmetric key cryptography is the preferred choice, simply because of its high performance. The hard problem for deploying symmetric cryptography is the distribution and management of secret keys, the aptly named "Key Distribution Problem."

The Key Distribution Problem, i.e. the definition of a process securely to distribute unique secret keys throughout a network, to every pair of persons or programs that needs to communicate in confidence, is very complex. Entire systems have been built solely to perform this function. The "Kerberos"[184] system developed by MIT, based upon the work of Needham and Schroeder, dedicates entire servers simply to the task of being trusted third parties for distribution of secret keys. We shall not go into the details of Kerberos. We simply observe that it is a workable symmetric key distribution system, that it is employed in Microsoft's security strategy, that it has evolved to its current Kerberos Version 5, and that in many cases, the need for a key distribution system such as Kerberos entirely can be avoided through the use of asymmetric key encryption, which is the subject of the next section.

Asymmetric Key Encryption

For asymmetric key encryption, the key used to encrypt data is a different key from that used to decrypt data. Unlike symmetric key encryption, which uses the same secret key both for encryption and decryption, asymmetric key encryption uses two different keys. Why is this important? It is important because only one of the keys needs to be kept private (i.e. secret). The other key can be widely known, i.e. can be made public. It is for this reason that asymmetric key encryption popularly is called "public/private" key encryption. Asymmetric ciphers greatly facilitate problems of key distribution.
Symbolically:

$$\text{Cipher-text} = \text{Encrypt}(\text{ Plain-text, public-key });$$

$$\text{Plain-text} = \text{Decrypt}(\text{ Cipher-text, private-key });$$

One can appreciate the power of having two keys by considering how one orders items over the Internet, such as books from Amazon.com. The ordering process used by such websites uses a protocol called SSL,[185] to assure that a secure session is established between the customer's computer and the website. An SSL session begins with a "handshake" protocol. The customer's computer sends a "hello" message to the Amazon web server, and web server's reply includes a Certificate containing an Amazon public key. The customer's computer checks that the Certificate is valid,[186] and then uses Amazon's public key to encrypt data that both the user's computer and the web server will use to construct a symmetric key for the session. Only the Amazon web server has the private key needed to construct the symmetric session key. After some further checking, the session continues using the symmetric key to encrypt/decrypt messages. The order information—credit card number, shipping address, gift-wrapping, greeting message, and items ordered—then can be sent confidentially to Amazon.

The most widely used asymmetric cipher is called "RSA," an acronym composed of the first letters of the last names of its inventors: Ron Rivest, Adi Shamir, and Leonard Adleman, who first

---

184. "Kerberos" is the name of the three-headed dog that guards the gates of Hades.
185. "Secure Sockets Layer," deployed in nearly every web browser and web server throughout the Internet. For details, see: Eric Rescorla, *SSL and TLS*, Addison-Wesley, 2001.
186. This is done by validating the digital signature of the Certificate. The public key for this validation is that of the Authority issuing the Certificate, which normally is stored within the browser in the customer's computer.

published their work in the summer of 1977.[187] Patent protection for the algorithm expired in September 2000, and it now is in the public domain. RSA operates upon very large integers modulo the product of two secret prime numbers. RSA public and private keys each are pairs of such large integers. For good security today, 1024 to 2048 bit integers are used, although some applications continue to use 512 bit integers. The cryptographic strength of RSA derives from the difficulty in finding the two secret primes given only their product.

More recent work has shown that finite groups of points lying on an "elliptic curve" provide a perhaps stronger base than RSA for asymmetric cryptography. The security of the schemes based upon elliptic curves derives from the difficulty in solving the discrete log problem over elliptic curves.[188] The keys needed for computations are shorter than those needed for RSA. The elliptic curve key equivalent in strength to a 1024-bit RSA key, for example, would be less than 200 bits in length. The computations, however, are more complex than those for RSA.

The primary difficulty for asymmetric encryption is that it requires much, much more computation. In other words, it is a lot slower than symmetric encryption. For example, AES on the Itanium 2 microprocessor operates at approximately one bit per cycle. For a 1024-bit value, AES would require about 1024 cycles to encrypt or decrypt. In contrast, on the same microprocessor, 1024-bit RSA would require about 20,000 cycles for a public key encryption, and over 250,000 cycles for a private key decryption.

Because of the relative strengths and weaknesses of symmetric and asymmetric cryptography, a common practice is to use asymmetric key cryptography for key distribution, and symmetric key cryptography for the bulk of the transferred data. This is what is done within the SSL protocol- asymmetric cryptography is used to establish a newly created symmetric key, which then is used for the data transfers within the SSL session.

One-Way Hash Functions

One-way hash functions[189] are algorithms that transform an arbitrary input bit stream into a fixed-size result. They are called "One-Way" because while it is straightforward to perform the hash function, it is provably impossible to compute the inverse of the hash function—that is, to compute the input bit stream given only the fixed-size hash function output.

Further, secure hash functions are designed so that, to the extent possible, the value of every bit of the output of the function is affected by the value of every bit of the input, and that for a given hash output value it is a prohibitively difficult task to find another input bit stream that would produce the identical hash function output. These properties of secure hash functions permit one reasonably to use the hash output value as an identifying "signature" or "digest"[190] for the input bit stream. In Bruce Schneier's parlance, hash function outputs are like "digital fingerprints" of the input bit stream.[191] Others have characterized hash outputs as "unforgeable check sums."

Secure hash functions typically operate in two phases. First, the arbitrary-length input bit stream is padded in a specific manner to a multiple of a fixed block size. Usually, the bit length of the entire input stream appears as the final 64-bit value in the last 64-bit double word of the final padded block. Second, the padded input is processed a block at a time by the hash function, using output values from each block as initial input values to the processing of the next block. The combined result after processing the final block is the output of the hash function.

---

187. It was later learned that Clifford Cocks, of the British General Communication Headquarters (GCHQ), independently in late 1973 had discovered the same algorithm.

188. For details, see: Blake, Seroussi, Smart, *Elliptic Curves in Cryptography*, Cambridge Univ. Press, 1999.

189. Also called "Secure Hash Functions."

190. For this reason, the output of a secure hash function also is called a "Message Digest."

191. B. Schneier, *Secrets & Lies – Digital Security in a Networked World*, John Wiley & Sons, 2000.

Symbolically:

$$\text{Message Digest} = \text{Hash-Function}(\ \text{Pad-Function}(\ \text{Input-Bits}\ )\ );$$

The two most widely used secure hash functions are "SHA-1" and "MD5". SHA-1 is the U.S. Governments' standard hash function. The acronym "SHA" stands for "Secure Hash Function"; the algorithm is documented in the publication: "Secure Hash Standard", FIPS PUB 180-1. The output of SHA-1 is 160 bits in length. RIPEMD-160 is a similar European algorithm. The recently defined SHA-256, SHA-384, and SHA-512 functions produce hash outputs of 256, 384, and 256 bits respectively. MD5 stands for "Message Digest 5", and was invented by Ron Rivest. MD5 produces a 128-bit hash output. Although still in use, MD5 has shown some cracks and now is seldom used for anything new.

Hash functions are one of the most versatile and widely employed cryptographic tools. They are used in nearly every Internet protocol. Whenever it is necessary logically to associate a number of elements, the common practice is to concatenate the byte-strings representing the elements and hash the total result. This produces a digital fingerprint reflecting every element as well as the entire association. Hash values of documents, data structures, and code images are crucial for digital signatures, which are discussed below.

Message Authentication Codes

Message Authentication Codes (MACs) are designed to protect the authentication and integrity of messages and data rather than to protect their confidentiality. A MAC is a value appended to a message or data that permits one to assure that the content of the message or data has not been modified in any way.

MACs, like symmetric key encryption, use a secret key. If it is not important to protect the content of a message, but only to insure its integrity, the secret key is used to compute a MAC, which then is appended to the message. Any party who knows the secret key can recalculate the MAC from the received message, and compare the newly calculated value with the MAC appended to the received message. If the newly computed and transmitted values match, the message has been transmitted correctly. MACs are used in secure IP (IPSec) to assure that packet contents have not been modified during transmission. They also are used in transfer protocols between banks to authenticate messages. MACs also can be attached to data stored in files or databases. In all cases any one knowing the secret key can verify that the data over which the MAC was calculated has not been altered. Computations of MACs utilize symmetric key encryption over the data, or sometimes over secure hashes of the data.

For confidential storage or transmission of data, both MACs and encryption must be employed. For example, first a MAC is calculated using a secret key and then appended to the block of data; second, the data and its appended MAC are encrypted using a second secret key. This assures both that the data remains unintelligible to unauthorized parties and that its integrity remains intact. It is becoming generally accepted that this combined protection is the proper way to secure network transmissions.

Digital Signatures (PKI)

Digital signatures are similar to MACs in providing a guarantee of the integrity of stored or transmitted data. But digital signatures differ from MACs with respect to the secrets employed and the distribution of those secrets.

For MACs there is a non-empty set of persons who know the secret key used to compute the MAC. Any of the people in the set can verify a MAC computed with the secret key. At the same time, any of these persons also can compute a MAC for different messages or data, or can forge a MAC for an altered message or data. All the persons who know the secret must trust each other—both to keep the secret and to employ it properly.

MACs work well when there is but a single individual who holds the secret. This person can use the secret to protect his or her data and to assure its integrity. It also works well for sets of two persons. These folks trust each other not to reveal the secret, and can send messages back and forth knowing that the integrity of each message has not been compromised. These models fit many important situations.

Digital signatures are an integrity protection mechanism where there is but a single party who is capable of constructing the signature, but everyone then is able to verify the signature. In this model, one specified party, the sole holder of the enabling secret, becomes responsible for computing and appending the signature to the data. This is called "signing" the data. After the data has been "signed", anyone can verify that the specified party in fact did compute the signature. This model fits many important commercial and practical situations.

Digital signatures are computed by using a remarkable property of asymmetric key cryptography. Namely, it also works in reverse. In the previous section on asymmetric key cryptography we wrote symbolically:

$$\text{Cipher-text} = \text{Encrypt}(\text{ Plain-text, public-key });$$

$$\text{Plain-text} = \text{Decrypt}(\text{ Cipher-text, private-key }).$$

But it turns out that the keys can be used in the reverse order, namely:

$$\text{Cipher-text} = \text{Encrypt}(\text{ Plain-text, private-key });$$

$$\text{Plain-text} = \text{Decrypt}(\text{ Cipher-text, public-key }).$$

In the first case the owner of the secret key does the decrypting, and anyone can do the encrypting. In the latter case, the owner of the secret does the encrypting, and anyone can do the decrypting.

Digital signatures often are used by themselves, rather than in combination with encryption designed to protect confidentiality. Usually, it is not important that the data contents be confidential, but it is extremely important that the data be accurate. Digital signatures are not computed by encrypting all of the data with the private key, but rather are computed by encrypting a secure hash of the data by the private key. In effect, we first take a digital fingerprint of the data, and then encrypt the digital fingerprint with the private key. Symbolically:

$$\text{Digital-Signature} = \text{Encrypt}(\text{ Hash-Function}(\text{ Input-Bits }), \text{private-key });$$

$$\text{Digital-Fingerprint} = \text{Decrypt}(\text{ Digital-Signature, public-key }).$$

Digital signatures also are verified in two steps. First the digital fingerprint of the data contents is recomputed using the hash function. Then the appended digital signature is decrypted using the *public* key. If the recomputed digital fingerprint and the decrypted digital signature match, the signature has been verified. The mathematics look very easy, but some delicacy is required to construct correct protocols around them. For example, if a digital signature is appended to a letter not including the identification of the intended recipients, an attacker may combine the body of the letter with a fictitious list of recipients and falsely claim that the original signer sent the letter to the fictitious list. Basically, digital signatures are used to protect the integrity of a collection of data. They often therefore are used as analogs of written signatures for documenting transactions, with and without the participation of trusted third parties. However, they are not exact analogs of written signatures, and certain niceties carefully must be observed.

There are several commonly used digital signature algorithms. RSA private key encryption applied to SHA-1 message digests of the signed material is the most common. The US government has defined as its digital signature standard a more complex algorithm known as DSA, which also operates upon an SHA-1 message digest.[192] Signature algorithms invented by Taher ElGamal[193] and based upon elliptic curves also are employed.

Random Number Generators

Random numbers are employed throughout cryptographic algorithms and protocols. They are used for keys, challenge values, pre-hashing appendages for passwords,[194] etc. Hardware devices based upon some form of physical randomness are beginning to appear. The problem with such hardware devices, of course, is testing them to assure they are operating correctly.

Solely computational means for generating truly random numbers do not exist. A favorite quote of John Von Neumann's, cited by Bruce Schneier, is "Anyone who considers arithmetic methods of producing random digits is, of course, in a state of sin." Fortunately, computational means do exist for computing numbers that are sufficiently unpredictable that they can be used in lieu of truly random numbers. Such numbers are called "Pseudo-Random Numbers" (PRNs). Some of the pseudo-random number generation methods employ values obtained by physical measurements of random events in a computer system, such as typing rates, arbitrary mouse motions, arrival times of I/O interrupts, etc. Others are based upon symmetric cryptography[195] or the difficulty of hard mathematical problems such as the factoring problem.[196] Pseudo random number generators (PRNGs) that produce sufficiently unpredictable values are called "Cryptographically Strong Pseudo Random Number Generators' (CSPRNGs).

A trusted system must include one or more CSPRNGs. Furthermore, it must provide means for storing any internal state needed by the CSPRNGs in a location that cannot be accessed as the result of any system penetration. The latter requirement is particularly difficult. In UNIX, Linux, and NT systems any hacker penetration into privileged mode permits code to examine all of physical memory, including stored CSPRNG state. A paper by Adi Shamir and Nicko van Someren[197] described the algorithms that permit detection of likely cryptographic keys and other random-looking materials in memory. Such results then can be forwarded over the network to an attacker's machine, and analyzed there for use in attacks against system data.

One of the easiest points of attack against encrypted data is its underlying pseudo-random number generation. The security of SSL V2, for example, was broken by Goldberg and Wagner[198] when, from a code listing, they discovered that the PRN was seeded with the time of day and process ID. These values were sufficiently predictable that the entire space could be searched in about an hour's computer time (less on today's computers). A Security Strategy must assure that all such avenues of attack are eliminated completely.[199]

Securing Servers

Best Practices

1. There should be no remote control and/or administration of host systems from other than the host system console unless explicit measures such as Secure Shell (SSH), Secure Socket Layer (SSL), or Virtual Private Network (VPN) have been made to secure both the

---

192. Digital Signature Standard, FIPS PUB 186. DSA always was in the public domain.

193. T. ElGamal, "A Public Key Cryptosystem and a Signature Scheme Based on Discrete Logarithms, "*IEEE Transactions on Information Theory*, volume, IT-31, 1985.

194. Called "salt."

195. E.g. ANSI X9.17

196. E.g. the Blum-Blum-Shub (BBS) algorithm, L. Blum, M. Blum, and M. Shub, "A Simple, Unpredictable Pseudo Random Generator," *SIAM Journal on Computing*, volume 15, no. 2, 1986.

197. Adi Shamir and Nicko van Someren, "Playing hide and seek with stored keys." 22 September 1998.

198. I. Goldberg and D. Wagner, "Randomness and the Netscape Browser," *Dr. Dobbs Journal*, January 1996.

199. The most common way encryption is compromised is that the password or phrase used is easy to guess, and the hacker simply lucks out and uses the correct password. The other way is through a fundamental flaw in the algorithm being used to encrypt the information, which allows for a successful attack.

network and host system environments. This includes, but is not limited to, system administrator access via modems, gateways, bridges, routers, switches, protocol converters, and other terminal-to-host connections.

2. All security functions and software changes/additions should be made only by authorized server administrator personnel; all changes should be documented.

3. The general user should not have access to the system console; system administrator logons should be done at the system console or any other end-user device if such capability exists.

4. There should be no access to the host system or to any system resources following diskette boot for those systems without physical security.

5. There should be no peer-to-peer communications between general-purpose end-user workstations unless authorized by the system administrator.

6. There should be only one user ID per user on a single system. There also should be only one user making use of any user ID, except as documented and approved in writing.

7. There should be no unauthorized or unsupervised use of traffic monitors/utilities (e.g., Data General Sniffer), recorders, or other customer premise equipment.

8. The host server and console should be physically and logically secured from unauthorized access and use. Maintenance performed on a host server by anyone other than authorized personnel must receive documented authorization from a system administrator.

9. Workstation sessions should be suspended and/or terminated after a predetermined period of inactivity, if technically possible.

10. In cases where session slippage occurs, or in instances where service requests require significant changes of access level privileges, user reauthentication should be required.

11. Successful logons should display the date and time (duration) of the end-user's last session. This is especially useful for super-user accounts.

12. The integrity of data should be maintained by using transaction locks on all shared data for both data files and databases.

13. Administrators should have the capability to constantly scan for viruses at the host server level, the workstation level, and so on.

Microsoft IIS Web Servers

The vulnerabilities inherent in remote data service (RDS) gave crackers the ability to exploit ODBC, which allows the execution of DOS commands within queries that result in a cracker's ability to run arbitrary commands.[200] The RDS vulnerability can be fixed by referring to the following URL: http://support.microsoft.com/support/kb/articles/q184/3/75.asp. Microsoft IIS Web servers continue to support many different programs such as HTR, STR, and IDC. These programs have a variety of associated vulnerabilities, "primarily the exposure of source to scripts." Also, "RDS, DOS commands, and HTR are all part of the default installation of IIS servers." In its effort to make its software more accessible to its technical support and to allow for easy entry into any entity's system to repair software problems, Microsoft created back doors or points of entry that are not published. However, this feature provides easy access for criminals as well as trained technicians. To mitigate the risk associated with these servers, it is necessary to remove all programs except those that are implemented exclusively within your own sites.

Microsoft Security Bulletins can be searched at the following website: http:///www.microsoft.com/technet/security/current.asp. The tragedy of September 11 made it clear that this host should not be located at headquarters. Instead, a remote secure facility should house all data backup servers.

---

200. The source for the information and quotes in this paragraph is "Secure Your Microsoft IIS Web Servers," a presentation of Trusecure on April 18, 2001.

The recent release of Security Assertion Markup Language (SAML) is supposed to "secure" all Windows 2000 operating systems. Security can never be guaranteed. In reality SAML is merely a "box full of patches" that will give users the illusion of safety when in fact it is merely a box full of Band-Aids. Silver bullet solutions do not exist.

Penetration Testing

Proper Systems Administration: Top 20 red flags

The following is a list of typical administrative failures within financial institutions and corporations.

1. Lack of training and expertise of administrators.
2. No time for or interest in reviewing log files.
3. No time for or interest in hardening machines.
4. Deployment of new technology without security peer review.
5. Failure to install software patches that fix security flaws.
6. Lack of strict requirements to use strong passwords.
7. Removal of security mechanisms because they cause user inconvenience. Restoration of systems from backups and failure to reload any patches that were previously installed.
8. Failure to remove administrative-level accounts that were added temporarily for service personnel.
9. Failure to install or use available security mechanisms such as password policy enforcement or system event logging.
10. Lack of daily audit of network logs for suspicious activity.
11. Setting up computer systems using the software defaults. These default settings are designed to get the system up and running with the least interference and are often very insecure.
12. Failure to perform routine backups of systems and then test those backups for viability.
13. Failure to properly install and update virus protection software.
14. Sharing administrative accounts and passwords over multiple systems.
15. Primary reliance on a firewall or public key infrastructure (PKI) system for security.
16. Use of SNMP, telnetd, ftpd, mail, rpc, rservices, or other unencrypted protocols for managing systems.
17. Assignment of passwords to users over the phone.
18. Failure to educate users about security problems and what to do when they see a potential problem.
19. Poorly written and implemented policies and procedures.
20. Improper documentation.

Best Practices

1. Network administrators should be responsible for installing and verifying patches and updates to operating systems weekly.
2. Onsite trained security staff should be present 24/7.
3. Employees should be required to use robust passwords (long in length; mix of letters, numbers, and symbols), which should be changed monthly.
4. Computer monitors should not be visible to anyone who is not an employee of the institution.
5. Network administrators should implement a profile procedure to process employees transferring to another office in the bank, termination of employees, and changes to an employee's level of access within the bank's systems.
6. Those who are responsible for large value transfers should utilize biometric identifiers as their password.
7. Backups should be maintained of all critical material that is stored in a different location.

8. An incident response capability and a plan that ensures continuity of operations and recovery from security breaches should be in place.
9. Strong authentication—preferably biometrics, smart cards, and cryptography—should be exercised for large value transfers.
10. Firewalls and intrusion detection systems should be installed.
11. Penetration testing/auditing should be performed on all of the institution's systems.
12. A login banner should be displayed stating that the system is only for authorized use and is subject to monitoring.
13. Patches must be updated weekly to both servers and remote access machines. See
14. http://www.microsoft.com/technet/security/current.asp
15. Critical operations should have two-person controls.
16. A security policy should be developed that mandates training for non-IT staff vis-à-vis an incident response plan and that prohibits instant messaging, voice-over IP, and wireless local area network (WLAN) installation without appropriate authorization and securitization.

What differentiates a good penetration test from a bad one[201]

Sound practices for a penetration test may include, but not be limited to the following:

1. Performed at least annually on all high-risk systems
2. Effective integration of Vulnerability Assessment ("VA") findings within the penetration testing scope
3. The scope may include: Performing a Network Survey, Port Scan, an Application and Code Review, Router, Firewall, IDS, Trusted System and Password Cracking
4. Exploitation of "VA" findings along with other common risk vulnerabilities identified through various databases and provided via software vendors and other sources
5. Identified Action (Remediation) Plans and Strategies to reduce risks (exploits)
6. Includes a comprehensive set of scenarios (i.e. Internal Employee & Consultant and External Party)
7. Includes realistic methods or approaches (i.e. Remote Network, Local Network and Stolen Computer)
8. Encompasses Social Engineering
9. Testing conducted on service providers network infrastructure
10. Outsourcing Pen tests are customized to the risk profile of the institution

A top ten list for Digital Forensic Procedures[202]

Sound practices for digital forensics may include, but not be limited to the following:

1. Inclusion within a comprehensive documented Incident Response Plan (IRP) or a separate Digital Forensic Policy, which addresses strategies for the protection of internal and external threats to the enterprise and a methodology which includes, but may not be limited to the following:

   ■ Detection of the incident
   ■ Escalation of the incident
   ■ Analysis of the incident
   ■ Containment and eradication of the problem
   ■ Provide workarounds or fixes
   ■ Prevent re-infection

---

201. Special Thanks to Kenneth C. Brancik for his insight on CyberSecurity risks
202. Ibid.

■ *Evidentiary Data* guidelines
■ Evidentiary Data Preservation requirements
■ Documentation requirements
■ Cyber Security post-mortem and apply lessons learned

2. Establishing an appropriate investigative strategy
3. Selection of the appropriate Forensic Tools
4. Comprehensive Digital Forensics training
5. A process which requires the timely and accurate completion of required regulatory guidelines which either directly or indirectly involves the collection and analysis of computer forensics related data
6. Completion of required law enforcement escalation and reporting of computer intrusions.
7. Evidentiary data criteria (i.e. Journalling, IDS Alerts, SYSLOGS, Firewall & Router Logs) is clearly defined prior to the collection and analysis of a computer incident
8. Effective event correlation analysis of evidentiary data generated as a result of a computer intrusion
9. Forensic analysis accurately differentiates between symptoms vs a root cause analysis of computer intrusion
10. A Post-Mortem analysis of lessons learned is conducted

Policy Management Software[203]

Given that good e-security is a combination of people, processes and technology, banks should be implementing a policy approach that is governed by system wherein the policy and enforcement are dynamic. Bank policy vis-à-vis computer usage necessitates enforcement by a software program. The verbal policy dimension should be translated into machine code. This method of policy enforcement mitigates the insider threat dimension both premeditated and accidental. Once policy is built and subsequently amended, users must be educated and then regulated by a ruleset which is modular not static. Computer Associates, Tumbleweed and Polivec vend effective policy management software. This security approach needs to take into account the privacy rights of the user on the system. Users should not only be identified once an alarm (policy violation) has occurred.

Incident Response[204]

The ability to react quickly to security incidents is an essential part of an overall security plan. An organization's ability to operate will depend on its ability to provide timely information to its clients in the form of electronic data.

It is also essential to categorize information. Information from critical systems will surely receive a more direct and focused response than, for example, electronic information stored for office supplies. An organization needs the ability to react to and recover from security incidents as they arise with an effective and coordinated response, which in turn will minimize the cost and damage to the organization's infrastructure and to its image within the banking industry.

A security incident can be defined as an event that changes the security posture of an organization or circumvents security polices developed to prevent financial loss and the destruction, theft, or loss of proprietary information. It is characterized by unusual activity that causes the organization to investigate because the activity cannot be explained through normal operations.

---

203. Contributed by Keith Schwalm, Director of Infrastructure Protection, The President's Critical Infrastructure Protection Board.
204. Contributed by Simon Martinez Sr., System Analyst at Integrated Management Services Inc.

Some possible classifications for security incidents are these:

- Virus attacks (unable to clean, rename, or delete);
- Denial of service attacks;
- IDS alert notifications (false positives possible);
- Automated scanning tools.

Banking organizations must share in the responsibility of coordinating their response efforts with those of other financial institutions. Networking in a trusted environment and sharing incident information and detection/response techniques can be important to all of these organizations in identifying and correcting weaknesses. Gathering intelligence information from all sources is a critical part of information infrastructure protection. Having an information-sharing network in place can also help government agencies alert other agencies to potential and/or actual threats directed at the critical information infrastructure of nations.

Incident response within any organization must begin with management. Management is responsible for providing the support, tools, personnel, and financial backing needed to ensure the success of the incident response team. An incident response team must be perceived well by all concerned. Security awareness training and briefings for senior management are key components of a successful deployment of an incident response team.

Sources of information for building a Computer Security Incident Response Team are as follows:

- SecurityUnit, Inc. (http://www.securityunit.com/pubs/index.htm)
- CERT Coordination Center (http://www.cert.org/csirts/)
- Creating a Computer Security Incident Response Team (http://www.cert.org/training/2002/creating_csirt.html)

To maximize the full potential of the team, members must be available 24/7. Attacks can come at any hour. Intrusion Detection Systems (IDS), network- and host-based, are playing a more critical role in identifying attacks and unusual activity. Alerts from such systems are generated at all hours of the day. An incident response team allows an organization to respond to alerts generated by automated systems 24/7. Monitoring systems and reviewing security alert information submitted by vendors is an important part of an incident response team's proactive duty. IDS systems, however, do not provide a complete solution to identifying and responding to incidents. An overall security plan is needed to ensure overall protection that would include an incident response mechanism.

An incident response team must also develop procedures. Clear definitions of each type of incident will enable members to react quickly and effectively. Procedures must detail the steps team members should take when alerted to an incident. Included within the procedures must be clearly defined investigative goals to be achieved before an incident can be closed. The team should also list and post contact information of key personnel and management to notify.

The team may need to contact other organizations to assist in the investigation. The bank must develop a policy that clearly describes the bank's position on the disclosure of incident information to the banking community as well as outside organizations such as the National Infrastructure Protection Center (NIPC), the Computer Emergency Response Team (CERT), FedCIRC, and commercial incident response teams. Bank organizations may designate an individual (job function) to coordinate the exchange of information. All team members must sign a nondisclosure form.

Tracking of security incidents can become a full-time job, because all incidents must be tracked. Incidents may remain open from a few hours to a few months, or even longer in some cases. The incident (case) record must contain all communications relating to the incident from the time it is opened to the time of closure. Depending on the type of incident, careful consideration should be given to collecting any data that may be relevant to the incident. Response team members should receive professional training in handling and collecting evidence (system logs and backup tapes) in case such evidence needs to be used in a court of law.

The Incident Response Plan

An incident response plan (IRP) is the primary document an organization uses to establish how it will identify, respond to, correct, and recover from a computer security incident. Every organization should have an IRP and should test it periodically.

All employees should be trained in the correct procedures to undertake in the event of a computer incident. An incident response plan might make the following points:[205]

1. The institution's security department, legal department, and public relations department should jointly develop and implement an incident response policy.[206]
2. You should contact incident response agencies responsible for your site. For example:

   - National Infrastructure Protection Center (http://www.nipc.gov)
   - Computer Emergency Response Team (http://www.cert.org)
   - European Computer Emergency Response Teams (http://www.cert.dfn.de/eng/csir/europe/certs.html)
   - Electronic Crimes Taskforce (http://www.ectaskforce.org/Regional_Locations.htm)
   - Forum of Incident Response and Security Teams, or FIRST, (http://www.first.org/team-info/)

3. Make communication via an out-of-band method (e.g., a phone call) to ensure that intruders do not intercept information.[207]
4. Document your actions (e.g., phone calls made, files modified, systems jobs that were stopped).[208]
5. Make copies of files the intruders may have left untouched (e.g., malicious code, log files) and store them offline.[209]
6. Contact law enforcement officials. To ensure proper reporting during an e-security incident, please refer to the following URL:
   http://www.nipc.gov/incident/cirr.htm

The term *incident determination*[210] describes the process used to define events as an "incident" and explains how each type of incident should be handled. Indicators that signal an incident may be categorized as Possible, Probable, and Definite. In addition, if there is a predefined set of conditions that constitute an incident, the incident will be handled in accordance with the plan once those conditions are determined to exist. Arguably, this is the most important section of the plan because it identifies certain situations or conditions and sets out in detail how to respond.

The term *incident notification* describes the procedures to be used in notifying the computer user population once an incident has been confirmed. This section of the plan identifies those who must be notified in the event of an incident and provides critical contact information and contact procedures. These are some elements that may be included in this portion of the plan:

---

205. Provided by Bob Weaver of the New York Electronic Crimes Taskforce.
206. Ibid.
207. National Infrastructure Protection Center's advice.
208. Ibid.
209. Ibid.
210. In the next paragraphs, the terms used for the plan, and the descriptions of the terms, were contributed by Galaxy Computer Services Inc.

- Internal components of the organization, including management, operations, security, public relations, and the general employee/user population
- Computer security incident response organizations
- Affected partners or other integrated entities
- The organization's insurer, if the organization is insured through an e-risk policy
- Law enforcement at the local, state, and federal levels
- News media and other public relations components

Incident containment is the third area of the plan. It addresses the measures that must be taken to halt/mitigate the effects of the incident and to regain control of the affected networks, systems, and related components.

Damage assessment is a critical step once containment has been achieved. This phase assesses the damage that has been inflicted on the institution's assets. It should determine the scope of damage, the duration of the incident, the cause of the incident, and the identification of the responsible party.

Incident recovery is the next key element of the plan. It requires a comprehensive approach to returning networks and systems to normal operations. The following are vital activities that must be addressed during the recovery phase of incident response. First, the vulnerability that allowed the incident to occur should be mitigated. If removal of the vulnerability is not possible, then safeguards should be improved to mitigate additional damage. Second, all out-of-date detection mechanisms should be updated. Software, data, and services should be restored in accordance with approved procedures. System and network activity should be followed closely after restoration for any signs of a follow-up attack. Finally, during recovery, efforts must be made to restore confidence in the organization by its users, partners, and clients.

Reflection, or lessons learned, is the final section of the plan. This requires the institution to conduct a postmortem of the incident. The institution reviews what occurred, how it occurred, how it could have been prevented, and what changes need to be made to ensure that such an event does not occur again. In addition, related plans should be reviewed to determine whether any changes in those plans are indicated also.

Cybernetic Intelligence

As proliferation of zero-day exploits make cybernetic intelligence a critical component of any network security system.[211] Proactive measures are critical to mitigating the risks inherent in a network system. CERT/CC estimates that eleven new vulnerabilities in software code are discovered daily. Without credible cybernetic intelligence these vulnerabilities can compromise even the most secure of systems. Cybernetic intelligence must be a frequent, and ongoing effort considering the rapid rate with which threats are created.

---

211. In a zero-day exploit, malicious users launch an attack on a system vulnerability the day of its discovery.

IDENTITY MANAGEMENT: AUTHENTICATION AND NON-REPUDIATION

The value of e-finance is defined, in part, by technology's ability to move information and to affect markets quickly, and as such, the underlying assumption is that the transferred information is reliable.[212] In order to construct a reliable e-finance system, transactions must be appropriately authenticated, verified, and authorized.[213] These access controls enable a dumb operating system to know whether an individual attempting to enter the system has permission to do so. Authentication is used to assure the system that the party attempting to engage in an activity is, in fact, the party so designated. Verification is the means used to confirm that the party claiming a certain identify is legitimate. Finally, authorization is the means used to determine that the party engaging in a transaction has the requisite authority to access that portion of the system or to engage in that type of activity.

Protecting information reliability is critical because customer interaction with financial institutions is migrating from in person, paper-transactions to remote access and transaction initiation. Moreover, these transactions have shifted from closed architectures to wide broadcast networks, including intranets and extranets, local area networks (LANs), WANs, virtual private networks

---

212. The value of information is based on its reliability and its integrity—whether the party was authorized to access or engage, whether the identity was authenticated, whether there is a risk of repudiation, whether there are any process restrictions for the particular transaction (specifically, whether the rules engine has any access controls), and whether there are any relationship constraints (specifically, whether privacy or confidentiality is protected). The process restriction and the relationship constraint are potential legal liabilities. However, the value of any information is directly related to the extent to which the information meets these criteria versus the extent to which it needs to meet this criterion. Thus, security is a value-added proposition and is a major business consideration in architecting an information system.

213. Reliable information is information that has not been manipulated, has not been corrupted, is intact, and is received as originally transmitted. Reliability is based, in part, on constructing a system and a process that keeps the percentage of repudiated transactions to a minimum.

(VPNs), satellite, microwave, and wireless. Websites such as http://astalavista.box.sk, reflect the growing pantheon of hacker search engines that disseminate critical weaknesses in existing hardware, software, encryption technologies, and wide area networks (WANs). As a result, is becomes increasingly difficult to protect assets, monitor operations, and respond to problems.

Most computer intrusions are perpetuated as a result of insufficient access controls and weak authentication mechanisms. There is widespread concern, especially among those in the law enforcement community, that the financial sector is not keeping up with the security side of technological change. For example, overall industry-wide use of passwords is outdated. A 1999 General Accounting Office (GAO) report[214] highlighted the reality of outdated access controls. It found access controls to be at the forefront of security weaknesses.[215]

Secure electronic service delivery is a key to providing consumers with improved, flexible, and convenient access to financial services, and to enhancing the efficiency of banking operations. One of the challenges in implementing secure electronic service delivery is building the appropriate non-repudiation mechanisms into the banking platform. Reliable customer authentication is imperative for financial institutions engaging in any form of electronic banking or commerce. The risks of doing business with unauthorized or incorrectly identified individuals in an e-banking environment could result in financial loss and reputational damage through fraud, corruption of data, unenforceable agreements, and the disclosure of confidential information. For further details please see the FFIEC guidance, which has been adopted by all members of the FFIEC. [216]

An effective access and authentication program should be implemented across the organizational structure, including affiliate entities, which requires the appropriate use of controls and authentication tools. Authentication processes should also maximize interoperability and offer consistency with the financial institution's assessment of the e-finance system risks. Before any financial service goes online, the financial institution should examine its business processes, undergo a data classification inventory as part of its risk management analysis, and configure its rules engines and access controls to support the data classifications. Annex E addresses the positive and negative attributes of passwords, tokens/smart cards, biometrics, and public key infrastructure authentication systems.

Access and Authentication Tools

Financial institutions can use a variety of access and authentication tools and methodologies to authenticate customers. Existing access control techniques and authentication methodologies involve three basic factors:

- Something the user knows (e.g., password or PIN)
- Something the user possesses (e.g., ATM card, smart card, or token)
- Something the user is (e.g., biometric characteristic, such as fingerprint or retinal pattern)

Biometrics

Biometrics appear to be the future of access controls. Biometric devices fulfill the non-repudiation element of layered security by authenticating a user by his or her physical characteristics. This can

---

214. Jack Brock, Director of Government-Wide Defense Information Systems for the General Accounting Office. Testimony in 1999 before the Senate on the proposed Government Information Security Act (S1993). Brock said the GAO found that users share accounts and passwords and often post passwords in plain view, making it impossible to trace specific transactions or modifications to an individual. Unfortunately, he said, as a result of these and other access control weaknesses, auditors conducting penetration tests of agency systems are almost always successful in gaining unauthorized access that would allow intruders to read, modify, or delete data for whatever purposes they had in mind.

215. Many of the GAO's reviews found that managers did not identify or document access needs for individual users or groups; instead, they provided overly broad access privileges to very large groups of people.

216. Federal Financial Institutions Examinations Council. "Authentication in an Electronic Banking Environment." Aug. 8, 2001.

be compared to PKI, which depends upon the safe management of the private key. Because of its reliance on a user's inherent characteristics, rather than on information that a user possesses, biometric technologies increases the likelihood that the person who initiates the communication or system access is who he or she claim to be. Moreover, PKI encrypts data from end to end, which does not solve the authentication issue. For instance, if a user stores the information to access the private key of PKI on a PIN, this can be compromised with relative ease, particularly if the PIN is stored on a computer's hard drive or a personal digital assistant (PDA).

Access Controls: Passwords and PINs

The entry of a username or an identification number and a secret string of characters, such as a password or a personal identification number (PIN), is the most common and vulnerable of all single-factor authentication techniques. The effectiveness of password security depends on three characteristics: length and composition, secrecy, and system controls.

Password Length and Composition. The appropriate password length and composition depends on the value or sensitivity of the data protected by the password. Password composition standards require the use of numbers and symbols in the password sequence, as well as upper and lower case alphabetic characters. This is necessary because those attempting to compromise the system may subject systems linked to the Internet to automated attacks. These automated attacks (e.g., Brute Force) can generate millions of alphanumeric combinations to garner a user's password.

Password Secrecy. The two most frequent ways of intercepting passwords are studying the user's behavior and catching passwords in transit. First, passwords can be compromised because of the user's behavioral techniques that capture passwords as they travel across the Internet. Attackers can also exploit server and system vulnerabilities to gain access to a financial institution or its service providers to obtain password files. Given these realities, passwords and password files should be encrypted with 128-bit encryption when stored or transmitted over the Internet.[217]

Password System Controls. At a minimum, system-wide policies on computer usage and access controls should be in place. These policies should address the following: evaluation of password length and composition requirements, verification of correct logon and lockout, password expiration and revocation, encryption requirements, and activity report monitoring. Using the following security measures is essential for minimum system access controls:

- Restrict the use of automatic logon features.
- Lock out users after three failed logon attempts.
- Establish an appropriate password expiration interval for sensitive internal or high-value systems.
- Terminate customer connections after a specified period of inactivity.
- Review password exception reports.
- Provide guidance on prudent, complex password selection.
- Incorporate a multifactor authentication method for sensitive internal or high-value systems.

The Inherent Weaknesses

Even with these precautions, the inherent weaknesses of passwords are technology and time. As a result of increased processor speeds, patient hackers can acquire an encrypted password file or session. A program named L0ftCrack is a random character generation program that, when used with a 1.8 gig processor, can run 1 million keyboard combinations per second.[218] The computer will execute L0ftCrack in logical progression, thus making it a matter of time before that terminal

---

217. Refer to Annex A, under the heading Access Controls, for "Best Practices."
218. Interview with Rick Fleming, Vice President of Security Operations, Digital Defense Inc.

is compromised. It may take months to set up an attack, but it takes seconds to execute a successful intrusion on a bank. Passwords can be compromised and thus provide no real level of non-repudiation.

Tokens/Smart Card

A token is an authentication method that makes use of something the user possesses. Typically, a token is a two-factor authentication process, complemented by a password or a biometric as the other factor. The device itself may authenticate static passwords or biometric identifiers used to authenticate the user locally. This process avoids the transmission of shared secrets over an open network.[219]

Physical devices such as credit cards, debit cards, and telephones may contain chips that generate passwords, possess credentials, or process information when brought into contact within receivers. Tokens using the chip technology embedded in cards are known as smart cards.[220] Some are designed to hold authenticating information, and others are capable of processing information obtained in a database.

Most so called "smart cards" are nothing more than a credit card sized device containing a microchip.[221] The sophistication of the chips varies, but most commercially available implementations are far from being secure. In considering the threat posed by criminals, it is not enough to deter the casual criminal through the inconvenience of basic security. New measures must be able to withstand the continuous and repeated efforts of a determined and well-funded adversary. Standard smart cards usually contain account numbers, encryption keys, and often additional stored information (such as biometric profiles) which can be extracted from the card and duplicated or altered. In so doing, the determined adversary can then present cloned or altered data smart cards as genuine, defeating the security and gaining access to critical infrastructure. For the use of smart cards to be effective, they must be able to dynamically respond to non-predictable challenges that defy duplication. They must not contain static, unchanging information such as accounts, encryption keys, biometric profiles, or other personal information. Failure in these regards leads to wide-spread distribution of system critical information that in turn becomes accessible to determined adversaries, including terrorists, and dramatically undermines the security demanded by the application in question.

A number of financial institutions use password-generating tokens to authenticate commercial customers to remotely access the institution's electronic banking system. Public key infrastructure (PKI) systems can incorporate smart cards that contain a user's credentials and digital certificate.

Therefore, the most important issues surrounding use of tokens that a financial institution needs to resolve are the following:

- Determine an appropriate expiration date and renewal and revocation process for tokens.
- Ensure that two-factor authentication processes that use tokens limit the number of login attempts.
- Educate customers about and require them to safeguard their tokens; include binding agreements on the rules of use, protection, and replacement.
- Design and implement a secure process for generating and distributing tokens.

Biometrics

Biometric authentication techniques can grant or deny access to networks by automatically verifying the identity of people through their distinctive physical or behavioral traits. A biometric identifier represents a physical characteristic of the user. The identifier is created from sources such as

---

219. Federal Financial Examinations Council. "Authentication in an Electronic Banking Environment." Aug. 8, 2001.
220. Ibid.
221. Interview with Mike Voorhees, CEO of Cryptodynamics Inc. www.cyonic.com

the user's face or hand geometry, voice, iris (or retina), or fingerprint. Once "captured," a biometric is translated algorithmically into a complex string of numbers and stored in a database as a template.[222] Later, this template is compared to any "live" biometric presented as proof of identity. Introducing a biometric method of authentication requires physical contact with each customer to initially capture and validate the biometric information. This corresponds to the "know thy customer" mantra of the Financial Action Task Force principles.

Verification Issues

In a verification system, an individual claims an identity, typically by using a name, an ID number, or an e-mail address, and then presents biometric data such as a fingerprint to verify this claim. This biometric data is compared to the user's existing record, typically stored in a database. If the two pieces of biometric data "match" when compared, the individual's identity claim is verified. These systems are deployed when it is necessary to verify rapidly that an individual is who he or she claims to be.

Verification requires at least two things. One is that the biometric came from the actual person at the time of verification. The other is that the biometric matches the master biometric on file. If the system does not do both, it is not secure. The use of biometrics for remote login authorizations can pose problems if the data transmission is not properly encrypted. End-to-end encryption is necessary, preferably with 128-bit or greater. If the biometric is not encrypted, it is susceptible to being copied over the network as easily as any other electronic file. Finally, tuning a system properly so that "false acceptances"[223] are more common in small value transfers and "false rejections"[224] are more common in large value transfers will mitigate certain elements of risk. What is essential to the viability of biometrics as preeminent authentication technology is the test for liveliness in real time.

Dorothy Denning, formerly a Professor of Computer Science at Georgetown University, reflects on biometrics:[225]

> What happens if someone snatches the biometric print used to validate you? Couldn't they just replay your biometric and pretend to be you? And wouldn't that make your biometric useless?" My response is, "No." A good biometrics system should not depend on secrecy. To understand why, think about how biometrics work in the physical world. Your friends and colleagues authenticate you by recognizing your face, voice, eyes, hands and so on. None of this is secret. Anyone who interacts with you sees these characteristics. Even your fingerprints can be lifted from surfaces. What makes biometrics successful is not secrecy, but rather the ability to determine "liveness." I can easily distinguish the living, flesh-and-blood you from a statue or photograph of you, or even someone wearing a costume and mask that looks like you.

Testing liveness is reasonably straightforward if the biometrics reader senses appropriate characteristics and is tightly coupled with the validation process and database of biometric prints. If the reader is remote from the validation process and database, encryption can be used to provide a secure path connecting the components. The encryption system, obviously, should protect against replays. Encryption can also be used to pass credentials from one system to another. For example, once a smart card validates a fingerprint, it may use a private signature key on the card to authenticate a user to services that use their public key for authentication. While the encryption system itself requires secret keys, in this context the secrets may be less prone to compromise because they do not require human intervention.

---

222. Security of the database is crucial. The database must be strongly encrypted and it cannot afford to be lost or inaccessible to both operational and emergency backup systems.

223. False acceptances are how often a system would let an imposter get through.

224. False rejections are occurrences wherein an authorized user is denied access because a system did not recognize that user.

225. Interview with Dr. Dorothy Denning, Georgetown University, August 21, 2001.

Types of Biometric Devices

Biometric devices are increasingly being explored as the solution to authenticate users more effectively. The biometric identifier represents something that the user is. The identifier can be created from sources such as the customer's or employee's face or hand geometry, voice, iris (or retina), and fingerprints.

Typical physical authentication methods identify a user by a comparing a person's live face against a photograph. Additional security measures may be provided, for example, by comparing a live signature to that on an ID card. Similarly in the digital world, validation of a user's biometric prints is conducted by checking for liveness of the reading. For example, the iris recognition system looks for the "hippus movement", the constant shifting and pulse that takes place in the eye. The liveness test ensures that the reading is fresh, so an adversary can not replay a previously recorded reading.

Applications of this type of technology include smart cards. Biometric iris codes can be stored on smart cards, and if these codes match the user's live iris scan, access to the banking network is granted. Such a system was implemented by the US Department of Defense. They recently begun passing out the first high-tech ID cards, and have proposed that these cards be in the hands of all 4 million military and civilian defense workers. Smart cards provide defense workers with access to Defense Web sites and computers, commerce capabilities, and facilitate secure communications.[226] Information stored on this credit card sized card include pictures, fingerprints, and identification numbers.[227]

For reasons of privacy and security, special protections must be in place when retaining, managing, and transferring biometric data. Institutions must understand the technical and legal challenges of using biometrics. The Federal Financial Institutions Examination Council says financial institutions need to consider the following when using biometric identifiers:

- First, design systems that encrypt biometric identifiers during storage and transmission.
- Second, design and implement a secure process for capturing biometric identifiers.
- Third, limit the number of failed logons a customer can attempt.[228]

In addition to the listed considerations, biometric authentication should not be stored in a database because of the threat of compromise. Security of the biometric signature is paramount. Once the biological feature has been scanned, it is converted into a data string, which like any other data can be copied and presented as genuine by unauthorized personnel. Furthermore, all biometric data must be encrypted using unique one-time keys. The use of static PKI or symmetric key encryption will ultimately be compromised and must be avoided at all costs, as the same or substantially similar biometric data will be encrypted time and again. This facilitates various cryptanalytic attacks that can compromise the encryption keys. Revocation of biometrics is virtually impossible, and thus when biometric devices are employed, either they should be live-scan-activated or storage of the image should be allocated to a smart card.[229] Smart cards coupled with a biometric PIN will solve the dilemma of storage of biometric identifiers. These considerations should ensure that intuitive biometric technologies replace traditional authentication mechanisms such as passwords, PINs, and tokens.

The Iris Scan.[230] The most effective methods of biometric authentication revolve around functional tests of liveness. Biometrics iris recognition involves identification of 266 detectable iris

---

226. Information provided by Defense Personnel Chief David S.C. Chu, on www.msnbc.com posted on Oct. 29, 2001.

227. Ibid.

228. Federal Financial Examinations Council. "Authentication in an Electronic Banking Environment." Aug. 8, 2001.

229. www.cyonic.com

230. Iridian is the sole developer of iris-based identification technologies.

FIGURE E.1: BIOMETRIC IRIS SCAN

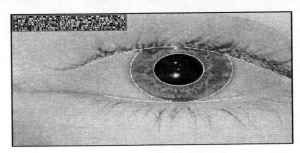

$$\max_{(r,x_0,y_0)} \left| G_\sigma(r) * \frac{\partial}{\partial r} \oint_{r,x_0,y_0} \frac{I(x,y)}{2\pi r} ds \right|$$

Localizing iris boundaries by differential operators

features that can be converted into digital code.[231] A video image of the iris of the eye is needed to produce a digitized 512-byte IrisCode™ record.[232] The image can be taken from up to 30 inches away, and therefore no physical contact is required. Iris recognition leverages unique features of the human iris to provide an unmatched identification technology. The algorithms used in iris recognition are so accurate that the entire planet could be enrolled in an iris database with only a small chance of false acceptance or false rejection. Iris recognition is based on visible (via regular and/or infrared light) qualities of the iris. Iris recognition technology converts these visible characteristics into a 512-byte IrisCode, a template stored for future verification attempts. The first step is location of the iris by a dedicated camera no more than three feet from the eye. After the camera situates the eye, the algorithm narrows in from the right and left of the iris to locate its outer edge. This horizontal approach accounts for obstruction caused by the eyelids. It simultaneously locates the inner edge of the iris (at the pupil), excluding the lower 90 degrees because of inherent moisture and lighting issues.

No video image of the iris is retained. Instead, the eye pattern is converted into a 512-byte IrisCode record. The IrisCode is hashed and encrypted as a security measure.

No two irises are alike, even in twins and even between the left and right iris of one individual. The iris is stable over one's entire life.[233] Iris-based biometrics would be the essential safeguard for employees of financial institutions who are responsible for large-value transfers.

The Fingerprint Scan. A functional alternative to the iris scan is the fingerprint biometric. Biometric imaging electronically captures forensic-quality fingerprint images for fraud prevention, employment processing, and customer access control. These systems are crucial when it is imperative to identify people unequivocally. Fingerprint bio-imaging technologies capture clear, sharp, grayscale digital fingerprints to ensure that important records are uniquely associated with one—and only one—person. The liveness test associated with these types of biometrics is that of a heat sensor under the imprint pad. The fingerprint imprint must be at least 96 degrees Fahrenheit for the device to send the authentication signal.

Once a high-quality image is captured, several steps are required to convert its distinctive features into a compact template. This process, known as feature extraction, is at the core of finger-scan technology. Each of the 50 primary finger-scan vendors has a proprietary feature extraction mechanism.

---

231. Bill Rogers Editor of Biometrics Digest. Interview. Jan. 3, 2001.
232. Ibid.
233. Ibid.

FIGURE E.2: BIOMETRIC FINGERPRINT SCAN

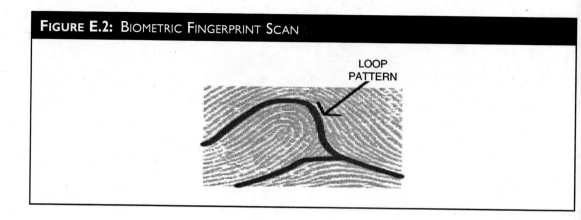

More advanced optical or non-contact fingerprinting systems (known as live-scan), which normally use prints from several fingers, are the current standard for forensic use. They require 250 kb per finger for a high-quality image. Finger-scan technology also acquires the fingerprint, but it does not store the full image. It stores particular data about the fingerprint in a much smaller template, requiring from 250 to 1,000 bytes. After the data is extracted, the fingerprint is not stored. Significantly, the full fingerprint cannot be reconstructed from the finger-scan template.[234] Increasingly sophisticated mechanisms have been developed to capture the fingerprint image with sufficient detail and resolution. The technologies in use today are optical, silicon, and ultrasound.

Optical technology is the oldest and most widely used. The finger is placed on a coated platen, usually built of hard plastic but proprietary to each company. In most devices, a charged coupled device (CCD) converts the image of the fingerprint, with dark ridges and light valleys, into a digital signal.

Silicon technology has gained considerable acceptance since its introduction in the late 1990s. Most silicon, or chip, technology is based on DC capacitance. The silicon sensor acts as one plate of a capacitor, and the finger is the other. The capacitance between the platen and the finger is converted into an 8-bit grayscale digital image. But a few firms have developed technology that employs AC capacitance and reads to the live layer of skin. Silicon-based sensors pick up electrical capacity that will serve as a functional liveness test. Sagem, Printrak, and Seimens all produce proven silicon-based fingerprint scanners.

Ultrasound technology, though considered perhaps the most accurate of the finger-scan technologies, is not yet widely used. It transmits acoustic waves and measures the distance based on the impedance of the finger, the platen, and air. Ultrasound is capable of penetrating dirt and residue on the platen and the finger, countering a main drawback to optical technology.

Voice Authentication.[235] Voice authentication technology makes use of distinctive qualities of a person's voice, some of which are behaviorally determined and others of which are physiologically determined. Voice authentication technology does not require specialized and expensive sensors or interface hardware. The entire system runs in software on conventional processors. The "infrastructure" required to implement most applications is already in place or available at low cost. In telephony applications, voice authentication technology works using the common corded, cordless, and cellular telephones. In computer-based applications, voice authentication technology works with a wide range of microphone/sound-card combinations on every standard desktop and laptop computer.

---

234. Provided by the International Biometric Group, www.biometricgroup.com.
235. Ibid.

FIGURE E.3: ACCESS CONTROL TERMINAL

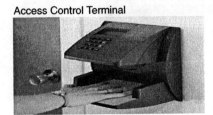

Access Control Terminal

There are certain inherent drawbacks to the implementation of this technology. Because of the prevalence of high-grade recording technology, one's voice can be recorded and used to garner a "false acceptance" from a secure network or banking system. To mitigate this risk, a "challenge response system" needs to be instituted as policy. A challenge response system asks users to verify their voice pattern by prompting them to respond with random number sequences. A randomly generated challenge response system will mitigate most of the risk inherent in recording technology. Nuance and BuyTel both provide reliable, proven voice recognition systems.

Hand Scan.[236] A hand scan reads the top and sides of the hands and fingers, using such metrics as the height of the fingers, the distance between joints, and the shape of the knuckles. Although not the most accurate physiological biometric, the hand scan has proved to be an ideal solution for low- to mid-security applications where deterrence and convenience are as much a consideration as security and accuracy. The hand scan is easy to use—the submission of the biometric is straightforward, and with proper training it can be done with few misplacements. The unit also works fairly well with dirty hands. The only problems may be with elderly clientele or people with arthritic hands, who may be unable to spread their fingers easily and place their hand on the unit's surface.

A hand scan is resistant to fraud. Short of casting a model of an enrolled person's hand and fingers, it would be difficult and time-consuming to submit a fake sample. Recognitions Systems Inc. (RSI), as the standard bearer of hand scan,[237] uses a template size of 9 bytes, which is extremely small—orders of magnitude smaller than in most other biometric technologies. By contrast, fingerprint scan biometrics require 250 to 1,000 bytes, and voice scan biometrics commonly require 1,500 to 3,000 bytes. The RSI technology facilitates storage of a large number of templates in a stand-alone device, which is how many hand scan devices are designed to work. It also facilitates card-based storage, because even magstripe cards have ample room for 9-byte samples. One drawback is that the design is static; in contrast to other biometrics, which can take advantage of technological breakthroughs such as silicon development or camera quality, hand scan has remained largely unchanged for years. Its size precludes its use in most logical access scenarios, where compact design may be a prerequisite. The second drawback is cost. Hand scan readers cost approximately $1,400 to $2,000 apiece, placing them toward the high end of the authentication security price spectrum.

Facial Scan. Facial scans map characteristics of a person's face into a multidimensional image. Face comparisons are made in real time. Identification involves a one-to-many comparison of an individual's face against all faces in a database in order to determine identity, and verification is characterized as a one-to-one match of an individual's face to his or her stored image for the

---

236. Ibid.
237. According to the International Biometric Group, Recognition Systems Inc. is the leading manufacturer of hand scans.

FIGURE E.4: BIOMETRIC FACIAL SCAN

purpose of confirming identity. Just as with finger scan and voice scan biometrics, there are various methods by which facial scan technology recognizes people. All facial scan technologies have certain commonalities,[238] such as emphasizing those sections of the face that are less susceptible to alteration, including the upper outlines of the eye sockets, the areas surrounding one's cheekbones, and the sides of the mouth. Most technologies are resistant to moderate changes in hairstyle, because they do not use areas of the face near the hairline. The International Biometric Group considers three firms to be in the first tier of facial scan technology: Viisage, Visionics, and BioID.

Signature Scan. Signature scan, also known as dynamic signature verification, is a biometric technology that has not seen broad use. Measuring the manner in which a user signs his or her name, password, or pass-phrase, signature scan examines stroke order, speed, pressure, and other factors that relate to the actual behavior of signing a tablet.

The biometrics of a handwritten signature are based not only on the shape of the signature but also on selected signature dynamics. The signature is captured, along with timing elements (speed, acceleration) and sequential stroke patterns (did the "t" get crossed from right to left and did the "i" get dotted at the very end). These unique dynamics derived from a person's muscular dexterity are usually referred to as "muscle memory." The brain, with no particular attention to detail, automatically controls these nerve impulses. These "muscle memory" dynamics yield accuracy results that are comparable to, and less intrusive than, the best alternative biometric technologies such as retinal eye scans or fingerprints. The signature and the data relevant to the transaction are collected and then bound to the signed document. There are three industry leaders in this field: Topaz Systems, Cyber-sign, and CIC.

Keystroking: BioPassword. BioPassword uses two methods (or factors) to accurately identify individuals before they are granted access to critical information and resources. First, the user must know both the correct user name and password. Second, the user's typing speed and rhythm must match a biometric template. Together, these two methods dramatically reduce the chance that unauthorized users can access resources. Keystroking biometrics verify a person's typing rhythm along with his or her knowledge of a unique user ID and secret password. Other than a standard keyboard and a 300 KB 32-bit Windows DLL, no special hardware or software is needed to realize this tenfold improvement in security.

Net Nanny's BioPassword[239] 4.5 ($100 direct per seat for 50 users, $40 per seat for 4,000 users[240]) is a software alternative to hardware biometrics solutions (such as retina or fingerprint scanners), which tie a unique physical characteristic to an individual's network account to provide a positive user identification. BioPassword links the user's specific typing style and patterns to the user's password for a flexible and secure solution, without the hassle of added components.

---

238. The International Biometric Group, www.biometricgroup.com.
239. Net Nanny Software Inc. is the only firm to provide keystroking technology.
240. Net Nanny Software Inc., http://www.biopassword.com/home/technology/technology_overview.asp.

FIGURE E.5: KEYSTROKING

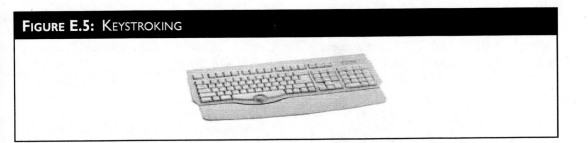

FIGURE E.6: GLOBAL POSITIONING BIOMETRICS

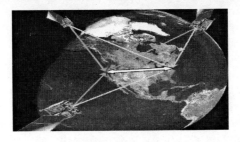

Once you are logged on, BioPassword requires you to train the system by entering a user name and password repeatedly (15 times by default). The administrator can set the amount from 1 to 20 times, but the more iterations, the better the user profile. The administrator can also establish the accuracy required for each user with the security setting. The security setting ranges from 1 to 10, with a default of 3. The higher the number, the more accurate the user must be.[241]

Global Positioning Biometrics. The Global Positioning System (GPS) is a network of satellites operated by the U.S. government that provides highly precise position and timing signals worldwide. The standard positioning service signals from the GPS are freely available for civil commercial and scientific use, and they comprise a stable and reliable standard for precise positioning and timing applications around the world. Authenticating locations involves the ability of IT personnel to authenticate the exact place and time at which access to a secure network is requested.[242]

A Colorado firm, Cyberlocator Inc., is the only firm that provides location authentication services worldwide. The client's sensor acquires the signals sent from GPS satellites that are in orbit overhead at a given moment. These raw, unprocessed signals are used to create a secure location signature. This location signature, once presented to a Cyberlocator server via the network, can be used to verify that the device is located at a specific geographical point. Both the client and the server can then use this authenticated location information for any number of purposes, including network access, location-based services, and asset tracking.[243] Cyberlocator implements GPS signals for robust network access authentication and location authentication using precise position and time signatures, and for determining the precise GPS positions of wireless devices of all types without the space, weight, and power burden associated with putting a GPS processor into the wireless device.

241. Jay Munro. BioPassword 4.5: Hardware-Free Biometrics. *PC Magazine*, Sept. 24, 2001.
242. A Colorado firm, Cyberlocator Inc., is the only firm that provides these services worldwide.
243. Input provided by Peter MacDoran, cofounder of Cyberlocater Inc.

Biometric Usage Worldwide

The following is a list of financial services providers that use biometrics to secure some of their systems: Ak Bank (Turkey), U.S. Department of Treasury, Bank United (Texas), Citibank, Dresdner Bank (Germany), Takefuji Bank (Japan), ING Direct, BACOB, Bank Belgium, Chase Bank, United Bank, Wells Fargo, NedCorp (South Africa), ABSA (South Africa), and Charles Schwab.

- Since the early 1990s, millions of South African citizens have received pension payments through a biometric smart card. Biometrics have proved very effective in overcoming problems of issuing benefits, such as a low literacy rate and the absence of a strong nationwide identification system.
- In 1998, the Philippines Social Security System commissioned Sagem to implement a large-scale ID application using biometrics. The new ID was designed to allow for the eventual electronic transmission of funds via ATMs.
- In July 2000, the Mexican government commissioned Visionics to create a face recognition system that would alert election officials whenever an individual attempted multiple registrations in the voting system.

Public Key Infrastructure

In a PKI system, the fundamental function of a certification authority is to verify the association between a particular person and a particular public/private key pair. A certification authority functions in effect as an online notary, a trusted third party that confirms the identities of parties sending and receiving electronic payments or other communications. Because banks already have a traditional role as a trusted third party in financial and commercial transactions, they are in this respect a natural fit for the certification authority business.[244] PKI allows users to interact with other users and applications, obtain and verify identities and keys, and register with certificate authorities (CAs), which act as trusted third parties and vouch for users and their identities. This technology has existed for more than 20 years. The certificates issued by the CAs are an encrypted package containing the identity of the end recipient together with details of the chain of trust through which the recipient was recognized. It is important to note that these certificates require compliance to policies and procedures where a high level of assurance can be provided as to the authenticity of the identity of the end recipient and that the certificate is available only for his or her use. The international standard for the implementation of functional PKI networks was a creation of the International Telecommunications Union (ITU).

Digital Signatures, Certificates, Certificate Authorities, and Public Key Infrastructures

The most widely accepted format for certificates is defined by the ITU-T X.509 international standard. X.509 is viewed throughout the information technology industry as the definitive reference for designing applications related to public key infrastructures (PKIs). The elements defined within X.509 are widely used—from securing the connection between a browser and a server on the Web to providing digital signatures that enable one to conduct electronic transactions with the same confidence one has in a traditional paper-based system.[245] This new edition, developed in close cooperation with ISO/IEC and the ISOC/Internet Engineering Task Force, supersedes and replaces the 1997 publication.[246]

- It contains specific enhancements to public key certificates to support the correct processing of certification paths that involve multiple certification authorities within multiple enterprises, as well as enhancements in the area of certificate revocation.[247]

---

244. Office of the Comptroller of the Currency (OCC) Bulletin 99-20 on certificate authority systems.
245. International Telecommunications Union, http://www.itu.int/ITU-T/news/sg7-x509.html.
246. Ibid.
247. Ibid.

FIGURE E.7: GENERATION OF DIGITAL SIGNATURES

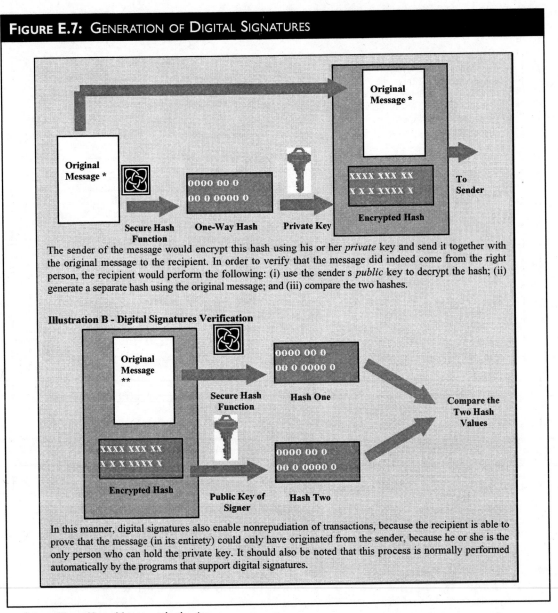

The sender of the message would encrypt this hash using his or her *private* key and send it together with the original message to the recipient. In order to verify that the message did indeed come from the right person, the recipient would perform the following: (i) use the sender s *public* key to decrypt the hash; (ii) generate a separate hash using the original message; and (iii) compare the two hashes.

In this manner, digital signatures also enable nonrepudiation of transactions, because the recipient is able to prove that the message (in its entirety) could only have originated from the sender, because he or she is the only person who can hold the private key. It should also be noted that this process is normally performed automatically by the programs that support digital signatures.

Source: Hong Kong Monetary Authority.

■ It contains a significant enhancement to attribute certificates and definition of the framework for privilege management infrastructure (PMI). Attribute certificates will play a major role in globally addressing the complex security issues of access control and authorization. They are a standardized mechanism for defining user access privileges in a multivendor and multi-application environment. These issues are just now coming to the attention of IT planners, as organizations move their mission-critical business relationships to the Web.

Digital signatures use asymmetric-crypto systems in ensuring that they efficiently discharge the role of a good signature system. Both a private key and a public key are involved. The private key is used for creating a digital signature or transforming data into a seemingly unintelligible form. The public key is used for verifying a digital signature or returning the message to its

FIGURE E.8: AUTHENTICATION USING DIGITAL CERTIFICATES AND CERTIFICATE AUTHORITIES

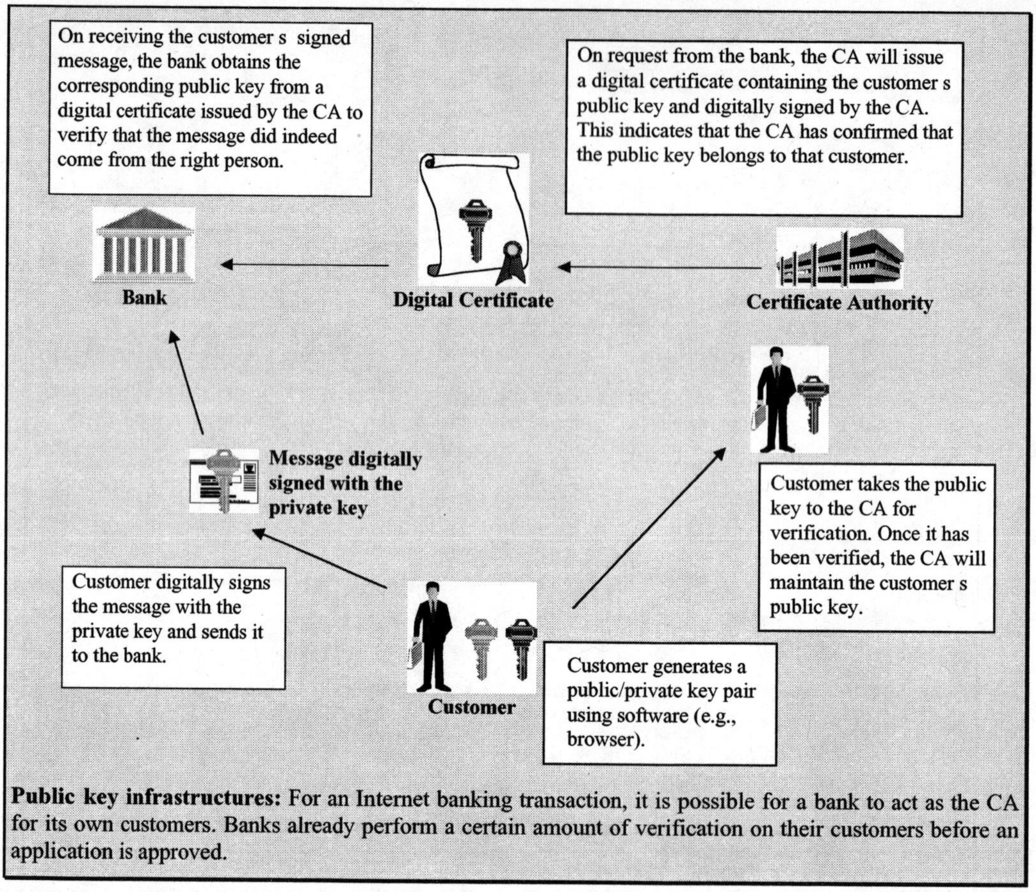

On receiving the customer's signed message, the bank obtains the corresponding public key from a digital certificate issued by the CA to verify that the message did indeed come from the right person.

On request from the bank, the CA will issue a digital certificate containing the customer's public key and digitally signed by the CA. This indicates that the CA has confirmed that the public key belongs to that customer.

Bank

Digital Certificate

Certificate Authority

Message digitally signed with the private key

Customer takes the public key to the CA for verification. Once it has been verified, the CA will maintain the customer's public key.

Customer digitally signs the message with the private key and sends it to the bank.

Customer

Customer generates a public/private key pair using software (e.g., browser).

Public key infrastructures: For an Internet banking transaction, it is possible for a bank to act as the CA for its own customers. Banks already perform a certain amount of verification on their customers before an application is approved.

Source: Hong Kong Monetary Authority.

original form. The authentication process consists primarily of key exchange. A key is a numerical value that, according to a protocol (X.509) used by both parties, allows the receiving party to decrypt the encrypted messages. After a successful key exchange, the system sets up a security association, which permits secure (encrypted) communication between the two parties. The private key is known only to the signer and is used to create the digital signature. The public key is more widely known and is used by a relying party to verify the digital signature. If many people need to verify the signer's signature, the public key must be available or distributed to all of them, perhaps by publication in an online repository or directory where it is easily accessible. The private key and the public key are mathematically related. However, in an efficient and secure system, one cannot derive the private key from knowledge of the public key. Thus, though many people may know the public key of a given signer, they cannot find out the signer's private key and use it to forge digital signatures.

Those who advocate the use of PKI should recognize that biometric technologies are superior to PKI in terms of the security levels they are able to provide during the transfer of data. "Whereas PKI's security rests entirely on the management of the private key, biometrics register users by their inherent characteristics, thus making it more difficult to assume the identity of the user."[248] PKI encrypts data from end to end, which does not solve the authentication issue. For instance, if a user stores the information to access the private key of PKI on a PIN, this can be compromised with relative ease, particularly if the PIN is stored on a computer's hard drive or a personal digital assistant (PDA).

The effectiveness of PKI, however, depends on the integrity of the public key and on the fact that some verification has initially been performed to associate the public key to its rightful owner. This can be achieved with the use of *digital certificates*.[249] A digital certificate is an electronic document that binds an identity to a public key. It contains certain information, such as the name of the owner, the validity period of the certificate, and the public key. This set of information is verified by a certificate authority, which digitally signs the certificate using the CA's private key to affirm the integrity of the certificate. A person who obtains a public key from a certificate issued by a CA can rely on the fact that the CA has performed the necessary verification of the identity of the key owner and rely on this knowledge to transact using the keys. The CA thus acts as a "trusted" party and itself must maintain a very high level of security to protect its own private keys and to maintain the list of valid certificates issued. It is possible for a bank to act as the CA for its customers.

Banks already perform a certain amount of verification on their customers before an application is approved. But a bank acting as a CA would need to establish strong security systems, because it takes on the responsibility for maintaining the public keys of its customers. Such a scheme might be considered adequate where customers deal only with their own bank. But this could become impractical for services across banks if individual institutions adopt different standards with no interoperability between them. Customers might also be required to hold a number of certificates associated with different banks. These factors can detract from the convenience that electronic banking aims to offer. Even outside the area of banking, this is an issue at the broader level of electronic commerce, where public key systems would also be the preferred means of authentication. Root certificate authorities form the very foundation on which public key infrastructures are built. Successful vendor interoperability testing is an important milestone in a PKI that purports to be open. Trust is the key element in any certification system. Because CAs may not be trusted by everyone who uses a given PKI, the CAs themselves are certified by other CAs. Moreover, because these "superordinate" CAs may have a different scope or set of requirements, they may not be trusted by everyone in a given PKI either. At some point, then, each PKI has a single trusted "root," from which all certification disseminates. Examples of root CAs are the VeriSign Digital ID Center and the U.S. Postal Service's Root CA. The aim of a public key infrastructure is to allow the adoption of common standards by all certificate authorities. The process of cross-certification can be further simplified by having a single entity take on this role. Such a "root authority" would establish the standards and certify subordinate CAs that comply with its standards. A root authority would also be in a position to establish cross-certification with other recognized root authorities overseas.

The Role of PKI in Singapore and Hong Kong

In Singapore, the Electronic Transaction Act (ETA) of 1998 has put in place a voluntary licensing scheme for certification authorities. It is possible to verify the identity of a person online through digital certificate and signature, if approved by the certificate authority that certifies a given public key with a given individual. Netrust is the first CA to issue keys for digital signatures in Singapore. PKI applications exist in Singapore. The ETA facilitates the setting up of authentication and certificate authorities. It also sets the guidelines that will be observed by all CAs. The liability of a licensed CA is limited under the ETA.[250] "The CA will not be liable for any loss

---

248. Interview with Raj Nanavati, partner at International Biometrics Group, Dec. 3, 2001.
249. Hong Kong Monetary Authority (HKMA).
250. New Singapore PKI Regulations Online, http://www.fitug.de/debate/9902/msg00182.html.

caused by reliance on a false or forged digital signature of a subscriber so long as the CA has complied with the requirements under the act and the regulations."[251] There are regulations stipulating when a digital signature will qualify as a secure digital signature (i.e., legally binding).

Meanwhile, in China, Hong Kong, the Hong Kong Postal Authority has established a PKI and, since January 31, 2000, has acted as a public certification authority. The Electronic Transactions Ordinance (ETO) gives the same legal recognition to digital signature that has been accorded to its paper-based counterpart. Different types of electronic signatures can be used in commercial dealings, based on agreement between the contracting parties. Where a digital signature is chosen to meet a legal requirement for a signature, only a digital signature (electronic signature based on the PKI technology) supported by a recognized certificate can be used to satisfy the requirement.

- The ETO establishes a voluntary recognition scheme for CA operations in Hong Kong. Government recognition is given only to those CAs that have attained a specified level of security and trustworthiness.
- A Certification Authority Recognition Office has been established to process applications for CA recognition and to monitor compliance by recognized CAs with the provisions of the ETO and the code of practice issued by the government.
- The electronic service delivery scheme launched by the government in December 2000, whereby public services involving financial and non-financial transactions are performed via the Internet, also provides for the use of PKI and digital certificates for securing transactions between the public and the government. The establishment of a public CA through the Hong Kong Postal Authority provides the foundation for the public key infrastructure.

In fact, since the first Digital 21 IT Strategy back in 1998, the HKSAR Government has made substantial progress to the improvement of Hong Kong's information security infrastructure, e.g. the enactment of Electronic Transactions Ordinance, development and promotion of PKI and e-cert, increase in the number of recognized certification authorities (total of 4 CAs in Hong Kong now), establishment of the Hong Kong Computer Emergency Response Team Coordination Center (HKCERT/CC) and the Inter-departmental Task Force on Computer Related Crime.

Best Practices for Administration of PKI

PKI builds on, but is distinct from, public key cryptography. It enables an encrypted communication to be wrapped in an electronic "envelope," so that the recipient can verify its origin and be sure that it has not been altered while en route. The basic encryption of the communication gives confidentiality. The future of PKI lies in scaling down expectations and focusing on closed domains, such as large enterprises and groups of trading partners. PKI is one step in the layered process of functional and effective layered security.

The PKI must be structured to be consistent with the types of individuals who must administer the infrastructure. Providing these administrators with unbounded choices not only complicates the software required but also increases the chances that a subtle mistake by an administrator or software developer will result in broader compromise. Similarly, restricting administrators with cumbersome mechanisms will cause them not to use the PKI. Management protocols are *required* to support online interactions between PKI components. For example, a management protocol might be used between a CA and a client system with which a key pair is associated, or between two CAs that issue cross-certificates for each other.

---

251. Ibid.

- Before specifying particular message formats and procedures, one must first define the entities involved in PKI management and their interactions (in terms of the PKI management functions required). Then these functions should be grouped in order to accommodate different identifiable types of end entities. The entities involved in PKI management include the end entity (the entity to whom the certificate is issued) and the certification authority (the entity that issues the certificate). A registration authority *may* also be involved in PKI management.
- In general, the term "end entity," rather than subject, is preferred in order to avoid confusion with the field name. It is important to note that the end entities here will include not only human users of applications but also applications themselves (e.g., for IP security). This factor influences the protocols the PKI management operations use; for example, application software is far more likely than human users to know exactly which certificate extensions are required. PKI management entities are also end entities in the sense that they are sometimes named in the subject or Subject/Alt/Name field of a certificate or cross-certificate. All end entities require secure local access to some information—at a minimum, their own name and private key, the name of a CA that is directly trusted by this entity, and that CA's public key. The form of storage will also vary from files to tamper-resistant cryptographic tokens.
- Any CA system used for banking transactions should be a "closed system restricted to participants that have agreed to meet the minimum operating standards, to operate according to common business practices, and to abide by that provider's rules and regulations."[252]

Validation of Certificates[253]

When relying on certificates, end-users must be able to determine whether the certificate is valid. There are a number of ways to accomplish this.

Certificate revocation lists (CRLs). Most early PKI models relied on CRLs to determine certificate validity. If a certificate was no longer valid, the CA would revoke it and add it to the CRL. CRLs are somewhat static-if a certificate has been revoked since the last CRL was issued, there is no record of the fact, nor will there be until the next CRL is issued. Quick and permanent revocation of certifications is the most important attribute to truly functional CAs.

CRL distribution points. In some cases, a CA may want to partition its CRLs to identify the reason a certificate was revoked. The Open CRL Distribution Process (OpenCDP) was designed to support this concept.

Online Certificate Status Protocol (OCSP). Just as credit booklets have given way to online verification scanners, CRLs have begun to give way to real-time verification mechanisms such as OCSP. OCSP relies on the existence of real-time "responders," which can be queried to check a certificate's validity. OCSP has also given rise to similar protocols, such as Real-time Certificate Status Protocol (RCSP), which attempt to improve on OCSP.

The Inherent Technical Weaknesses of PKI

Two important security questions arise about PKI. First, where are the certificates to be held? PC browsers are not safe as storage points. Web sites like http://astalavista.box.sk instruct their patrons on how to gain access to computers and networks by manipulating cracks in their browsers' programming codes. These problems make proliferation of smart cards necessary. Second, should the existing certification system be revamped to include the ability to track/audit all those who use it? In sum, operation over a wide area network forces individuals to accept certain

---

252. Excerpt taken from the Office of the Comptroller of the Currency's November 1999 Statement of Conditional Approval #339, www.occ.treas.gov.
253. Contributed by Verisign Inc.

losses to their privacy in order to ensure the security of their virtual identity and that of their business. Creating audit logs is critical in maintaining the system. Audit logs are tools that can help monitor the certification process by tracking what a certified user does; the user can and will sign the log for an audit trail that cannot be forged. "It is this feature that is the basis of the legal enforceability of the electronic contract," says Verisign.[254] Implementing biometric technologies would lessen the chances of an unauthorized user manipulating the passwords of an unsuspecting individual. The audit log's accuracy would be much less fallible if biometric technologies were implemented as private keys.

The largest drawbacks associated with PKI deployment came from imprecise definitions of trust. Some Certificate Authorities (CA) defined trust to mean that they maintain security only when handling their own private keys; it had no bearing on their procedures for the handling of other companies' keys. No authority has the power to grant accreditations, leaving the risk in the hands of the verifier of the certificate. The inherent problem here stems from the worldwide saturation of certificate authorities who maintain the power to handle private keys. Another issue is protection of the private signing key. Most enterprises will not own a secure computing system with physical access controls and air wall network security. The key is potentially open to attack by viruses and other malicious programs, and it could be misused while vulnerable, with disastrous consequences.

Existing Vulnerabilities Associated with PKI

A nefarious individual can manipulate PKI systems by executing the following attack methodologies:

1. One can place a Trojan virus in a word document and send it to a user's private key file.
2. One can flood PKI with fictitious user IDs and names. The net effect is that any typo gets the user one of your prepositioned keys. One then decrypts their messages and forwards them encrypted to the intended recipient.
3. One can use social engineering[255] to get a person to encrypt items that you provide them, and use it to get their private key.
4. One can break into a server that holds public keys and change them to ones that you specify.
5. One can crash a few key servers that form the base of a PKI tree for the users you want to defeat and they will only be able to communicate in plain text.
6. One can generate tons of key traffic so that the system overloads with requests and shuts down.
7. One can use the "Van-Eck attack" to observe secret messages after they are encrypted.
8. One can use video-viewing to observe the keyboard of users as they type in their keys or messages before encryption.
9. One can use a parallel processor to break keys of limited length. This has been successful against systems of common key lengths.
10. PKI in its purest sense is not an authentication technology but rather an encryption technology. All private keys are protected by either a token or a password, both of which are easily compromised.

---

254. Ibid.

255. In this context, social engineering is used to describe an occurrence when an unauthorized person attempts to gain access to a system through deception or other means. For example, a hacker calls a user claiming to be the systems administrator. He claims they are trying to update the system and asks the user for his/her password. (S)he gives it, believing the person to be a legitimate systems administrator.

WIRELESS VULNERABILITIES[256]

It was 1876 when Alexander Graham Bell's patent, the telephone, made its first successful voice transmission between Bell and his assistant, Thomas A. Watson. Bell probably did not foresee an era when the telephone would be wireless and subsequently utilized to facilitate commerce globally. Rather than spending the vast amount of resources and time to establish fixed-line infrastructure to facilitate telecommunications, countries around the world are substituting hard-wired infrastructure for the relatively cheap and easy to develop wireless towers. These towers facilitate e-finance and e-commerce, which will lead to lower costs and greater access to markets. Although tremendously beneficial to the economies of the developing world, wireless e-financial and e-commerce platforms can present operational and systemic risks to the financial sector at large.

Wireless networks are available in three basic formats: high-powered microwave systems used by telephone companies for long-haul, line-of-sight communications; CDMA/TDMA/GSM (Groupe Spécial Mobile), cellular and PCS networks used for wireless phones and personal digital assistants (PDAs); and wireless LANs using the 802.11b protocol. While all of these are common throughout the world, they all suffer from the same basic security flaw. They use radio frequency (RF) technology to transmit their information. The result can be the compromising of their transmissions.

Wireless technology is built around the 802.11b IEEE standard in the United States and the Global System Mobile (GSM) standard in Europe. This chapter depicts the security issues raised by both of these forms of wireless technology and provides a glimpse into the future of third generation wireless (3G) and satellite based platforms.

---

256. See Kellermann. 2002. *Mobile Risk Management*. World Bank.

TABLE F.1: THE WIDE RANGE OF MOBILE SERVICES

Cellular and PCS Services	GSM (TDMA), CDMA, digital cellular, and 3G
WLANs	The 802.11a and b standards, as well as the new 5.7 GHz wireless LAN band.[257]
Satellite Systems[258]	Ka-band desktop services[259] and the Astra satellite network[260]

WLAN (wireless local area network): The US standard

Wireless networks (WLANs) have seen explosive growth in their deployment. With cost savings at an all-time high and with the simplicity of installation, WLANs have been deployed rapidly. Wireless networks were supposed to do what traditional Ethernet LANs do without cables. Convenience for the customer is paramount in the proliferation of wireless. Wireless LANs make use of the IEEE 802.11b technology, which is a system that transmits and receives in the 2.4GHz range and is capable of a maximum network capacity of 11Mbps. WLANs implement the Wireless Equivalent Protocol (WEP), which was designed to offer the same security features as a physical wire: confidentiality, access control, and data integrity. The 2001 *Black Hat Briefing* made public that hackers have a multitude of ways in which they can crack, interject, or modify WEP messages on a wireless network. There is a particular problem with devices using the 802.11 wireless network standard. The encryption can easily be broken, and once broken it can provide easy access to corporate networks for anyone listening in. Furthermore, if a wireless gateway is located on the corporate Ethernet network, that network will broadcast all the data passing through it over the airwaves. If someone cracks the encryption, that person can intercept everything. But the immediate points of vulnerability are the mobile devices themselves, including notebooks, which tend to be poorly protected and which often contain sensitive but unencrypted data. The danger to financial and corporate networks is very real. The 802.11b standard includes a provision for WEP encryption. Depending on the manufacturer and the model of the NIC card and access point, there are two levels of WEP commonly available—one based on a 40-bit encryption key (also called 64-bit encryption because it uses a 24-bit initialization vector (IV) and is considered very insecure) and the other using a 104-bit key plus the 24-bit IV (also called 128-bit encryption).

A recent technical paper titled "Weakness in the Key Scheduling Algorithm of RC4"[261] laid out several fundamental flaws in how the RC4 encryption algorithm was used in the WEP encryption scheme. This paper proposed a method for determining the master WEP key that would allow a hacker to pose as a legitimate user of the network. Shortly after that, a program called AirSNORT appeared on the Internet.[262] AirSNORT takes advantage of the flaws outlined in the "Weakness" paper and, after monitoring a wireless network for some time, can discover the WEP key. The essential problem with WEP is that the underlying clear text message used to frame the information in the 802.11 header is predictable and repeatable. Given enough cipher text coupled with clear text, a cryptographer can find the key.

---

257. This new LAN is now being used for many new applications that involve financial transactions, from toll highways in Europe to banking and bank-to-bank transactions.
258. These systems provide for both trunk-line Internet transmissions and digital video broadcast services for video streaming and cache updating, as well as direct access services.
259. These systems began in Europe.
260. Hughes Spaceway System.
261. Scott Fluhrer, Istak Mantin, and Adi Shamir.
262. Input provided by Rick Fleming, Vice President of Security Operations, Digital Defense Inc.

When designing a wireless network, one should keep in mind a number of important security concerns. These are the seven basic categories of wireless network security risks:[263]

1. **Insertion Attacks**—The intruder attempts to insert traffic into your network, typically through an unsecured mobile access point.
2. **Jamming**—This is a DOS (denial-of-service) attack, where the attacker tries to flood the radio frequency spectrum of your wireless network by broadcasting packets at the same frequency as your network.
3. **Encryption Attacks**—The IEEE 802.11b wireless network standard uses a WEP encryption method. This standard uses weak encryption and initialization vectors and has been cracked successfully many times.
4. **Traffic Interception and Monitoring** (war driving)—Wireless packets using the 802.11b standard have an approximate transmission distance of 300 feet. This means that anyone with the proper standard equipment can receive that signal if he or she is in transmission range. Equipment to extend that range further is easily available, so the area of interception can be quite large and hard to secure properly.
5. **Mobile Node to Mobile Node**—Most mobile nodes (laptops, PDAs) are able to communicate directly with each other if file-sharing or other TCP/IP services are running. This means that any mobile node can transfer a malicious file or program rapidly throughout your network.
6. **Configuration Issues**—Any wireless device, service, or application that is not correctly configured before installation and use can leave an entire network at risk. Most wireless devices and applications are preconfigured to accept any request for services or access. This means any passing mobile client can request and receive telnet sessions or ftp.
7. **Brute Force Attacks**—Most wireless access points use a shared password or key for all devices on that network. This makes wireless access points vulnerable to Brute Force dictionary attacks against passwords.

War Driving

Industrial espionage and white-collar crime have reached new heights with the advance of new technologies. War dialing, the hacking practice of phoning up every extension of a corporate phone network until the number associated with the firm's modem bank is hit upon, has been replaced by *war driving*. War driving involves motoring between targeted financial institutions and corporate headquarters with a laptop fitted with a WLAN card and trying to record network traffic (sniffing). According to Dave Thomas, the Chief Investigator of the FBI Computer Crimes Division, war driving is a widespread phenomenon that jeopardizes the security of all institutions and corporations that implement WLANs.

When testing and deploying WLANs, a network administrator may find that the institution's laptops can only connect to the access points within a certain distance and may therefore assume that the signals do not travel beyond this point. This is a flawed assumption. In fact, these signals may travel for several thousand meters if there is nothing in the way to deflect or interrupt the signal. The reason for this misconception is that the small antennas in the laptops cannot detect the weaker signals. But if external antennas are used, the range can be vastly extended. The wireless segment is usually omni-directional, so a potential adversary need not gain physical access to the segment to sniff (or record) the packet traffic. As a result, WLANs are susceptible to message interception, alteration, and jamming.

These considerations raise the issue of how to better secure wireless networks. This will be as critical as securing fixed-line Internet systems in the emerging markets, as highlighted above.

---

263. Chris Bateman of CERT Analysis Center contributed the seven wireless vulnerabilities.

Each of these security breaches and associated risks can be minimized or negated with the proper use of security policy and practices, network design, and system security applications, and with the correct configuration of security controls.

Fifteen Steps to Securing WLANs

Wireless network security is much like the physical security at the entrance of a building. Someone with enough interest, resources, and time is going to be able to gain access. First and foremost, it is important to treat your wireless network as though it were a publicly accessible network. A system administrator should not make any assumptions that traffic on that network is private and secure.

Financial institutions should create an institution-wide policy on wireless devises which should tailor the corporate security policy to address network use guidelines. The following security recommendations, compiled from a host of industry leaders, offer some simple rules that can provide a foundation for securing a WLAN:

1. Take Inventory: Track how many employees have WLANs at home.
2. Disable all unneeded services and applications on each client and server.
3. Change the default settings of your products. This includes the default password on your access point.
4. Plan your coverage to radiate out to the windows but not beyond.
5. Provide directional antennas for wireless devices.
6. Turn WEP on and manage your WEP key by changing the default key and changing the WEP key every week.
7. Use VPN tunneling between the network firewall and the wireless.
8. Deploy a network-based intrusion detection system (NIDS) on the wireless network.
9. Deploy enterprise-wide anti-virus software on all wireless clients.
10. Employ two-factor authentication.
11. Disable DHCP and use static IP addresses for your wireless NICs.
12. Purchase access points that have "flashable" firmware only.
13. Use a wireless firewall gateway
14. Access Points (AP) should be placed in secure areas and Layer 2 switches should be employed in lieu of hubs.
15. Ensure that AP Channels are at least five channels different from other nearby wireless networks to prevent interference.

Proper System Administration and Auditing

The proper administration of a wireless network is one of the main components of achieving reliable security. The system administrator should routinely perform the following tasks:

1. Reconfigure any wireless device from its factory settings before it is deployed on the network. Turn off all unnecessary services.
2. Obtain the latest security fixes from the vendor and install appropriately before deployment.
3. Review all firewall logs weekly, and scan critical host logs daily.
4. Review all ACLs and user accounts on a monthly basis. System administrators should remove all access privileges for terminated employees.
5. Scan automatically all downloads, using enterprise antivirus software.
6. Set password content and length policy to at least 10 alphanumeric characters.
7. Review all IDS logs weekly.
8. Maintain an inventory of all mobile devices.
9. Prohibit all unauthorized wireless devices.

10. Develop a standard wireless access point configuration, and use it on all nodes.
11. Change all access point SSIDs (server set IDs). These are the shared passwords that come factory-installed on all wireless access points.
12. Disable SNMP community passwords on all access points.
13. Enable 128-bit WEP encryption.
14. Move or encrypt the SSID password and the WEP key. Most wireless clients store the SSID password and a shared WEP key in the Windows registry file.

Also, at least biannually, a penetration test or risk assessment should be performed. The results should be used to drive new policy, equipment, and network configuration changes. A wireless network is relatively easy to test for vulnerabilities, and a war-driving system can identify key security risks cheaply and quickly. A more comprehensive risk assessment methodology called OCTAVE (Operationally Critical Threat, Asset, and Vulnerability Evaluation) is available from the Software Engineering Institute at http://www.cert.org/octave. There are several freeware war-driving software packages available now, such as AirSNORT), and several made by wireless technology companies (e.g., IBM's WSA) that will provide the organization with a solid picture of the network's vulnerabilities.[264]

The European Cellular Standard: GSM

In 1982, the Conference of European Posts and Telegraphs (CEPT) formed a study group called the Groupe Spécial Mobile (GSM) to study and develop a pan-European public land mobile system. Today, GSM is the world's most widely deployed and fastest growing digital cellular standard. GSM subscribers worldwide number nearly 600 million, more than two-thirds of the world's digital mobile population. The numbers are increasing by four new users per second. GSM covers every continent, being the technology of choice for 400 operators in more than 170 countries. But this is only the beginning of the wireless revolution. The industry predicts more than 1.4 billion GSM customers by the end of 2005.[265]

GSM phones have a small smart card inside them that holds the identity of the cell phone. This small smart card is called a Subscriber Identification Module (SIM). The SIM must keep the identity inside secret and uses cryptography to protect it.

The North American GSM system operates at 1900mhz in conjunction with digital PCS services. The data services associated with GSM are Short Message Service (SMS), Analog Cellular Switched Data (CSD), and General Packet Radio Service (GPRS). Most European cellular carriers use a form of GSM, in either 900mhz or 1800mhz. Europeans also have the option of using High Speed Circuit Switched Data (HSCSD), which combines several channels into a single channel capable of 38.4 KBPS. GPRS is also available in most countries.

GSM Vulnerabilities

SIM Card Vulnerability. In both European and American GSM systems, the network access method is the same. Removable smart cards in the phone (SIM cards) are used to store phone numbers, account information, and additional software such as wireless Web browsers. The data on the cards is encrypted, but the COMP128 algorithm that protects the information on the card has been compromised, making these cards susceptible to duplication. War driving is not a substantial issue for cellular subscribers using GSM. Regardless of frequency, cellular signals can easily be jammed. There is a widely known method for recovering the key for an encrypted GSM conversation in less than a second using a PC with 128 MB of RAM and 73 GB of hard drive space.

---

264. Ibid.
265. ETSI (European Telecommunications Standards Institute), http://www.etsi.org/search/frameset/home.htm?CiScope=%2F&CiMaxRecordsPerPage=10&TemplateName=query&CiSort=rank%5Bd%5D&HTMLQueryForm=search.htm&UserRestriction=GSM

FIGURE F.1: A GSM HACK

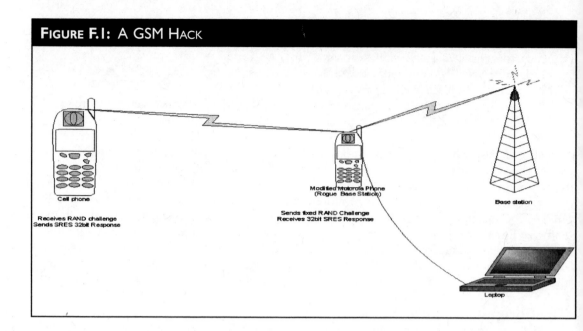

The security of GSM phone technology is limited. It is possible to clone GSM SIM cards. The hack attack is possible because critical algorithms are flawed, making it possible to dump the contents of the SIM cards and then emulate them using a PC. This latest problem could render GSM phone conversations totally insecure. For a bank, there are other issues. For example, a remote teller machine could be tricked into communicating with a fake mobile tower because it cannot reach a real one. This would allow the perpetrator to remotely control the transmissions of funds via the teller machine. In the figure below, a modified GSM cell phone and laptop are being made to act as a base station. All that is necessary is to make a few software and hardware modifications to the phone and to be within closer range than the actual tower. The mobile phone must authenticate itself to the base station, but the station does not have to authenticate to the phone at all. To eliminate the unknown variables, a fixed RAND challenge is sent out to all mobile phones in range. The received responses are the SRES and IMSI. These are recorded and used later, along with the COMP 128 algorithm, to derive the shared secret key K that is used. This key is then copied to a smart card and can be used to act as a person or to eavesdrop on a person.

The SMS Vulnerability. GSM offers Short Message Services (SMS). SMS is used in GSM systems for many reasons, such as voicemail notification, updating the subscriber's SIM, sending short text messages, and communicating with e-mail gateways. Although these services are convenient, they pose an additional risk to the security of the network. There is freely available software that can spoof SMS messages, send SMS bombs to both handsets and SMS gateways (used to communicate between devices both on and off the network), and corrupt SMS packets that can crash the software on most handsets.

The GPRS Vulnerability. General Packet Radio Service (GPRS) is an IP packet-based service that allows an always-on connection to the Internet. The main problem with this is that it still relies on SMS for Wireless Application Protocol (WAP) push requests. A spoofed (cloned) SMS packet can be sent to the phone requesting a redirected site and fooling users into entering their information into a fake site that they believe is a secure order form. Many GPRS-enabled phones also support Bluetooth, IBM's wireless programming language. Each Bluetooth device has a unique address, allowing users to have some trust in the person at the other end of the transmission. Once this ID is associated with a person, by tracking the unscrambled address sent with each message it is possible to trace individuals and easily log their activities. For Bluetooth devices to communicate, an initialization process uses a PIN for authentication. While some devices will allow you to punch in an ID number, you can also store a PIN in the device's memory or on a hard disk. This is highly problematic if the physical security of the device cannot be guaranteed. Also, most PINs use four digits and half the time they are "0000."

The security of Bluetooth is based on keeping the encryption key a secret shared only between participants in the network. But imagine that you and I are having a conversation using our Bluetooth cell phones. To keep the conversation secure, I use your secret key. Later that day, a friend calls you again and you use your key. Knowing your key, I can use a faked device address, determine the encryption, and listen to your phone conversations. I could also masquerade as you or your friend. Bluetooth authenticates only devices, not users.

WAP Weaknesses. The common flaw in any of these devices, no matter what network, is the Wireless Application Protocol standard, which also includes Wireless Markup Language (WML) and Handheld Device Markup Language (HDML). For the sake of convenience, developers try to require the least amount of keystrokes when entering in credit card number or personal or account information. This means that most of this information is still stored on a server, but the password to access that server is stored in a cookie on the handheld device, requiring only a PIN or sometimes nothing at all to shop online or transfer funds. This means that the actual mechanism used to transport sensitive information end-to-end in these untrusted public cellular networks, is left to Wireless Transport Layer Security (WTLS).[266] Unless 128-bit SSL for mobile commerce or IPSEC for Enterprise access is being used, which most handsets cannot support because they lack processing power and bandwidth, there will be a weak link somewhere in the network that can be exploited. Even then, this only pushes the weakness out to the end devices that are communicating, and it can be easily lost. GSM uses the Wired Application Protocol and also the Wireless Transport Layer Security. This is equal to Secure Socket Layer, but it has weaker encryption algorithms. WTLS is not compatible with SSL, which is the industry standard. Wireless messages travel through a "gateway"[267] that channels them to a wired network for retransmission to their ultimate destination. At the gateway, the WTLS message is converted to SSL. For a few seconds, the message is unencrypted inside the gateway, which in turn makes the communication vulnerable to interception.[268]

Security Solutions for GSM

The inherent problems affecting GSM are not easily corrected. The telephones and PDAs that use GSM technology typically cannot upload protective firmware and software. Users are at the mercy of the telephone developer. Whereas GSM is not vulnerable to war driving like its American counterpart, 802.11, it is suffering from several core vulnerabilities. The 802.11 standard is geared to computers, not handhelds, and thus security can be improved much more drastically for 802.11 than for the GSM protocol. Virtual private networks are the common thread between the two. The establishment of VPNs is commonly referred to as the solution for the existing vulnerabilities of GSM and 802.11. However, when it comes to proper layered security, there are no magic bullets.

To protect information systems that may use any of these technologies, users should deploy virtual private network technology at each and every trusted gateway into their networks and ensure that every user accessing the trusted network uses VPN technology. A virtual private network is essentially a private connection between two machines that sends private data traffic

---

266. In his paper *Attacks Against the WAP WTLS Protocol*, Saarinen describes in detail a number of security problems with WTLS. Although the WTLS protocol is closely modeled on the well-studied TLS protocol, a number of security problems have been identified with WTLS. These problems include vulnerability to datagram truncation attack, message forgery attack, and a key-search shortcut for some exportable keys.

267. A gateway is a device that translates the WAP to LAN from wired to fixed-line communication. Hackers have cracked the security for gateways.

268. Input provided by Dave Thomas, Chief Investigator for the National Infrastructure Protection Center.

FIGURE F.2: DIAGRAM OF VIRTUAL PRIVATE NETWORKS

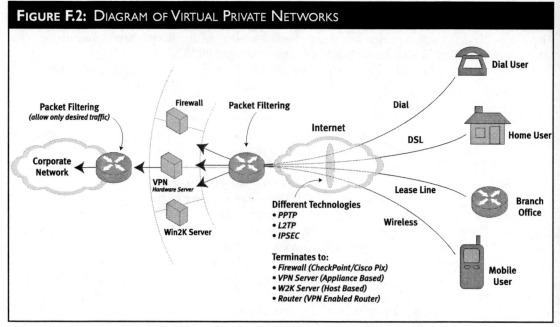

Source: Linda McCarthy, Vice President of Systems Engineering at Recourse Technologies.

over a shared or public network, the Internet. VPN technology lets an organization securely extend its network services over the Internet to remote users, branch offices, and partner companies. In other words, VPNs turn the Internet into a simulated private wide area network (WAN). VPNs allow remote workers to access their companies' servers.

To use the Internet as a private WAN, organizations may have to overcome two main hurdles. First, networks often communicate using a variety of protocols; VPNs provide a way to pass non-IP protocols from one network to another. Second, data packets traveling the Internet are transported in clear text. Consequently, anyone who can see Internet traffic can also read the data contained in the packets. This is clearly a problem if banks desire to use the Internet to pass important, confidential business information. VPNs overcome these obstacles by using a strategy called tunneling. Instead of data packets crossing the Internet out in the open, they are first encrypted for security and then encapsulated in an IP package by the VPN and tunneled through the Internet.

Many vendors—Nokia, Cisco, Nortel, Checkpoint, and Microsoft, among others—have viable, secure VPN technologies[269] that can be deployed at multiple locations in a corporate network. While VPNs provide content protection for that information traversing the network, depending on how they are deployed, they may not provide any protection from extraneous users accessing the network itself. In other words, an unauthorized user may not be able to see the content because of the VPN, but that user can still access the network resources and use the bandwidth, causing network congestion and possibly denial of service to authorized users. Access control, authentication, and encryption are vital elements of a secure connection. The Point-to-Point Protocol (PPP) has long been used as the Internet's universal link layer for creating tunnel links between devices, but in recent years, the Point-to-Point Tunneling Protocol (PPTP) and Layer 2 Tunneling Protocol (L2TP) have prevailed.[270]

---

269. The standards for VPN are currently in revision by the Internet Engineering Task Force to make IP Security more secure, but also to make it compatible with satellite communications.

270. Karen Bannan's article "Safe Passage" in *PC Magazine* August 2001 reviews seven VPN providers for products that would suit a medium-size business with a budget of $10,000 that needed a VPN for its central and branch offices. The article is available at http://www.pcmag.com/print_article/0,3048,a%3D12352,00.asp.

A View into the Future: 3G Technology
The third generation of wireless communication technology (3G) refers to pending improvements in wireless data and voice communications through any of a variety of proposed standards. The immediate goal is to raise transmission speeds from 9.5K to 2M bit/sec. In systems and communications security, the goal is not to design a flawless system, but to design a system that can adapt to security enhancements as the need for them is identified. Several of the attacks that were possible on other networks have been addressed and eliminated in the 3G environment.

The Strengths of 3G's Security Structure
3G security is based on GSM security, with the following important differences:[271]

- A change was made to defeat the false base station attack. The security mechanisms include a sequence number that ensures that the mobile device can identify the network.
- Key lengths were increased to allow for the possibility of stronger algorithms for encryption and integrity.
- Mechanisms were included to support security within and between networks.
- Security is based within the switch, rather than in the base station as in GSM. Therefore, links are protected between the base station and the switch.
- Integrity mechanisms for the terminal identity have been designed in from the start, whereas they were introduced late into GSM.
- The authentication algorithm has not been defined, but guidance on choice will be given.
- When roaming between networks, such as between a GSM and 3GPP, only the level of protection supported by the smart card will apply. Therefore, a GSM smart card will not be protected against the false base station attack when it is in a 3GPP network.

The 3G system is far more secure than its GSM counterpart. That said, the ingenuity of nefarious individuals should never be underestimated. Certain attacks are theoretically possible on a 3G network. They are described below.

Camping on a False Base Station
This is an attack that requires a modified base station/mobile station (BS/MS) and exploits the weakness that a user can be enticed to camp on a false base station. A false BS/MS can act as a repeater for some time and can relay some requests between the network and the target user but modify or ignore certain service requests or paging messages related to the target user.

The security architecture does not prevent a false BS/MS from relaying messages between the network and the target user, nor does it prevent the false BS/MS from ignoring certain service requests or paging requests. Integrity protection of critical messages may help, though, to prevent some denial of service attacks, which are induced by modifying certain messages. Again, the denial of service in this case only persists for as long as the attacker is active, unlike the other kinds of attacks, which persist beyond the moment where intervention by the attacker stops. These attacks are comparable to radio jamming, which is very difficult to counteract effectively in any radio system.

Forcing Unencrypted Communications
This attack requires a modified BS/MS. While the target user camps on the false base station, the intruder pages the target user for an incoming call. The user then initiates the call setup procedure, which the intruder allows to occur between the serving network and the target user,

---

271. The evaluation of relevant strengths and weaknesses associated with 3G technology was provided by Rick Fleming, Vice President of Security Operations, Digital Defense Inc.

modifying the signaling elements so that it appears to the serving network that the target user wants not to enable encryption. After authentication, the intruder cuts the connection with the target user and then uses the connection with the network to make fraudulent calls on the target user's subscription.

Integrity protection of critical signaling messages protects against this attack. More specifically, data authentication and replay inhibition of the connection setup request allows the serving network to verify that the request is legitimate. In addition, periodic integrity-protection messages during a connection help protect against hijacking of un-enciphered connections after the initial connection is established. Hijacking the channel between periodic integrity-protection messages is still possible, but this may be of limited use to attackers. In general, connections with ciphering that has been disabled will always be vulnerable to some degree of channel hijacking.

Again it should be pointed out that these attack profiles are theoretical, based on an understanding of how the technology will be deployed. All in all, 3G systems have enhanced and improved security technology in place, but continued vigilance is necessary to maintain their security to set up a mobile-originated call.

Satellite

In 1945, Arthur C. Clarke wrote an article titled "Extraterrestrial Relays" which theorized the ability for wide-range communication devices to be placed in orbit, 22,300 miles above the equator. About 30 years later, by the mid-1970, private companies were investing in satellite technologies to not only host voice communications, but cable television signals as well.[272] Increasingly, satellite capabilities are integrated into daily functions. Information has gone digital, and as a result, communications technologies can converge. Dr. Joseph Pelton calls this phenomenon "the Pelton Merge," referring to "open systems merging and webbing together."[273] As an illustration of this, recently the United States Federal Communications Commission (FCC) passed legislation whereby satellite telephones could use ground spectrum to boost their transmission.[274]

The Pelton Merge is occurring within the financial sector. Global positioning systems (GPS) are being increasingly used for the precise pointing and operation of many communications satellites that are today used to support Electronic Funds Transfer. Several of the newest verification systems for e-commerce related transactions depend on verification of the customer's location to with a meter or so of the indicated transaction site. The cost savings to aircraft flight operations, to satellite system operation and transaction verification potentially available from GPS and the Galileo space navigation systems in the future are truly enormous (i.e. in the many billions of dollars). However the heavy dependence upon the GPS creates a potential single point of failure in our critical infrastructure in the event the GPS or other space navigation systems are somehow attacked or its signals rendered unusable or unreliable.

There are many ways to begin an assessment of the extent and nature of this vulnerability. At the most simplistic level one might consider the fact that a search of the Web on two elements "GPS, jamming" yields 9,420 links to this topic area alone. Web searches on the topics of "GPS, spoofing" and "GPS, signal simulators" yields multiple thousand of additional links. It is indeed these three possibilities, namely jamming, spoofing and signal simulation that could be used to undermine the reliability and functionality of the current GPS system. Even relatively low level jamming at the level of a few watts could render a fairly wide area inoperable. Today jamming (either intentional or accidental) could prevent the operation of GPS receivers for any and all

---

272. Orbit Communication Corp. "About Satellite TV", accessed at: http://www.orbitsat.com/AboutSat/history1.htm#2. Originally, "A Dream In The Making" by Harry W. Thibedeau, first appeared in Private Cable & Wireless Cable magazine, August 1996.

273. See Dr. Joseph Pelton (George Washington University) http://www.tfi.com/pubs/ntq/articles/view/95Q2_A2.html.

274. Yuki Noguchi, "Satellite Phone Firms Win Ruling," Washingtonpost.com, 1/31/2003, accessed at: http://www.washingtonpost.com/wp-dyn/articles/A3671-2003Jan30.html.

applications. More sophisticated spoofing or signal simulation attacks could create bogus positioning indications and thus constitute serious risk exposures. In light of the billions of dollars invested or to be invested in GPS and the new Galileo system suggests that a serious commitments needs to be made to insure the integrity of space navigation systems. It is possible to design critical continuous RF surveillance facilities to provide warnings of RF attacks or other integrity compromises to the existing GPS system.

Other steps should be taken to ensure the integrity of the GPS that could potentially come from interference from future navigation systems such as the Galileo Satellite Navigation System or in time from the ultra wide band (UWB) commercial wireless communications architectures being pursued around the world. The likelihood of successful attacks against the GPS satellite space segment has only increased in the past decade. Devices that can jam, undertake signal simulation and/or spoofing have already be designed. Although the greatest current dangers apply to military, air navigation, satellite positioning and other "velocity related applications", the ability to use GPS spoofing to fool electronic verification and authorization systems should not be ignored as financial security systems increasingly apply GPS location determination techniques in the future.

GPS Simulator
GSP Simulators were originally created and distributed so to test GPS receivers under a wide-range of circumstances. One example is that these simulators are sued to simulate a plane on final approach. The concern is that someone can utilize a simulator to override the signals going into a receiver. Other more advanced receivers that are commercially available can issue source acquisition codes. These cost between $5,000-30,000 U.S.

Deployment of GPS by Financial Sector
Rocket Agent for OS/390 and z/OS's two-factor authentication is supposed to ensure greater security than traditional static passwords, which are subject to surveillance, guessing or discovery through carelessness. With RSA SecurId two-factor authentication, randomly generated token codes literally change each end user's password once per minute. This creates a small opportunity for intrusion by another party, and even prevents accidental disclosure of passwords through end user carelessness. Because the clock in the token is based upon the server and the corresponding GPS signal, hackers can and have manipulated the server clock redeploying the number in order to grant themselves access to the system. Due to the reality that the servers know what algorithm is running in each tag it is possible to manipulate the server and thus the tag with a GPS attack.

Trading of Commodities and Currency Exchanges
Financial institutions around the world have utilized GPS signals to time-tag large currencies flows. This is necessary due to the fluctuation of the value of currencies due to international currency markets. In addition, time-stamped transactions are typical in commodity exchanges around the world due to the fluctuations in the market price. The behavior of traders is absolutely time critical which is why they utilize GPS to verify the correct values of the trades. GPS simulators can be legally purchased that emulate the constellation (e.g. satellite signal). Since GPS has an inherently weak signal. It is relatively easy to flood a receiver with a new time and thus back-up the clock that creates the time-tag and change the value of the currency.

- **The fraud scenario** would be if a nefarious individual put in a transaction that is predated so that the currency transaction is worth more, with fluctuations being on a time scale of a few seconds a 20 sec back stamp could be worth millions.
- **A denial of service attack scenario**[275] since GPS receivers are linked into the server network of the exchanges one could flood the system with so much information that it would

---

275. Websites like astalavista.box.sk will endow a visitor with over 8,000 hits once the phrase GPS Jamming is entered. Methodologies on how to hack GPS servers are widespread on the Internet.

crash essentially taking the capital market of currency exchange offline. The potential financial losses are tremendous.

Because many place so much faith in the GPS system there is a lack of proper monitoring and risk mitigation. GPS applications in the business sector seem to be focused on time synchronization. The GPS timing system accuracy can be shown to be quite impressive at better that a tenth of a millionth of a second (better than 100 nanoseconds) and is likely to be trusted implicitly.

Currency Trading Scenario

Consider now the situation of currency trading. Suppose that the Euro drops in value relative to US dollars effective at 12:00:00 UTC on a particular day. The holder of Euros is likely to wish that they had sold Euros before the drop in value. Suppose now that the server that is time tagging the buy/sell orders is being controlled by the reception of GPS positioning and timing signals. A GPS spoofing electronic attack is then conceivably possible against the GPS time controlled transaction server. The attack consists of microwave signal waveforms centered at 1575.42 MHz derived from a C/A channel GPS simulator (either commercially available (1) or from Internet based information (2)). These spoofing signals would be adjusted in power level so as to override the real GPS signals that are typically quite weak (−160 dBW). The simulator would be configured so that positioning values (pseudoranges) would be approximately correct (determining the location of the GPS timing antenna to within several meters may not be very difficult). However, for purposes of "back-dating" and fulfilling of the wish to have sold before the Euro's decline, the spoofing attacker alters the GPS timing (for example, 11:59:50 UTC) and then the order to sell Euros is time stamped at a time prior to the decline in the Euro's value. The electronic attacker then turns off the GPS spoofing signal and the GPS timing system once again receives the real GPS signals and returns to the correct time in the server.

Secure ID Hack Scenario

RSA has the SecurID random token user authentication system that creates a new six digit number every 60 seconds as determined by an internal clock operating within the small form-factor of the token, sometimes referred to as a smart card. The fundamental concept is that both the client's random token and the server share the same random number generation algorithm and have synchronized time so that the six digit random numbers will increment simultaneously. However, timing accuracy becomes an issue. The timing accuracy of the client's random token internal clock is no better than a wrist watch at perhaps plus or minus a few seconds per day. Therefore, after one month, the timing error in the client's token accumulates to perhaps plus or minus two minutes and accounting for the on-time value, actually requires that the server accept five possible six digit values, assuming that the server's clock is without error. Maintaining the server's time essentially without error is now a task accomplished by GPS. SecurID also requires a PIN.

Using a common hacker/cracker tool of a traffic-sniffer, the attacker captures a SecurID six digit token value and the associated PIN and notes the time of capture. The client/server connection is broken once the client is prompted by the server to manually enter the six-digit value/PIN thus avoiding the possibility of the server checking for one time use of the random token value. The attack proceeds by altering the GPS constrained server's clock to correspond to the time that the six digit token value was captured. The attacker then presets the token value/PIN and the server is then satisfied that the token value is arriving within an appropriate time window with the proper PIN and that the six-digit value has not been previously used. The attacker now is then judged to be authentic and the intrusion proceeds.

Three Steps to Preventing a GPS Attack

■ GPS receivers are integrated into the into the server network. They need to be tested for accuracy and monitored the signal to noise ratio (e.g. carrier to noise density c/n (o)). The carrier to noise density ration should be between the range of 48-50 bbhrtz an attack will have a carrier to noise density ratio of 60 bbhrtz or higher. The most effective method to avoid being fooled by the described electronic attack is to impose a type of "sanity check." For example, every GPS receiver has within its internal operations the computation of the signal strength for each of the GPS satellites that it is processing. Typically the highest signal levels to be expected from real GPS signals, in terms of dispread GPS signals, carrier-to-noise density ratio (C/No) would 50 dB-Hz. The electronic attack against the GPS timing system will likely present a power level of at least −140 dBW so as to overwhelm the real GPS signals by 20 dB. The GPS receiver internal functions would then indicate a C/No of 70 dB-Hz and be too good and be the tip-off that an attack was in progress and should initiate an alarm to the system administrator. In a similar manner, if the C/No values are excessively low at less than 33 dB-Hz there should also be an alarm that a jamming/denial-of-service attack may be in progress.

- Backups need to be created so that internal clocks oscillation is concurrent with real time.[276]
- Finally, high levels of physical security should be maintained around GPS receivers. Incorporate site-specific characteristics that an electronic attacker is not likely to know a priori. Obscure the GPS antenna/receiver so that its actual location is not easily known or deduced. Deploy the GPS receiver so that some of the sky view is actually blocked. Thus, if a spoofing attack occurs that presents GPS signals from a direction that the GPS receiver has blocked from view, then that condition is enough to set an alarm flag and institute back-up timing procedures.

---

276. Other sanity-checking can also be done by using Internet time synchronization services operated by the U.S. Naval Observatory (4) and the National Institute of Standards and Technology (5) that can test that the timing is within a few milliseconds. This will guard against a time resetting at the seconds to minutes level. The inclusion of a good quality ovenized crystal reference oscillator (frequency accuracy of parts in 10^{10}) can support timing maintenance within 10 microseconds per day once it has been set by a properly operating external epoch timing source. Such external timing sources are, of course, GPS timing receiver or a satellite communications two-way time exchanges with another node).

GLOSSARY[277]

A

Abuse of privilege: An act or activity that is not permissible because it goes beyond a user's scope of authorized power as stipulated by an organization's law or policies.

Access: The ability and means to communicate with or otherwise interact with a system in order to use system resources to either handle information or gain knowledge of the information the system contains.*

Access authorization: To give permission to communicate with, or otherwise interact with any system.

Access control: The process of limiting access to the resources of an information technology (IT) product only to authorized users, programs, processes, systems (in a network), or other IT products.*

Access-sharing: To grant permission to two or more users to simultaneously interact with IT files, systems, or devices.

Alphanumeric key: A sequence comprised of letters in the alphabet, numbers 0 through 9, symbols, and blank spaces from one to eighty characters long.

The American National Standards Institute (ANSI): A private, not-for-profit association of users, manufacturers, and other organizations that administers U.S. private sector voluntary standards. Serves as the United States representative to both the International Standards Organization (ISO) and the International Electrotechnical Commission (IEC).*

---

277. We would like to thank the Anne and Lynn Wheeler Garlic Site Security Taxonomy <http://www.garlic.com/~lynn/secure.htm> and Secure Synergy <http://www.securesynergy.com/library/articles/it_glossary/glossary_a.php> for permission to use their definitions. Definition from Anne and Lynn Wheeler Garlic site Security Taxonomy are noted with a (*). Definition from Secure Synergy website are annotated with a (**).

Anonymous File Transfer Protocol (FTP): A guest account that allows anyone to login to the FTP server. It can be a point to begin access on the host server.

Application gateway firewall: A type of firewall system that runs an application, called a proxy, that acts like the server to the Internet client. The proxy takes all requests from the Internet client and, if allowed, forwards them to the Intranet server. Application gateways are used to make certain that the Internet client and the Intranet server are using the proper application protocol for communicating.*

Application level gateway: A firewall system in which service is provided by processes that maintain complete TCP (Transmission Control Protocol) connection state and sequencing. Application level firewalls often re-address traffic so that outgoing traffic appears to have originated from the firewall, rather than the internal host.*

Application logic: The computational aspects of an application, including a list of instructions that tells a software application how to operate.**

Audit: An independent examination of a work product or set of work products to assess compliance with specifications, standards, contractual agreements, or other criteria.*

Audit trail: A set of records that collectively provide documentary evidence of processing used to aid in tracing from original transactions forward to related records and reports, and/or backward from records and reports to their component source transactions.*

Authenticate: To verify the identity of a user, device, or other entity in a system, often as a prerequisite to allowing access to resources in a system.*

Authentication: An authentication process consists of two steps: 1) Identification step, to present an identifier to the security system; 2) Verification step, to present or generate authentication information that corroborates the binding between the entity and the identifier.*

Authentication tool: A software or hand-held hardware "key" or "token" used during the user authentication process. See *key* and *token*.**

Authentication token: A portable authenticating device that uses techniques such as challenge/response and time-based code sequences.*

Authorization: Access privileges granted to a user, program, or process.*

Availability: The ability to use or access objects and resources as required. The property relates to the concern that information objects and other system resources are accessible when needed and without undue delay.*

B

Back door: A hole in the security of a computer system deliberately left in place by designers or maintainers. Synonymous with trap door; a hidden software or hardware mechanism used to circumvent security controls.* Malicious code, such as worms, can also contain back doors through which future system attacks can take place. Knowledge about a system's back door enables unauthorized users to gain entry and cause damage.

Bandwidth: A characteristic of a communication channel that is the amount of information that can be passed through it in a given amount of time, usually expressed in bits per second.*

Bastion host: A strongly protected computer that is in a network protected by a firewall (or is part of a firewall) and is the only host (or one of only a few hosts) in the network that can be directly accessed from networks on the other side of the firewall.*

Biometric access control: Using physiological or behavioral human characteristics, including (but not limited to) fingerprints, iris scans, signatures, and voice, in order to control access.

Blended threat: Types of malicious code, e.g. worms, that exploit software vulnerabilities in such a way as to circumvent perimeter defenses like firewalls, intrusion detection systems, virus scanners and encryption.

Business-critical applications: Any proprietary or off-the-shelf software application that is critical to a business and its business operations, such as accounting programs, customer relationship management (CRM), or human resource databases.

C

Capital Assets Management Equity and Liquidity (CAMEL): A system for periodic bank examination, based on a ranking of one to five, with one being the best.

Challenge/response: Prearranged procedure in which a subject requests authentication of another and the latter establishes validity with a correct reply.*

Chroot: A command or process in UNIX systems for changing root directory hierarchies, so that certain processes are restricted to an isolated subset of the file system.

Client/device: Any piece of hardware capable of establishing a connection to a server for the purpose of information or data retrieval.

Clustering: A group of independent systems working together as a single system. Clustering technology allows groups of servers to access a single disk array containing applications and data.**

Coded file: A file that contains information that encrypts, or otherwise alters the file so that it is unreadable to unauthorized users.

Combined evaluation: Method using proxy and state or filter evaluations as allowed by administrator.* See Stateful evaluation.

Communications server: Procedures designed to ensure that telecommunications messages maintain their integrity and are inaccessible by unauthorized individuals.*

Computer Emergency Response Team (CERT): CERT was established at Carnegie-Mellon University. After the 1988 Morris worm became the first instance of malicious code online, CERT was created in anticipation of cyber security needs. Their functions include risk alerts to educate the public, and incident response to current threats and vulnerabilities, as well as research into future ones.

Computer security: Measures and controls that ensure confidentiality, integrity and availability of information system assets including hardware, software, firmware and information being processed, stored, or communicated.*

Computer security audit: An independent evaluation of the controls employed to ensure appropriate protection of an organization's information assets.

Critical infrastructure: The Policy on Critical Infrastructure Protection: Presidential Decision Directive 63 (PDD-63), issued by the Clinton Administration in 1998, identified the critical sectors of an electronically dependent economy and assigned lead agencies to coordinate sector cyber security efforts. This directive identified eight critical infrastructure sectors: finance, transportation, energy, water, government, aviation, telecommunications, and emergency.

Cryptographic checksum: A one-way function applied to a file to produce a unique "fingerprint" of the file for later reference. Checksum systems are a primary means of detecting file-system tampering on UNIX.**

D

Data-driven attack: A malicious act in which attack code is encoded in seemingly innocuous data so that it can slip through security controls, such as firewalls that perceive it to be mere data. Once the malicious code slips through the security measure, the attack code can be unwittingly executed by a user, or automatically launched along with other software programs.

Data encryption standard (DES): A U.S. National Institute of Standards and Technology (NIST) Federal Information Processing Standard and commonly used secret key cryptographic algorithm for encrypting and decrypting data and performing other functions.*

Decode: Convert encoded data back to its original form of representation.*

Decrypt: In encryption terms, to convert encoded text, or ciphertext, back into its original, plain text form.

Dedicated: A special-purpose device that, although capable of performing other duties, is assigned to only one.**

Defense-in-depth: A two-fold approach to securing an information technology (IT) system: (1) layering security controls within a given IT asset and among assets, and (2) ensuring appropriate robustness of the solution as determined by the relative strength of the security controls and the confidence that the controls are implemented correctly, are effective in their application, and will perform as intended. This combination produces layers of technical and non-technical controls that ensures the confidentiality, integrity, and availability of the information and IT system resources.*

Demilitarized Zone (DMZ) : A network segment or segments located between protected and unprotected networks. As an extra security measure, networks may be designed such that protected and unprotected segments are never directly connected. Instead, firewalls (and possibly public resources such as HTTP or FTP servers) reside on a so-called DMZ network. DMZ networks are sometimes called perimeter networks.*

Denial of service: A type of electronic attack in which malicious code is used to execute any type of system overflow or jam, thereby causing the server to shut down and deny service to its users.

DNS spoofing: To assume the Domain Name Server (DNS) name of another system. Hackers will often use DNS spoofing to conceal their true identity, and to create the appearance of being a legitimate user.

Dual-homed gateway: A firewall consisting of a bastion host with two network interfaces, one of which is connected to the protected network, the other of which is connected to the Internet. Internet traffic forwarding is usually disabled, restricting all traffic between the two networks to whatever passes through some kind of application proxy.*

E

Electronic Banking Group (EBG): The Basel Committee on Banking Supervision's Electronic Banking Group (EBG) was formed to make recommendations for needed additions, changes, or improvements in supervision and examination to accommodate the new technologies.

Electronic Benefits Transfer (EBT): Electronic benefits transfers (EBT) is the third oldest channel for conducting electronic finance. This entails the electronic transfer of benefits, such as food stamps, Social Security payments, and child assistance benefits. EBT has been in existence for over a decade in more than 37 countries worldwide. In the United States alone, EBT moves $500 billion in these cash entitlements.

Electronic Data Interchange (EDI): A channel for electronic finance, Electronic Data Interchange (EDI) is the second oldest form of electronic money movement. It is used to effect money payment orders and bar coding. Bar coding is operational in more than 70 countries worldwide.

Electronic Funds Transfer (EFT): Electronic funds transfer (EFT) is one of four primary channels for conducting electronic finance. EFT began in the early 1960s, and is the oldest form of electronic money transmittal. The amount of money moving by EFT is $2 trillion per day and growing. The volume of EFT usage worldwide is 677,411,204 transactions.

Electronic finance: The use of electronic means to exchange information, to transfer signs and representations of value, and to execute transactions in a commercial environment. E-finance comprises four primary channels: electronic funds transfers (EFTs); electronic data interchange (EDI); electronic benefits transfers (EBTs); and electronic trade confirmations (ETCs).

Electronic payment: Any digital, financial payment transaction involving currency transfer between two or more parties.

Electronic security: Policies, processes, and technology needed to enable electronic transactions to be carried out with a minimum risk of breach, intrusion, or theft. Also, any tool, technique, or process used to protect a system's information assets. E-security enhances or adds value to a naked network and is composed of soft and hard infrastructure, and is a key component to the to the delivery of e-finance benefits.

E-mail bombs: Code that when executed sends many messages to the same address for the purpose of using up disk space or overloading the e-mail or Web server.**

Encrypting router: See Tunneling router and Virtual network perimeter.

Encryption: Cryptographic transformation of data (called 'plaintext') into form (called 'ciphertext') that conceals the data's original meaning to prevent it from being known or used.*

End-to-end encryption: Continuous protection of data that flows between two points in network, provided by encrypting data when it leaves its source, leaving it encrypted while it passes through any intermediate computers (such as routers), and decrypting only when the data arrives at the intended destination.*

Enterprise Resource Planning (ERP): ERP systems permit organizations to manage resources across the enterprise and completely integrate manufacturing systems.

Environment: Aggregate of the external procedures, conditions, and objects affecting the development, operation, and maintenance of an information system.*

Extranet: An intranet that is accessible or partially accessible to authorized users outside the organization.*

F

Fat client: A computing device, such as a PC or Macintosh, that includes an operating system, memory, a powerful processor, and a wide range of installed applications that can execute on either the desktop or the server. Fat clients can operate in a server-based computing environment.**

Fault tolerance: The ability of a processor to maintain effectiveness after some subsystems have failed.*

File Transfer Protocol (FTP): File Transfer Protocol, a standard Internet protocol, is the simplest way to exchange files between computers on the Internet. Like the Hypertext Transfer Protocol (HTTP), which transfers displayable Web pages and related files, and the Simple Mail Transfer Protocol (SMTP), which transfers e-mail, FTP is an application protocol that uses the Internet's TCP/IP protocols. FTP is commonly used to transfer Web page files from their creator to the computer that acts as their server for everyone on the Internet. It's also commonly used to download programs and other files to your computer from other servers.**

Financial Action Task Force (FATF): The Financial Action Task Force provides guidance for the implementation of measures to prevent criminal exploitation of financial systems. The FATF established their Forty Recommendations as a universal framework for anti-money laundering efforts.

Firewall: An internetwork gateway that restricts data communication traffic to and from one of the connected networks (the one said to be 'inside' the firewall) and thus protects that network's system resources against threats from the other network (the one that is said to be 'outside' the firewall).*

Flooding programs: Code that is intended to bombard a target computer system with more data that it can process, thereby causing the system to slow down or crash.

FSA: The Financial Services Authority (see http://www.fsa.gov.uk/).

G

Gateway: A bridge between two networks that run on different service protocols. The gateway allows for interoperability, usually by translating data transmissions between the two networks.

Generic utilities: General purpose code and devices—that is, screen grabbers and sniffers that look at data and capture such information as passwords, keys, and secrets.**

Global security: The ability of an access-control package to permit protection across a variety of mainframe environments, providing users with a common security interface to all.**

Granularity: Relative fineness or coarseness to which an access control mechanism or other IT product aspect can be adjusted.*

Groupe spécial mobile (GSM): Groupe Spécial Mobile, the European Union's digital cellular standard.

Guidelines for the Management of Information Technology Security (GMITS): The ISO/IEC 13335, better known as the Guidelines for the Management of IT Security (GMITS) established processes for securing the hostile online environment.

H

Hack: Unauthorized use, or attempts to circumvent or bypass the security mechanisms of an information system or network.*

Hackers: Any unauthorized user who gains, or attempts to gain, access to an information system, regardless of motivation.

HKMA: Hong Kong Monetary Authority (see http://www.info.gov.hk/hkma/).

Host: Any entity that serves as an information storage or service provider unit.

Host-based security: The technique of securing an individual system from attack. Host-based security is operating system- and version-dependent.*

Hot standby: A computer system that is configured and maintained so that, in case of disaster, it can act as a backup without any loss of service continuity to users.

Hybrid gateway: An unusual configuration with routers that maintain the complete state of the TCP/IP connections or examine the traffic to try to detect and prevent attack (may involve host). If very complicated, it is difficult to attach, maintain, and audit.**

Hyper Text Transfer Protocol (HTTP): A Transfer Control Protocol (TCP) based, application-layer, client-server, Internet protocol used to carry data requests and responses in the World Wide Web.*

I

Independent Computing Architecture (ICA): An acronym for Citrix's Independent Computing Architecture, a three-part server-based computing technology that separates an application's logic from its user interface and allows 100 percent application execution on the server.**

Information systems technology: All the electronic and human components involved in the collection, processing, storage, transmission, display, dissemination, and disposition of information. An information system may be automated (e.g., a computerized information system) or manual.*

Insider attack: Any network attack that originates from within an organization's protected network, such as by employees.

International Standards Organization (ISO): The global, non-governmental standards-setting body, composed of a network of national standards setting body representatives.

Internet: A decentralized, global network of computers (Internet hosts), linked by the use of common communications protocols (Transmission Control Protocol/Internet protocol, or TCP/IP). The Internet allows users worldwide to exchange messages, data, and images.*

Internet Engineering Task Force (IETF): A public forum that develops standards and resolves operational issues for the Internet. IETF is purely voluntary.

Internet Protocol (IP): A Internet Standard protocol (version 4 and version 6) that moves datagrams (discrete sets of bits) from one computer to another across an internetwork but does not provide reliable delivery, flow control, sequencing, or other end-to-end services that TCP provides.*

Internet Service Provider (ISP): Any entity that provides access to the Internet. They themselves are connected through Network Access Points, and together form the backbone of the Internet.

Inter-operability: Seamless interconnectivity between network components, including both physical hardware, software applications, and user functions.

Intranet: A computer network, especially one based on Internet technology, that an organization uses for its own internal, and usually private, purposes and that is closed to outsiders.*

Intrusion detection system: A system that detects and identifies unauthorized or unusual activity on the hosts and networks; this is accomplished by the creation of audit records and checking the audit log against the intrusion thresholds.*

IP sniffing: Intercepting or reading Internet data packets in order to steal critical information, such as network addresses, user names, and passwords.

IP splicing: An attack whereby an active, established session is intercepted and co-opted by the attacker. EP splicing attacks may occur after an authentication has been made, permitting the attacker to assume the role of an already authorized user. Primary protections against IP splicing rely on encryption at the session or network layer.

IP spoofing: An attack resulting from a system impersonating another system by using its Internet Protocol (IP) network address.*

ISO 17799: An information security standard that addresses e-security issues in ten major sections, including: business continuity planning, system access control, system development and maintenance, physical and environmental security, statutory, regulatory, or contractual obligation compliance, personnel security, security management for third-party access or outsourcing to a third-party service provider, computer and network management to safeguard information assets, asset classification and control, and security policy management support. The ISO 17799 is heavily regarded to assess level of security implementation, when insurers underwrite e-risk policies.

Information Systems Security Association (ISSA): The ISSA is a non-profit organization of information security professionals providing educational and networking opportunities for its members.

J-K-L

Key: A long string of seemingly random bits used with cryptographic algorithms to create or verify digital signatures and encrypt or decrypt messages and conversations. The keys must be known or guessed to forge a digital signature or decrypt an encrypted message.*

Layered security: The implementation of multiple modes of defense. Because the network is only as secure as its weakest link, it is recommended that twelve core layers of proper security are a fundamental component for maintaining the integrity of data and mitigating the risks associated with open architecture environments.

Least privilege: A principle that requires that each subject be granted the most restrictive set of privileges needed for the performance of authorized tasks. For certain applications, the most restrictive set of privileges could pertain to the lowest clearance. The application of this principle limits the damage that can result from accident, error, or unauthorized use of a system.*

Local area network (LAN): A communication system designed for intra-building data communications. A group of computers and other devices dispersed over a relatively limited area and connected by a communications link that enables a device to interact with any other on the network.*

Logging: The recording of user requests made to the firewall. Firewalls typically log all requests they handle, both allowed and rejected.*

Log processing: How audit logs are processed, searched for key events, or summarized.**

Log retention: The length of time that audit logs are kept and maintained.

M

Market failure: Market failures are instances in which demand is inaccurately represented by the mechanisms of the market, generally as a result of incomplete information. With regards to e-security, market failure occurs when inadequate incentives exist within the workplace, as well as within the regulatory and enforcement arenas, to require the timely and accurate reporting of e-breaches.

MAS: Monetary Authority of Singapore (see http://www.mas.gov.sg).

Mobile code: A program downloaded from the Internet that runs automatically on a computer with little or no user interaction.**

Money transmitter: Generally speaking, a money transmitter is any commercial enterprise engaged in the transfer and exchange of monetary instruments and currency. Often these non-depository entities are involved in the "money service business" and serve as third-party automated clearinghouse providers. These services may include money order issuance, wire transfers, and currency exchange.

Multi-user capability: The ability for multiple concurrent users to log on and run applications from a single server.**

N

National Infrastructure Protection Center (NIPC): NIPC brings together representatives from U.S. government agencies, state and local governments, and the private sector in a partnership to protect the nation's critical infrastructures. NIPC's mission is to serve as the U.S. government's focal point for threat assessment, warning, investigation, and response in cases of threats or attacks against electronic critical infrastructures.

Network computer (NC): A computer with minimal processing power, that generates most of its memory, storage, and processing power from the network servers to which they are connected.

Network computing architecture: A computing architecture in which components are dynamically downloaded from the network into the client device for execution by the client.**

Network-level firewall: A firewall in which traffic is examined at the network protocol packet level.**

Network worm: A worm is an acronym for "write once, read many". It is a self-contained piece of computer code, that can replicate and spread through the network to an many computers. Network worms are generally intended for malicious purposes, such as crashing or disrupting service. They can create back doors for future attacks or thefts on a computer.

Non-repudiation: A form of accountability in which both the sender and receiver of a message can confirm the integrity of transmitted digital information. Through such mechanisms as digital signatures, the recipient is able to prove that the message in its entirety could only have originated from the sender, because he or she is the only person who can hold the private key.

O

Office of the Comptroller of the Currency (OCC): Formed in 1863 as a branch of the U.S. Treasury, the Office of the Comptroller of the Currency (OCC) charters, regulates, and supervises all national banks, the federal branches, and agencies of foreign banks.

One-time password: Not capitalized: A 'one-time password' is a simple authentication technique in which each password is used only once as authentication information that verifies an identity. This technique counters the threat of a replay attack that uses passwords captured by wiretapping. Capitalized: 'One-Time Password' is an Internet protocol programmed to generate one-time passwords for use as authentication information in system login and in other processes that need protection against replay attacks.*

Open architecture: Any system whose architecture includes public access, open specifications, and the freedom to add any end-node to the network.

Operating system: Software required by every computer that: a) enables it to perform basic tasks such as controlling disks, drives, and peripheral devices; and b) provides a platform on which applications can run.*

Operational risk: Consistent with the Basel Committee on Banking Supervision Consultative Document, it is the threat of any internal person(s) or processes, or external event, that results in a direct or indirect loss for an organization. This monograph identifies three ways to measure operational risk: (1) the basic indicator approach, (2) the standardized approach, and (3) the internal management approach.

Operationally Critical Threat, Asset, and Vulnerability Evaluation (OCTAVE): CERT's comprehensive, risk assessment methodology, available from the Software Engineering Institute at http://www.cert.org/octave.

Orange book: An alternate name for the Department of Defense Trusted Computer System Evaluation Criteria. It provides information to classify computer systems, defining the degree of trust that may be placed in them.**

Outsourcing: The process of hiring a commercial third party, e.g. application service provider, to manage portions of an organization's responsibilities.

P

Password: A secret data value, usually a alphanumeric string, that is used as authentication information.*

Performance: A major factor in determining the overall productivity of a system, performance is primarily tied to availability, throughput, and response time.**

Perimeter-based security: The technique of securing a network by controlling access to all entry and exit points of the network. Usually associated with firewalls and/or filters.*

Personal Identification Number (PIN): A alphanumeric string used as a password to gain access to a system resource.* (See Challenge/response; Two-factor authentication.)

Policy: Organizational-level rules governing acceptable use of computing resources, security practices, and operational procedures.**

Portal: In particular, a series of ordered steps involving computing and communication that are performed by two or more system entities to achieve a joint objective. Agreed-upon methods of communications used by computers.*

Private key: The element of a public/private key pair that is kept secret by the key pair owner. The private key is used to decrypt messages that have been encrypted by the corresponding public key. It also is used to construct a digital signature – the document to be signed first is hashed using a secure hash algorithm; then encrypting the hashed value using the private key forms the digital signature.

Protocols: Agreed-on methods of communications used by computers.

Proxy: A firewall mechanism that replaces the Internet Protocol (IP) address of a host on the internal (protected) network with its own IP address for all traffic passing through it.*

Public key: The element of a public/private key pair that can be known by anyone. The public key is used to encrypt information that is to be intelligible only to the holder of the corresponding private key. It also is used to decrypt a digital signature in order to compare the decrypted digital signature and the hashed value of the signed document.

Public-Key Instrastructure (PKI): A system of Certificate Authorities (and, optionally, RAs and other supporting servers and agents) that perform some set of certificate management, archive management, key management, and token management functions for a community of users in an application of asymmetric cryptography.*

Q-R

Remote access: Use of a modem and communications software to connect to a computer network from a distant location via a telephone line or wireless connection.*

Remote presentation services protocol: A protocol is a set of rules and procedures for exchanging data between computers on a network. A remote presentation services protocol transfers user interface, keystrokes, and mouse movements between a server and a client.**

Risk analysis: The analysis of an organization's information resources, existing controls, and computer system vulnerabilities. It establishes a potential level of damage in dollars or other assets.**

Risk management: A broad based framework based upon CERT's OCTAVE paradigm for managing assets and relevant risks to those assets.

Risk mitigation: The act of minimizing the level of threat to a system.

Rivest-Shamir-Aldeman (RSA): RSA stands for its inventors, Rivest-Shamir-Aldeman. A public-key cryptographic algorithm that hinges on the assumption that the factoring of the product of two large primes is difficult.*

Rogue program: Any illicit program, such as a Trojan horse or worm, specifically designed to crash, disrupt, or otherwise inflict damage upon a computer system.

S

Salami slice: A hacker method for the acquisition of funds. A database of account information is copied. Then on a later date all accounts are charged a minimal amount, so as not to arouse suspicion.

Scalability: The ability to move application software source code and data, without significant modification, into systems and environments that have a variety of performance characteristics and capabilities.*

Screened host gateway: A host on a network behind a screening router. The degree to which a screened host may be accessed depends on the screening rules in the router.**

Screened subnet: Conceptually, it is similar to a dual-homed gateway, except that an entire network, rather than a single host is reachable from the outside. It can be used to locate each component of the firewall on a separate system, thereby increasing throughput and flexibility.*

Screening router: Synonymous to a filtering router, it is used to implement part of the security of a firewall by configuring it to selectively permit or deny traffic at a network level.*

Server: A server is a computer system, or a set of processes on a computer system providing services to clients across a network.*

Server-based computing: An innovative, server-based approach to delivering business-critical applications to end-user devices, whereby an application's logic executes on the server and only the user interface is transmitted across a network to the client. Its benefits include single-point management, universal application access, bandwidth-independent performance, and improved security for business applications.**

Server farm: A group of servers that are linked together as a "single system image" to provide centralized administration and horizontal scalability.**

Service-level agreement: Contract that guarantees network functionality 99.999% of the time, but significantly, this does not necessarily pertain to data integrity and subsequent layered security of the servers.

Session shadowing: A feature of Citrix WinFrame and MetaFrame that allows administrators and technical support staff to join remotely or take control of a user's session for diagnosis, support, and training.**

Session stealing: See IP splicing.

Single-point control: Helps to reduce the total cost of application ownership by enabling applications and data to be deployed, managed, and supported at the server. Single-point control enables application installations, updates, and additions to be made once, on the server, and then instantly made available to users anywhere.

Smart card: A credit-card sized device containing one or more integrated circuit chips, which perform the functions of a computer's central processor, memory, and input/output interface.*

Social engineering: An attack based on deceiving users or administrators at the target site. The manipulation of people and processes for the purpose of unauthorized access to a system or information. Social engineering attacks are typically carried out by telephoning users or operators and pretending to be an authorized user to attempt to gain illicit access to systems.

Stateful evaluation: An assessment methodology using a mixture of proxy or filtering technologies intermittently, depending on perceived threat (or need for speed.) **

Stateful packet filtering: The process of forwarding or rejecting traffic based on the contents of a state table maintained by a firewall. Packet filtering and proxy firewalls are essentially static, in that they always forward or reject packets based on the contents of the rule set. In contrast, devices using stateful packet filtering will only forward packets if they correspond with state information maintained by the device about each connection.*

Symmetric key: The secret key used for both encryption and decryption with a symmetric cipher such as DES, triple DES, or AES.

Systemic risk: Special characteristic of certain types of financial securities, that are subject to reverberations from other parts of the financial system. Also known as market risks.

T

Transmission Control Protocol/Internet Protocol (TCP/IP): TCP/IP is a standard network protocol. The IP is responsible for packets. The TCP is responsible for exchanging and reassembling these packets between two host computer systems.

Thin client: A low-cost computing device that works in a server-centric computing model. Thin clients typically do not require state-of-the-art, powerful processors and large amounts of memory because they access applications from a central server or network. Thin clients can operate in a server-based computing environment.**

Third party provider: An entity employed to be an objective and neutral outside party to fulfill a particular function or conduct a specific transaction.

Token: An object that is used to control access and is passed between cooperating entities in a protocol that synchronizes use of a shared resource. Usually, the entity that currently holds the token has exclusive access to the resource. In authentication, it is a data object or a portable, user-controlled, physical device used to verify an identity in an authentication process. See Key.*

Total Cost of Ownership (TCO): A model that helps information technology professionals understand and manage the budgeted (direct) and unbudgeted (indirect) costs incurred for acquiring, maintaining, and using an application or a computing system. TCO normally includes training, upgrades, and administration as well as the purchase price. Lowering TCO through single-point control is a key benefit of server-based computing.**

Trojan horse: A malicious program such as a virus or a worm, hidden in an innocent-looking piece of software, usually for the purpose of unauthorized collection, alteration, or destruction of information.*

Tunneling router: A router or system capable of routing traffic by encrypting it and encapsulating it for transmission across an untrusted network, for eventual de-encapsulation and decryption.*

Turn commands: Commands inserted to forward mail to another address for interception.**

Two-factor authentication: Two-factor authentication is based on something a user knows (factor one) plus something the user has (factor two). In order to access a network, the user must have both "factors," just as he or she must have an ATM card and a PIN to retrieve money from a bank account. In order to be authenticated during the challenge and response process, users must have this specific (private) information.**

U

Uniform Electronic Transactions Act (UETA): The UETA is a legal framework that addresses all consumer-related financial transactions and records, including electronic signatures and electronic transaction. UETA is the preferred framework in the U.S., as promulgated by the National Conference of Commissioners on Uniform State Laws (NCCUSL). The objective is to promote electronic commerce and to ensure that electronic signatures have the same effect under the law as manual signatures.

United Nations Commission on International Trade Law (UNCITRAL): The United Nations Commission on International Trade Law (UNCITRAL) is a model for assessing electronic commerce law. Though UETA and UNCITRAL have significant differences, such as defined terms, they are similar in their objective to promote electronic commerce and to ensure that electronic signatures have the same effect under the law as manual signatures.

User: Any person who interacts directly with a network system. This includes both those persons who are authorized to interact with the system and those people who interact without authorization.*

User ID: An alphanumeric or symbol character string that is unique to a user, and used for identification purposes.

User identification: User identification is the process by which a user identifies herself to the system as a valid user—as opposed to authentication, which is the process of establishing that the user is indeed that user and has a right to use the system.**

User interface: The part of an application that the user interacts with. They can be either text-driven (such as DOS) or graphical (such as Windows).**

V

Virtual network perimeter: A network that appears to be a single protected network behind firewalls, but actually encompasses encrypted virtual links over untrusted networks.**

Virtual private network (VPN): A private connection between two machines that sends private data traffic over a shared or public network, such as the Internet. VPN technology lets an organization securely extend its network services over the Internet to remote users, branch offices, and partner companies.

Virus: Self-replicating malicious program segment that attaches itself to an application or other executable system component and leaves no external signs of its presence. Viruses may or may not contain attack programs or trapdoors.*

Voice over Internet Protocol (VOIP): Voice over Internet Protocol is the transmission of voice through digital, packet-based, Internet channels.

W

Windows-based terminal (WBT): A fixed-function thin-client device that connects to a Citrix WinFrame or MetaFrame server and terminal server to provide application access. The key differentiator of a WBT from other thin devices is that all application execution occurs on the server; there is no downloading or local processing of applications at the client.

Wireless Equivalent Protocol (WEP): A wireless protocol designed to be implemented over wireless local area networks (WLANs) to offer the same security features as that offered in a physical network: confidentiality, access control, and data integrity.

Wireless Local Area Network (WLAN): A wireless network that corresponds to wireless laptops.

Write Once, Read Many (WORM): A type of malicious code that, once written to disk by an author, can self-replicate multiple times, over many machines, and execute whatever illicit activity it is programmed to launch. Worms generally contain back doors that create entry ways for future attacks.

X-Y-Z

Y2K: An acronym for the year 2000 problem, which involved three issues: two-digit data storage, leap-year calculations, and special meanings for dates.

REFERENCES

Allen, Julia. 2001. *CERT Guide to System and Network Security Practices.* Indianapolis, Ind.: Addison-Wesley.

American Bar Association. 2003. International Corporate Privacy Handbook. August.

———. 2003. International Strategy for Cyberspace Security. August.

Arkin, Ofir. 2002. "Why E.T. Can't Phone Home? Security Risk Factors with IP Telephony-based Networks." Sys-Security Group, November. http://www.sys-security.com/archive/papers/Security_Risk_Factors_with_IP_Telephony_based_Networks.pdf

Asia Pacific Economic Cooperation (APEC). 2002. *APEC Working Group on Electronic Financial Transactions Systems (E-FITS) Final Report.*

Associated Press. "FBI Seeks Hacker Who Stole Credit Card Numbers From eBay Users." *The Mercury News*, February 7, 2003.

Bajkowski, Julian. "Australian Amex site made 'unusable' by Slammer worm." *Computerworld*, February 3, 2003.

Bank of International Settlements. 2003. *Basel Committee on Banking Supervision: Risk Management Principles for Electronic Banking.* July.

———. 2001. *Electronic Finance: A New Perspective and Challenges.* BIS Papers No. 7., Basel, Switzerland.

Bank Secrecy Act Advisory Group. 2003. *The SAR Activity Review. Trends, Tips & Issues.* Issue 5 (February).

Bannan, Karen. 2001. "Safe Passage." *PC Magazine*, August.

Basel Committee on Banking Supervision. 2001. *Risk Management Principles for E-Banking*, May.

———. 2001. *Basel Committee on Banking Supervision Consultative Document: The New Basel Accord.* January.

Bator, Francis. 1958. "The Anatomy of Market Failure," *QJE.*

Bellis, Mary. "Selling the Cell Phone: History of Cellular Phones." About.com. Undated.

Berinato, Scott. 2002. "Finally, a Real Return on Security Spending." *Chief Information Officer (CIO) Magazine*, February 15.

Blake Ian, Gadiel Seroussi, and Nigel Smart. 1999. *Elliptic Curves in Cryptography*. Cambridge Univ. Press.

Blum, L., M. Blum, and M. Shub. 1986. "A Simple, Unpredictable Pseudo Random Generator." *SIAM Journal on Computing* 15(2).

Borneo Post, The. "Scam Big Blow to Embanking in Australia." July 22, 2002.

Bossone, Biagio and Larry J. Promisel. 1999. *The Role of Self-Regulation in the Financial Sector*. World Bank.

Calomiris, Charles, and Robert Litan. 1999. *Financial Regulation in a Global Marketplace*. Brookings Institution, Washington, D.C.

CERT Coordination Center. 2002. *Overview of Attack Trends*.

Claessens, Stijn, Thomas Glaessner, and Daniela Klingebiel. 2002. *Electronic Finance: A New Approach to Financial Sector Development*. World Bank Discussion Paper No. 431. Washington, D.C.

———. 2001. *E-Finance in Emerging Markets: Is Leapfrogging Possible?* World Bank Financial Sector Discussion Paper No. 7. Washington, D.C.

———. 2000. *Electronic Finance: Reshaping the Financial Landscape around the World*. Financial Sector Discussion Paper 4. World Bank, Washington, D.C.

Claessens, Stijn, and Daniela Klingebiel. 1999. *Alternative Frameworks for Providing Financial Services*. Policy Research Working Paper 2189. World Bank, Washington, D.C.

Claessens, Stijn, and Marion Jansen, eds. 2000. *The Internationalization of Financial Services*. Boston, Mass.: Kluwer Academic Press for the World Bank and the World Trade Organization.

Computer Security Institute. 2003. *CSI/FBI Computer Crime Report*. CSI, San Francisco.

Crockett, Andrew, and William McDonough. 1998. *Managing Change in Payment Systems*. BIS Policy Paper 4. Bank for International Settlements, Monetary and Economic Development, Basel, Switzerland.

Cunningham. 2001. "Digital Security: Heightened Risks Demand Innovation," *Red Herring* (July).

Department of Health and Human Services. 2003. *Health Insurance Portability and Accountability Act (HIPAA)*.

El Gamal, T. 1985. "A Public Key Cryptosystem and a Signature Scheme Based on Discrete Logarithms." *IEEE Transactions on Information Theory*, volume IT-31.

European Central Bank. 2003. *Electronic Money System Security Objectives. According to the Common Criteria Methodology*. May.

European Union. 2000. EU directive 2000/46/EG.

Federal Bureau of Investigations and Computer Security Institute. 2003. "2003 CSI/FBI Computer Crime and Security Survey." Eight Annual Report, by Computer Security Institute.

Federal Direct Insurance Corporation. 2001. "Authentication in an Electronic Banking Environment." August 8, 2001.

Federal Financial Institutions Examination Council (FFIEC). 2002. *FFIEC's Information Systems IT Examinations Handbook*. Document downloadable on the World Bank E-Security/E-Finance website at http://www1.worldbank.org/finance/, see "Key Readings."

Federal Trade Commission. 2001. *ID Theft. When Bad Things Happen to Your Good Name*.

Furst, Karen, William W. Lang, and Daniel E. Nolle. 1998. "Technological Innovation in Banking and Payments: Industry Trends and Implications for Banks." *Quarterly Journal* 17 (3): 23-31.

———. 2000. "Internet Banking: Developments and Prospects." Working Paper 2000-9, Comptroller of the Currency Administrator of National Banks, Washington D.C.

General Accounting Office. 2003. *Critical Infrastructure Protection: Efforts of the financial Services Sector to Address Cyber Threats*.

———. 2003. *Potential Terrorist Attacks: Additional Actions Needed to Better Prepare Critical Financial Market Participants.*

———. 2002. *Commercial Satellite Security Should Be More Fully Addressed.*

Gilbride, Edward. 2001. "Emerging Bank Technology and the Implications for E-Crime." Presentation, September 3.

Glaessner, Thomas. 1992. *External Regulation vs. Self-Regulation: What is the Right Mix? The Perspective of the Emerging Securities Markets of Latin American and the Carribean.* Regional Studies Program Report. World Bank, Latin America and Caribbean Technical Department, Washington, D.C.

Glaessner, Thomas, and Tom Kellerman, and Valerie McNevin. 2002. "Electronic Security: Risk Mitigation in Financial Transactions." Processed.

Goldberg, I. and D. Wagner. 1996. "Randomness and the Netscape Browser." *Dr. Dobbs Journal* (January).

Group of 8. 2003. "Principles for Protecting Critical Information Infrastructure." May.

Haber, Lynn. 2001. "Biometrics Locks Down PCs." ZDNet (December 28).

Hanley, Robert. "Former H&R Block Manager Accused in Identity Theft Ring." *The New York Times,* January 3, 2003.

International Standards Organization (ISO). 2002. *Banking and Related Financial Services-Information Security Guidelines.*

Internet Security Alliance. 2002. *Common Sense Guide for Senior Manager. Top Ten Recommended Information Security Practices.* First Edition.

International Telecommunications Union. 2002. "ITU Internet Reports 2001: IP Telephony." Summary. http://www.itu.int/ITU-D/ict/publications/inet/2000/

———. 2000. "ITU Announces New Edition of X.509 Recommendation Which Accelerates Global E-commerce Through Enhancements to Authentication and Authorization Specifications." March 31, 2000.

International Trade Administration. 2001. "E-banking: Brazil Leads Latin America."

Kahn, Alfred E. 1998. *The Economics of Regulation: Principles and Institutions.* Cambridge, Mass.: MIT Press.

———. 1970. *The Economics of Regulation: Principles and Institutions.* John Wiley & Sons, Inc.

Kahn, David. 1996. *The CODE-BREAKERS.* Scribner.

Kellermann, Tom. 2002a. *Mobile Risk Management: E-Finance in the Wireless Environment.* World Bank, Washington D.C. http://wbln1023.worldbank.org/html/FinancialSectorWeb.nsf/(attachmentweb)/Mobile_Risk_Management/$FILE/Mobile_Risk_Management.pdf.

———. 2002b. *Electronic Security: Risk Mitigation in Satellite-Based Networks.* World Bank, Washington D.C.

Kellermann, Tom and Yumi Nishiyama. 2003a. *Blended Electronic Security Threats: Code Red, Klez, Slammer, and Bugbear.* World Bank, Washington, D.C.

———. 2003b. *Phishing in the Digital Streams: The Growing Threat of Cyber Social Engineering to the Financial Sector.* World Bank, Washington, D.C.

Konda, Suresh, and Soumyo Moitra. 2000. "The Survivability of Network Systems: An Empirical Analysis." Carnegie Mellon Software Engineering Institute, Pittsburgh.

Krebs, Brian. 2003. "Internet Worm Hits Airlines, Banks." *The Washington Post,* January 26, 2003.

Krim, Jonathan. 2003. "8 Million Credit Card Accounts Exposed." *The Washington Post,* February 19, 2003.

La Repubblica. 2003. "Major Italian Banking and Credit Card Hacking Organization Smashed by Police." SNP Security News Portal, January 29, 2003.

Lemon, Sumner. 2001. "'Code Red' worm exploits Windows NT flaw." *Info World.* July 10, 2001. http://iwsun4.infoworld.com/articles/hn/xml/01/07/20/010720hnwormup.xml.

Mason, John. 1995. "Banks' Security Chains Rattled." *Financial Times.* September 20, 1995.

McAndrews, James. 1997. "Banking and Payment System Stability in an Electronic Money World." Working Paper 97-9. Federal Reserve Bank of Philadelphia, Philadelphia.

McAndrews, James, and William Roberts. 2000. "Payment Intermediation and the Origins of Banking." *Journal of Economic Literature Classification.*

McCormick, John. 2003. "Sapphire/Slammer Worm Attacks." *ZD Net UK,* January 28, 2003.

McGuire, David and Brian Krebs. 2002. "Attack on Internet Called the Largest Ever." *The Washington Post,* October 22, 2002.

McKinsey, Kitty. 2001. "In the Cards." *Far Eastern Economic Review,* January 12, 2001.

Merton, Robert C. 1995. "A Functional Perspective of Financial Intermediation." *Journal of the Financial Management Association* 24(2).

Microsoft Corporation. 2000. "SQL Server Fast Facts." August 17, 2000.

Mishkin, Frederic, and Philip Strahan. 1999. "What Will Technology Do to Financial Structure?" In Robert E. Litan and Anthony Santomero, eds., *Brookings-Wharton Papers on Financial Services.* Washington, D.C.: Brookings Institution.

Mobile Commerce World Magazine. 2001. "Dial M for Banking." January.

Mondex. 1999. "17 Central Banks Make Mondex E-Cash Standard in Africa." [http://mondex.com]

Monetary Authority of Singapore. 2003. *Technology Risk Management Guidelines for Financial Institutions.*

Munro, Jay. 2001. "BioPassword 4.5: Hardware-Free Biometrics." *PC Magazine,* September 24, 2001.

Mussington, David, Peter Wilson, and Roger C. Molander. 1998. "Exploring Money Laundering Vulnerabilities Through Emerging Cyberspace Technologies: A Caribbean Based Exercise." Rand and Critical Technologies Institute (CTI).

National Conference of Commissioners on Uniform State Laws. 2000. "Uniform Money Services Act." Conference, July 28-August 4, 2000.

National Fraud Center. 2000. *The Growing Global Threat of Economic and Cyber Crime.*

National Infrastructure Protection Agency. 2003. "Worm Targets SQL Vulnerability." Advisory 03-001.1, January 27, 2003.

————. 2002. "Microsoft SQL Worm Spida." Advisory 02-003, May 22, 2002.

National Institute of Standards and Technology (NIST). 2003. "Standards for Security Categorization of Federal Information and Information Systems." Draft, May.

Neustar. *ENUM: Driving Convergence in the Internet Age.* ENUM.org. Undated.

Nishiyama, Yumi, 2003. "Vulnerabilities in Electronic Communication: IM & VOIP." Unpublished, World Bank, Washington D.C.

Noguchi, Yuki. 2003. "Satellite Phone Firms Win Ruling." *The Washington Post,* January 31, 2003.

Office of the Comptroller of the Currency (of the U.S. Treasury). 2001a. "Bank Provided Account Aggregation Services." OCC Bulletin 2001-12, February 28, 2001.

————. 2001b. "Examination Procedures to Evaluate Compliance with the Guidelines Safeguarding Customer Information." OCC Bulletin 2001-35, July 18.

————. 2001c. "Guidelines Establishing Standards for Safeguarding Customer Information." OCC Bulletin 2001-8.

————. 2001d. "Network Security Vulnerabilities." OCC Alert 2001-4, April 24.

————. 2000a. "Distributed Denial of Service Attacks." OCC Alert 2000-1, February 11.

———. 2000b. "Intrusion Risks." OCC Bulletin 2000-14, May 15.

———. 2000c. "Risk Management of Outsourced Technology Services." OCC Advisory Letter 2000-12, November 28.

———. 1999d. OCC Statement of Conditional Approval #339. November.

Organization for Economic Cooperation and Development (OECD). 2002. *OECD Guidelines for the Security of Information Systems and Networks.*

Pelton, Joseph. 1993. "Five Ways Nicholas Negroponte is Wrong About the Future of Telecommunications." *Telecommunications* 11(4).

Poulsen, Kevin. 2003. "Slammer worm crashed Ohio nuke plant network." SecurityFocus, accessed August 19, 2003 at: <http://www.computercops.biz/article2793.html>.

Predictive Systems. 2001. "Global E-Review." August.

Rescorla, Eric. 2001. *SSL and TLS.* Addison-Wesley.

Reuters. "SQL Slammer Worm Spread Worldwide in 10 Minutes." February 4, 2003.

Rosencrance, Linda. 2002. "Identity Theft Case Seen as Largest in U.S. History." *Computerworld*, November 26, 2002.

Saarinen, Marrku-Juhani. "Attacks Against the WAP WTLS Protocol." University of Jyvaskyla. Undated.

Schneier, Bruce. 2000. *Secrets & Lies—Digital Security in a Networked World.* John Wiley & Sons.

Schumaker, Troy. 2002. *Cover Your Assets.* Denver, Colorado: North Atlantic Books and Frog Limited.

Shamir, Adi, and Nicko van Someren. 1998. "Playing hide and seek with stored keys."

Shapiro, Carl, and Hal Varian. 1999. *Information Rules: A Strategic Guide to the Network Economy.* Boston, Mass.: Harvard Business School Press.

Shu-Pui, Li. 2002. E-Security: Risk Mitigation in Financial Transactions. Presentation at the World Bank Global Dialogue on E-security, September 25. http://www1.worldbank.org/finance/html/dl11bkgd.html

Simons, Katerina, and Joanna Stavins. 1998. "Has Antitrust Policy in Banking Become Obsolete?" *New England Economic Review* (March/April). Federal Reserve Bank of Boston, Boston, Mass.

Sirtaine, Sophie. 2001. "On the Services Offered by Post Offices in Various Countries." World Bank, Finance and Private Sector Development, Washington, D.C.

Soo Hoo, Kevin 2001. "Tangible ROI through Secure Software Engineering." *Secure Business Quarterly* (October).

Stenger, Richard. 2001. "'Code Red' worm spreads, Pentagon reacts." *CNN.com*, August 1, 2001.

Sullivan, Bob. 2001. "Massive Credit Heist Fraud Reported." MSNBC Online. Retrieved on December 22, 2001, from http://www.msnbc.com.

———. 2003. "Virus-like attack slows Web traffic." MSNBC Online, January 27, 2003.

Summers, Bruce, and Akinari Horii. 1994. "Large-Value Transfer Systems." In Bruce Summers, ed., *The Payments System: Design, Management, and Supervision.* Washington, D.C.: International Monetary Fund.

Symantec. "Securing Instant Messaging." White Paper, Undated.

Teeraruangchaisri, Kittipong. 2001. "Code Red and Code Red II: Double Dragons." SANS Institute.

Thibedeau, Harry W. 1996. "A Dream In The Making." Cable & Wireless Cable, August.

Trusecure. 2001. "Secure Your Microsoft IIS Web Servers." April 18, 2001.

Tzekov, Lubomir. 2002. "E-security Risk Mitigation in Financial Transactions." Presentation at the World Bank Global Dialogue on E-security, September 25. http://www1.worldbank.org/finance/html/dl11bkgd.html

United Nations. 2001. UNCITRAL Model Law on Electronic Signatures. Article II, Subsection A. United Nations Commission on International Trade Law.

U.S. Department of Justice. 2002. "McNeese" Press Release. Retrieved on March 1, 2002, from http://www.cybercrime.gov/mcneeseArrest.htm.

U.S. Securities and Exchange Commission. 2000. "Federal Regulation of Securities Activity on the Internet." Division of Market Regulation, Washington, D.C.

Vijayan, Jaikumar. 2002. "VOIP: Don't overlook security." *Computerworld*, October 7.

Vorhees, Mike. 2002. *The Myth of Online Payments.*

Wallman, Steven. 1999. "The Information Technology Revolution and Its Impact on Regulation and Regulatory Structure." In Robert E. Litan and Anthony Santomero, eds., *Brookings-Wharton Papers on Financial Services.* Washington, D.C.: Brookings Institution.

Weinberg, John. 1997. "The Organization of Private Payment Networks." *Economic Quarterly Volume* 83(2). Federal Reserve Ban of Richmond, Richmond, Va.

Werthamer, N. Richard, and Susan Raymond. 1997. "Technology and Finance: The Electronic Markets." In *Technological Forecasting and Social Change: An International Journal.* New York: Elsevier Science.

White House. 2000. *Defending America's Cyberspace: National Plan for Information Systems Protection Version 1.0.* White House, Washington D.C.

————. 2003. *The National Strategy to Secure Cyberspace.* White House, Washington D.C. Document downloadable on the World Bank E-Security/E-Finance website at http://www1.worldbank.org/finance/, see Key Readings.

————. 1998. "The Policy on Critical Infrastructure Protection." Presidential Decision Directive 63 (PDD-63).

Wang Jun. 2002. "What's happening in the area of E-security for the Financial Transactions in China." Presentation at the World Bank Global Dialogue on E-security, September 25. http://www1.worldbank.org/finance/html/dl11bkgd.html

Woochan Kim. "E-security in Financial Transaction: Case of Korea." Presentation at the World Bank Global Dialogue on E-security. September 25. http://www1.worldbank.org/finance/html/dl11bkgd.html

World Bank. 2001. "Finance for Growth: Policy Choices in a Volatile World." Financial Sector Policy Research Report. Washington, D.C.

Zeichick, Alan. 2001. "Smart Cards Explained." *Red Herring* (January): 82–83.